ANTONIO VIVALDI

His Life and Work

By the same author

Anton Webern: an introduction to his works

I. Portrait of a Musician, by an anonymous master (Liceo Musicale G. B. Martini, Bologna), identified by Francesco Vatielli as probably Antonio Vivaldi. One of the clues to identification is a lock of natural auburn hair, visible by the edge of the peruke at the left temple.

- WALTER KOLNEDER

ANTONIO VIVALDI

His Life and Work

Translated by
Bill Hopkins

UNIVERSITY OF CALIFORNIA PRESS

Berkeley and Los Angeles

1970

UNIVERSITY OF CALIFORNIA PRESS
Berkeley and Los Angeles, California

ISBN: 0-520-01629-7
Library of Congress Catalog Card Number: 71-101341

Originally published in Germany
Breitkopf & Härtel, Wiesbaden; 1965

Printed in Great Britain

To my Italian friends

CONTENTS

CONTENTS

ILLUSTRATIONS

ILLUSTRATIONS

INTRODUCTION

When, on July 28, 1741, 'Herr Antonj Vivaldi, Weltl. Priester, alt 60 Jahr' was laid to rest in a mean grave in St. Stephen's cemetery, Vienna, he had long since left behind him the summit of a glorious career as composer, violinist, *maestro di cappella* and teacher. Little notice was taken of his death. The musical world which in former times had listened insatiably to his concertos had now turned its affections to new idols. In the works of Tartini, Locatelli, Sammartini, Pergolesi and others, a new style had made its appearance, at first in isolated traits and afterwards consolidating itself more and more. It was felt to be more modern, more progressive, and better suited to the rapidly changing tastes of the public.

A year after the composer's death, during the celebrations and festivities that followed Charles VII's coronation at Frankfurt, the 'famous virtuoso Stamitz'—a young musician of only 25 years—was giving performances on the 'violin, viola d'amore, violoncello and double-bass'. His manner of playing, and probably also the style of his early compositions, created such a stir at the time that in the previous year the Elector Palatinate Karl Philipp had engaged him at Mannheim, where in a few years he rose to the position of concert-master and director of the chamber music. His music, with its novel melodic lines inspired by Bohemian and Austrian folk-music, its new formal methods and orchestral presentation, rapidly spread through the whole of Europe, as is shown by the numerous transcripts of his works in Italian and Austrian libraries and by the fact that his music was printed and performed in Paris. During the time when Stamitz was in effect founding a school in Mannheim with his circle of selected musicians, Bach's sons on the other hand were maturing into composers who worked in a style that made the elder Bach's music seem to them antiquated and old-fashioned. And when, five years after

I

INTRODUCTION

the death of Johann Sebastian Bach, the 23-year-old Joseph Haydn wrote his first string quartet, a great era of European music finally saw its last days. Today it is difficult for us to grasp the pace at which musical development progressed in those times. A public which heard music without any sort of historical perspective and which felt itself intimately involved only with the art of the present was undoubtedly bound to feel that a work was outmoded once it was even as few as a dozen years old. Handel's oratorios were among the rare exceptions, and even the *Well-Tempered Clavier* lived on only in circles of real connoisseurs. But Vivaldi's music remained dead for some hundred years, shrouded in the dust of archives and libraries. Leopold Mozart's violin method, published in 1756 —the year his son was born—might contain the odd example from Tartini, but already has nothing by Vivaldi, a fact that is symptomatic of this state of affairs.

In the middle of the nineteenth century, work was begun on a collected edition of the music of Bach whose basis was to be one of scholarly thoroughness; it was then found that among these works were the master's reworkings of Vivaldi, and interest in the latter began to grow. Essays by Julius Rühlmann (1867) and Paul Graf Waldersee (1885) were the first fruits of this interest, and in his great book on Bach (1873–80) Philipp Spitta pointed to further aspects of that singular phenomenon, the impression Vivaldi made on Bach. For Rühlmann, however, Vivaldi's music was still 'almost entirely dead'. Then Nachéz and others took it upon themselves to prepare the first performing editions of Vivaldi's original works. Stylistically these arrangements, amply garnished with trimmings, are today extremely dated, but they deserve credit for having made Vivaldi's concertos known—particularly to amateur violinists. As a result of the labours of Schering (1902–6) and Fischer (1924) the composer's historical significance gained recognition, particularly with regard to the development of instrumental music, and a catalogue drawn up by Altmann (1922) listing the works printed in his lifetime completed the first stage of the efforts made on behalf of his work; and at first it might well have been regarded as the final, conclusive stage.

But in the years 1926–30 the Director of the National Library of Turin, Luigi Torri, and the Turin Professor of Musicology, Alberto Gentili, succeeded in securing a hitherto unknown collection of music which contained no less than 300 concertos, 8 sonatas, 14 complete operas, 5 volumes of sacred works and 2 volumes of secular vocal works by Vivaldi. The story of this discovery is itself a subject worthy of a novel, and since it has never been set down on record we shall give it here in a version based on Gentili's own accounts of it and on documents in his family's possession.

During the eighteenth century there existed in Turin a distinguished court orchestra whose performing style was based in all its essentials on that of the violinist Giovanni Battista Somis (1686–1763) and his school. At the time of the Napoleonic wars this orchestra accompanied the court to Sardinia, and since its enormous musical archives could not be taken there too they were hidden before the flight—and unfortunately hidden so well that they could not be traced after the musicians returned. Oral tradition had it that they were in a Piedmontese monastery. Gentili, who died at an advanced age in 1954, sought this hoard for decades and with incomparable tenacity followed up every report pertaining to old music manuscripts. He thought he had come to the end of his investigations when in the autumn of 1926 Monsignore Emanuel, rector of the Collegio S. Carlo in the small region of S. Martino (Monferrato, province of Alessandria, to the north of Genoa and to the east of Turin), approached the Turin National Library with a request for the evaluation of a collection of musical manuscripts and old prints. The Salesian monks were obliged to sell them in order to undertake necessary repairs to their monastery, and to rooms there that had once been occupied by Don Bosco. The collection comprised no fewer than 95 volumes, including manuscript scores of Alessandro Stradella and 14 volumes with works by Vivaldi. These treasures had been presented to the monks by the heirs of one Marchese Marcello Durazzo of Genoa. This family had achieved some importance in musical history through the Genoese Conte Giacomo Durazzo (1717–94) who from 1749 on had been active in Vienna as envoy extraordinary for his home town. Through his marriage to Aloisa Ernestine Ungnad von Weissenwolff he came into relation with the highest circles of the nobility and in 1752 was transferred to the Austrian Imperial service as an honorary privy councillor. By reason of his artistic interests, his theatrical gifts (shown by his gallant performances), and his skill as an organizer, he soon became 'General Superintendant of Spectacles', and later also 'Musikgraf', in other words, director of the court theatre and chief administrator of the court orchestra. In that capacity he earned lasting merit by his patronage of Gluck and of the latter's collaboration with the librettist Calzabigi, culminating in 1762 with the first performance of *Orfeo*. Durazzo was a man of great resourcefulness and he had the wholly modern idea of covering the opera's losses by means of a gaming-table, which was installed in the opera house itself. This enterprise flourished for a while, but soon it was held that in his calculations of the receipts Durazzo was beginning to make really generous allowances in his own favour—the reason was supposed to be that numerous love affairs with singers and ballerinas were costing him more money than he had at his disposal. Thus he soon incurred the displeasure of the puritanical Empress Maria Theresa, and the opposition group—at that time already a traditional feature of Viennese operatic life—succeeded in engineering his overthrow. However, this was not Durazzo's downfall, indeed it was rather the contrary: in 1765 he became the richly-paid Austrian ambassador in Venice, occupied a large palace with its own private theatre, and by his encouragement of Mozart in 1771 was once more to give proof of his sound judgment in musical matters. But above all he was now active as a collector, and in 1784 his friend Conte Bartolomeo Benincasa was able to publish in Parma a printed work *Descrizione della raccolta di stampe di S. Conte Jacopo Durazzo, esposta in una dissertazione sull'arte dell'intaglio a stampa*. We may well suppose that Durazzo had bought from the Ospedale della Pietà, in whose music department Vivaldi had been active for nearly forty years, all the composer's works in their possession for which they could no longer find a use.

Gentili needed only a brief glance through the pages of the first volume to realize the actual value of what he had been given to estimate. In order to keep the valuable collection intact and above all in a place where it would remain accessible for practical and scholarly use, it was necessary to prevent it at all costs from reaching the dealer who had already been chosen as the agent. Since the normal resources of the Turin Library did not stretch to anything like the cost of the volumes, Gentili set about looking for a private patron—an enterprise that had to be undertaken with the greatest secrecy, since there was a constant risk that some affluent foreign manuscript-hunter might appear on the scene. After several fruitless efforts, the Turin banker Roberto Foà declared himself prepared to buy the collection and to present it to the Turin National Library in memory of his deceased son Mauro. The purchase and presentation were effected on February 15, 1927, and the latter was ratified by the Italian government on March 23, 1927. Then on January 28, 1928, works from the Mauro Foà Collection were heard for the first time in a 'Concerto di musiche antiche italiane' that Gentili gave with the 'Gruppo Universitario Musicale' in the theatre at Turin, with the collaboration of some of the town's foremost artists.

On closer inspection of the collection Gentili made an exciting discovery: the Vivaldi scores, bound in stout pigskin, were numbered consecutively in pairs of works. However, many pairs lacked the even-

4

numbered volumes, and others the odd-numbered ones, so that Gentili supposed that the collection had originally been twice as large and had at one time possibly been divided between two heirs. Now Torri and Gentili decided to search systematically for the rest of the collection. This undertaking demanded even more cunning and caution; for meanwhile the customary sensational announcements had appeared in the presses of the world, and already in many districts monastery libraries had begun to be ransacked. An experienced archivist, Marchese Dr. Faustino Curlo, was found for the task of investigating the Durazzo family tree with all its branches, and to trace any surviving members of the family; as a relative of a family of Genoese aristocrats he brought with him the best possible credentials for the job in hand. After many difficulties and with the assistance of the state police he was able to track down in Genoa a last scion of the famous family, Marchese Giuseppe Maria Durazzo, a whimsical and unsociable old man, who in his personal affairs would listen only to the counsel of high ecclesiastical dignitaries. Through them Curlo found his way to the old man's father confessor, the Jesuit father Antonio Oldra, who with much effort was able to put him in touch with the Marchese. Marchese Giuseppe Maria was in fact a nephew of the Durazzo from whom the Vivaldi collection of the Salesians of the Collegio S. Carlo had come. He had inherited from his father a large but quite disorganized library, which was of course totally impossible to evaluate; and, pathologically afraid of theft, he had strictly forbidden even the domestic servants all access to it. There was a good chance that, in accordance with the pattern of inheritances within the family, the complementary part of the great Durazzo collection might be found in this library. However, the Marchese was furious with the monks who, in his opinion, had had no right at all to sell the manuscripts. After extremely patient overtures, and with the constant support of the father confessor (who was himself a connoisseur), they managed gradually to wring from the old man his permission to enter the library and to study any musical manuscripts they might find there. After almost three years of endeavours, under a cloak of strict secrecy, Marchese Durazzo gave his written consent on January 30, 1930, stating that he would in principle agree to a sale of the second part of the collection, which had meanwhile been brought to light, in the event that a patron should declare himself prepared to contribute to the funds of the Turin National Library. For a second time Gentili drew up his petitions, and once more he was in luck: the Turin textiles manufacturer Filippo Giordano was disposed to pay the required sum, and on April 30, 1930, sale and donation were concluded. By a strange coincidence, he too had lost an infant son, Renzo; so from that time on the two parts of the collection were combined in Turin under the title *Collezione Mauro Foà e Renzo Giordano*. The volumes are embellished with charming vignettes showing the children in half-length portraits.

But old Durazzo fought to his dying day over his manuscripts. One of the conditions he laid down was that all publication, and hence all performance, of the works should be prohibited for ever. It was only possible to lift this ban after protracted proceedings in the civil and ecclesiastical courts. All these circumstances naturally hindered, and to a certain extent prevented, study and evaluation of the collection for a long time. In 1936, Olga Rudge, secretary of the Accademia Chigiana in Siena, laid out a catalogue of the Turin works, making a preliminary survey possible. Then in Siena, during a Vivaldi week in September 1939, works from the entire Durazzo collection were heard, having been prepared for performance by Alfredo Casella. In the programme book the initiator and patron of this week, Conte Chigi dei Saracini, could still say 'uno dei più grandi ma anche meno conosciuti fra i musicisti del Settecento' ('one of the greatest, but also one of the least known of eighteenth-century masters'). Since then the situation has changed radically. The Siena festival week heralded a Vivaldi renaissance which today is immediately evident from Vivaldi's ample representation in concerts, broadcasts, amateur music-making and in recordings. Hand in hand with this there has been research into his life and work. After the appearance of studies by Salvatori, Gallo, Abbado, Rinaldi and others, Marc Pincherle in 1948 brought out the standard work on the composer, representing the fruits of a preoccupation with Vivaldi that had lasted over forty years. An excellent thematic catalogue of the instrumental music completes this work, in which the composer is accorded recognition in his true role as one of the greatest influences on the development of music in the eighteenth century. And so the singular destiny of a musician has been fulfilled: after a meteoric rise, Vivaldi at thirty-five was already a composer of European significance, after his death he was completely forgotten for more than a hundred years, then was resurrected, even if only partially, from under the shadow of his great 'pupil' Johann Sebastian Bach, and today, after the discovery of what probably constitutes the essential part of his complete works, is once more in the limelight of the musical world.

HIS LIFE

In the year 1291 two men of Genoa, Ugolino and Vadino Vivaldi, died at sea after they had discovered the Canary Islands. Writers on music with a taste for grandiose conjecture have since spoken of the 'blood of bold Genoese seafarers' that 'flowed' in the veins of the composer. Now, however, thanks to the researches of Emil Paul, we know that the composer's paternal grandparents lived in Brescia as respected citizens, and Antonio's father Giovanni Battista (also Gianbattista) was born there in 1655. At the age of ten he went with his mother to Venice, where to begin with he learnt the barber's trade, and then set up business himself, at the same time becoming active as a part-time musician. This was not an unusual combination at the time, because as a rule there were instruments in Italian barbers' shops so that the clients could pass their time agreeably in the waiting room. Finally Giovanni Battista devoted himself entirely to the musical profession and soon must have found himself enjoying a certain esteem; for in 1685 we find his name among the founder members of a musical fraternity, the 'Sovvegno dei musicisti di Santa Cecilia', which had elected as its director the honoured composer of operas and sacred music, Giovanni Legrenzi. After the latter's engagement as *maestro di cappella* at St. Mark's, the orchestra was expanded as one of the first measures to be taken in reorganizing Venetian church music, and the elder Vivaldi, who received a substantial pay increase a few years later, found himself chosen as one of the supplementary musicians. It is interesting that, appearing for the first time in the records, he is referred to not by his family name, but is called G. B. Rossi. Thus the light red hair-colour that appears so striking in Italy seems to have been a family characteristic which the son inherited from his father, and which caused the son to be known by the nickname 'il prete rosso' ('the red-haired priest').

On August 6, 1677, Gianbattista married Camilla Calicchio, the daughter of a Venetian tailor, and Antonio came into the world as early as March 4, 1678. As a premature child he had such a weak constitution that 'per pericolo di morte' ('on account of the risk of death'), as the baptismal register has it, he had to be baptized by the midwife, and that only two months later could he be taken to the church of San Giovanni in Bragora for formal baptism. According to the records, Antonio had three sisters (Margherita Gabriela, Cecilia Maria and Zanetta Anna) and two brothers (Bonaventura Tomaso and Francesco Gaetano). These brothers were not professional musicians, but remained true to their father's traditional trade. The family appears to have been easy-going, temperamental and highly irascible. For instance, Francesco was banned from Venice in 1721 on account of a squabble that had taken place at daybreak after a night of carousal. One Iseppo Vivaldi—probably another brother or perhaps some relative of the composer—met with the same fate when on November 9, 1728, he had injured a chemist's errand-boy in a brawl on the public highway. In the statements of the witnesses, Antonio is mentioned in a peculiar way: one witness recognized Iseppo as an accessory and said: 'Iseppo, non so il cognome, fratelle de Prete rosso famoso che sona il violin' ('Iseppo, I do not know the surname, a brother of the famous red-haired Priest who plays the violin').

We know very little about Antonio's youth and musical education. He was probably a pupil of his father in violin-playing and is reputed to have worked in the Cathedral orchestra from as early as his tenth year, occasionally even deputizing for his father, who was temporarily occupied outside Venice in the years 1689–92. According to an older tradition Antonio was a pupil of Legrenzi in theory. Since the latter died as early as 1690, there is some doubt about this. However, if we consider the precocity of a Mozart or a Schubert there seems little basis for such doubt. A sacred vocal work in the Turin collection, 'Laetatus', dated 1691, may very well have been the product of this instruction.

His father's occupation as a Cathedral musician naturally brought the young Antonio into contact with the clerical orders, and so his decision to enter the clergy is understandable, particularly since in seventeenth- and eighteenth-century Italy it was not unusual for such an occupation to be combined with a career in music. On September 18, 1693—that is, at the age of fifteen and a half—he received the tonsure from the Venetian patriarch, and the following day he became an Ostario: in other words, he received the first of the so-called minor orders. Documents from the

8

Archivio Patriarcale in Venice give us precise details of the separate rites of priestly ordination:

September 18, 1693   Tonsure

    Minor Orders
September 19, 1693   Ostario
September 21, 1693   Lettore
December 25, 1695   Esorcista
September 21, 1696   Accolito

    Holy Orders
April 4, 1699   Suddiacone
September 18, 1700   Diacone
March 23, 1703   Sacerdote

In the records Vivaldi is referred to three times as 'Antonius filius Jo. Bap.tae Vivaldi Ecclesia S. Geminiani', in other words, as belonging to the parish of S. Geminiani, and five times as a parishioner of S. Giovanni in Oleo. In those days, in fact, it was possible to become a priest outside a seminary, as assistant to a minister to whom one was assigned, as it were, during one's time of study and apprenticeship. Antonio probably underwent this type of training and thus is likely to have been to a certain extent free to study where he liked. This proved very beneficial for his musical studies.

Vivaldi's virtuoso playing of the violin as well as many stylistic echoes of Corelli, particularly in the early sonatas, have given rise to conjectures that he was actually a pupil of that master in Rome, where Somis studied with him in 1703. However, no evidence has been found for any period of study with Corelli, although it would explain the strikingly long interval of three years that elapsed between his deaconship and his priesthood—one year being the minimum time prescribed by the Church. Besides, Corelli's works came out in print in Venice immediately after their appearance in Rome, and were thus well known there. No proof could be given either for a period of study with Somis in Turin, such as has likewise been suggested. Conversely there is also no support for the supposition that in addition to his stay in Rome Somis studied composition with Vivaldi in Venice. However, Vivaldi's father, whose name appeared together with his son's in a 'Guida dei Forestieri in Venezia' ('visitors' guide to Venice') of 1713 as one of the city's best violinists, must have been more than a capable orchestral violinist, and was evidently very well equipped to guide his pupil through to the highest grades of violin-playing.

In 1704 the composer's name appears for the first time on the accounts of the 'Ospedale della Pietà'; in fact, he received 30 ducats for the preceding term as 'Maestro di Violino'. From this we learn that in September 1703, thus a few months after his ordination as a priest, he had taken the post which caused him to be referred to occasionally in older publications as a 'conservatoire director'. However, this modern title is an apt description neither of the kind of institution in question nor of Vivaldi's occupation. In olden times Venice was a city of maritime commerce and for centuries, by virtue of firmly established bonds, had had the run of trade with the Orient, and consequently repeatedly found itself involved in severe conflicts, especially with the Turks. In such a city there was an abundance of orphans, foundlings, illegitimates and similarly needy folk. To take care of them, orphanages had been set up already in the fourteenth century, to which were attached infirmaries, hence the description 'Ospedale'. They were supported partly by public means, partly by grants and the townspeople's donations; the sums needed must have been very high, yet at times these institutions sheltered up to 6,000 children. For religious as well as educational reasons, choral singing soon occupied an important place in the syllabus, and in this way music courses were gradually developed: in other words, pupils of unusual talent were given instruction not only in basic theory and solo singing, but also in the playing of different instruments. Famous masters such as Caldara, Galuppi, Hasse, Legrenzi, Lotti, Domenico Scarlatti, Tessarini, Traetta and others played an active role in these establishments, four of which became renowned for the high standard of their regular Sunday and feast-day concerts. These were: 'la Pietà', 'i Mendicanti', 'gli Incurabili' and 'l'Ospidaletto' ('Charity', 'the Beggars', 'the Incurables' and 'the Little Hospital'), all of them housing girls exclusively. The directors of the institutions also gave the concerts a lot of backing because the receipts on the sale of seats contributed enormously to the costs of education. The level of accomplishment of both solo and choral singing as well as of instrumental playing must have been extraordinary; in letters, memoirs and travel diaries of the time there are repeatedly enthusiastic opinions of them. A few years before Vivaldi took up his duties, the Russian Petr Andreevič Tolstago, on an Italian journey, reported from Venice:

'In Venice there are convents where the women play the organ and other instruments, and sing so wonderfully that nowhere else in the world could one find such sweet and harmonious song. Therefore people come to Venice from all parts with the wish to refresh themselves with these angelic songs, above all those of the Convent of the Incurables.' (May 1698).

As late as 1790, Goethe did not neglect to visit the famous church performances of the Ospedali.

At first, Vivaldi was only a teacher of the violin, but doubtless he soon began to contribute to the performances with his compositions, and would also conduct them occasionally as 'Maestro del Coro' or 'Maestro de' Concerti'. This was all the more probable when the director of the music course, Francesco Gasparini, an important composer and the author of a widely used textbook on the figured bass, became very ill. The fact that soon the Ospedale della Pietà outshone the other institutions with its outstanding orchestra can doubtless be ascribed to the particular merits of Vivaldi.

A short time after enrolling on the course's teaching staff Vivaldi no longer celebrated mass. An angina pectoris from which he had suffered from birth must have sometimes manifested itself so violently that several times he had to leave the altar in the middle of mass. An anecdotal biography has seized imaginatively on these occurrences and goes on to elaborate that in moments of intense inspiration Vivaldi went into the sacristy to write down themes. Choron and Fayelle then even go somewhat further, and declare:

'He was referred to the Inquisition, which fortunately regarded him as a musician, in other words an idiot, and contented itself with forbidding him to celebrate the mass from that time on.'

In our own time, Farga too gave free rein to his imagination:

'So it was understandable that . . . Vivaldi finally renounced the cloth and devoted himself entirely to music.'

The composer told of his illness in a biographically important letter written during his last years, that is, when the Church reproached him with his sometimes very mundane way of life. He says:

'I have not now said mass for twenty-five years, and I shall never do so again, not because of a veto or a command, as His Eminence can confirm, but of my own accord, and this on account of an ailment I have suffered from since birth, which oppresses me greatly. When I had just been ordained a priest, I still said mass for rather more than a year and then gave it up, because three times I had to leave the altar without finishing mass on account of my illness.

For this reason I spend my life almost entirely at home, leaving my house only in a gondola or a carriage, because with my chest complaint, known as heart seizure, I cannot walk. No nobleman invites me to his house, not even our doge, because they all know of my ailment. I can usually leave the house immediately after breakfast, but never on foot. This is the reason that I do not say mass.' (Letter of November 16, 1737, to Marchese Guido Bentivoglio d'Aragona.)

For his first years as violin teacher at the Ospedale della Pietà we must imagine him as having been industrious in his activity as a pedagogue and composer; the institution's administrators soon acknowledged his successes: in 1708 he was given a pay rise, and in 1711 Vivaldi stepped into a vacated position which held a secure yearly wage. At that time the young master's reputation began to be firmly established in his home town, and was gradually spreading abroad too, fostered by foreign visitors to Venice. In fact, the city was at that time a centre of international tourist traffic at least as important as it is today, and the many princely personages, great and small, from Northern and Western Europe, bringing their entourages to visit the city of lagoons, never failed to hear Vivaldi's concerts. Thus in 1709 Frederick IV of Denmark was in Venice and attended the performance of an oratorio at the Ospedale della Pietà. On this occasion Vivaldi was probably presented to the guest, to whom he dedicated his twelve violin sonatas, Op. II.

There is a report of a visit made to Venice in 1712 by Gottfried Heinrich Stölzel, who was active as *Kapellmeister* in Breslau at only twenty-two, and was already a successful operatic composer. Thus, he was the first German musician to have personal contact with Vivaldi.

At this time changes of personnel came about at the Ospedale which had a favourable effect on Vivaldi's creative activities. In 1713 Gasparini took a long sick leave, never to return to his post. So Vivaldi became the official house composer, particularly since Dall'Olio, Gasparini's successor as director of the course, was hardly forthcoming creatively. It is surprising that Vivaldi was not called upon to take up this position. Perhaps it was denied him on account of the precarious state of his health, or maybe an older and more experienced master was preferred for the directorship. But the real reason should be sought in the fact of Vivaldi's turning to the theatre. For instance in 1713 he had even taken a month's leave, apparently for the première of his first opera, *Ottone in villa*, which took place that year in Vicenza. With the composer's second opera, *Orlando finto pazzo*, was begun in 1714 an evidently very successful series of performances of his stage works in Venice; for it comprised no less than eight operas in five years, including two in each of the years 1716 and 1718. In this connection Vivaldi would feel an inner liberation from the relatively strict confines of his activity in the seminary, and besides he apparently very quickly developed a certain skill in the business side of operatic life. The Frankfurt patrician's son, Johann Friedrich Armand von Uffenbach, who was later to become the mayor of his home town, was staying in Venice in 1715, and noted in his diary entry for February 4 a visit to the opera: 'Der entrepreneur davon war der berühmte Vivaldi' ('Its impresario was the famous Vivaldi'). It was no rarity in seventeenth- and eighteenth-century Italy for a minister to be active in opera. The libretto of the sacred opera *Il San Alessio* (1632) by Stefano Landi was by the subsequent pope, Clement IX; the Venetian Franciscan father Daniele Castrovillari was the composer of three operas that were performed between 1660 and 1662; and Cardinal Grimani wrote the text of Handel's *Agrippina*, which was performed in Venice in 1709. Finally Metastasio was an *abate*, and the participation of ministers in the theatre orchestra is recorded several times. Vivaldi's extensive operatic works—we know of 48 dramatic stage works by him—were certainly born of the urge for wide social recognition. But it may be supposed that Vivaldi was also very conscious of the antithesis between the world of musical theatre and that of *musica da chiesa e camera*, and he may also perhaps have suffered from this division of his attention. In any case, from 1713 on, a peculiar indecisiveness between his position at the Ospedale and his life as an operatic composer can be felt. After the first leave of one month's absence, the composer often left the institution for longer or shorter periods, but he invariably returned, even though he must surely have been offered posts that would have been more lucrative and carried more prestige. After many a deplorable artistic, and maybe even personal, experience in the theatre, he was probably drawn again and again to an unusual extent to the quiet atmosphere of the Ospedale which was entirely devoted to the best in music. It can be seen that Vivaldi's operatic works were also rooted in an inner urge towards mastery of larger forms of musical expression from the fact that he now took up a hitherto neglected genre, namely oratorio. Perhaps it was only Gasparini's departure that enabled him to do so. At any rate two of Vivaldi's oratorios were performed in the concerts of the Ospedale della Pietà, *Moyses Deus Pharaonis* in 1714 and *Juditha triumphans devicta Holofernis barbaris* in 1716.

Since up till 1718, the year when the opera *Scanderbegh* was performed in Florence, and with the exception of the first opera, all Vivaldi's stage works were produced in Venice, and the account books of the Ospedale mention the composer regularly, he probably lived in Venice throughout all these years. His fruitful activity in the seminary, which was also very successful in its effects on a wider public, now also brought him the official designation 'maestro dei concerti', which appears for the first time in a document of 1716. An important visit brought with it further proof of the esteem in which he was held: in April, 1716, Friedrich August III, the son of August the Strong, and later to be Elector of Saxony and King of Poland, came to Venice and brought with his entourage the violinist Johann Georg Pisendel. The latter, born in Karsburg (Franconia) in 1687, started his musical career as a court choirboy in Ansbach, and was also a pupil there of Torelli. He had been a violinist at Dresden since 1712, and in taking part in this journey he was enabled by his superiors to have a short, but apparently very intensive period of study with Vivaldi. A cordial relationship sprang up between Vivaldi and Pisendel, who was also a gifted composer, and this relationship bore musical fruit. No less than six concertos and three sonatas in the Dresden National Library bear the inscription 'fatto per il Sign. Pisendel' ('composed for Mr. Pisendel'). They come from the estate of Vivaldi's pupil and were bought in 1755 at the instigation of the music-loving Electress Maria Josepha of Saxony, together with the rest of the estate, for the repertoire of the Dresden court chapel. It is interesting, particularly with regard to the great number of uses to which a violin concerto might be put, that Hiller records that at a Venice opera performance of 1717, at the suggestion of the Elector, Pisendel played a violin concerto (P. 268) by his teacher as interval music. The Dresden National Library, whose large collection of Vivaldi is another indication of the Elector's high opinion of the composer, possesses a Vivaldi concerto in whose Adagio are shown several versions of possible ornamentations. It was Schering's guess that these were Pisendel's, and that perhaps he has thus handed down to us something of his teacher's performing practices.

1716 was also the year of the visit to Venice of Daniel Gottlieb Treu, who followed the fashion of the times by italianizing his name to Fedele. He had been sent to Italy by his employer, the Duke of Würtemberg, for training, and was Vivaldi's pupil for a short time. We have no evidence as to whether Johann David Heinichen, a composer and the author of a much-used textbook on figured bass, who was in Venice in 1715, and the important Bohemian composer Jan Dismas Zelenka, who stayed there from 1716 to 1717, were also personal pupils of Vivaldi; but this may well be inferred from the strong influence of Vivaldi shown in their works.

Aside from two operatic performances in Venice, the year 1718 saw the already mentioned production in Florence, proof enough that Vivaldi's fame as an operatic composer was now spreading outside his native city. From this time on there are no more entries referring to the composer in the books of the Ospedale for several years; his name does not appear again until July 2, 1723. However, in his letter of November 16, 1737, the master himself tells of a stay of several years in Mantua ('I was at Mantua for three years in the service of the exceedingly godfearing prince of Darmstadt'), and on the title page of the libretto for the opera *La Verità in Cimento*, performed in Venice in 1720, Vivaldi for the first time designates himself 'Maestro di Cappella di Camera di S.A. il Sig. Principe Filippo Langravio d'Assia Darmstadt', a title which also appears in publications of the time and was later retained. From this it has long been concluded that he was active in Germany, but this 'Langravio' was not the Prince resident at Darmstadt, but his brother the Margrave Philipp of Hessen-Darmstadt, who had marched into Mantua in 1707 as the general in command of the imperial troops, and had then been in command of the occupation forces in Naples. In 1714 he returned to Mantua as commandant and lived there until the year 1735. Vivaldi's period of work in the service of this prince, whose family is known for its cultivation of music, must have been in the years 1719–22. A Vivaldi opera performed in 1720 at a carnival at the Teatro Arciducale in Mantua may have marked the beginning of his period of service, though it cannot have been too exacting, for during this time the composer had two operas performed in Venice and two more in Vicenza and Milan. A cantata bearing the dedication 'In lode di Monsignor Di Bagno, Vescovo di Mantua' ('To the praise of M.D.B., Bishop of M.') is perhaps another hint as to the time Vivaldi took up work in Mantua. The dedicatee was appointed Archbishop in 1719.

It was during his stay in Mantua that he met the singer Anna Giraud (Italian style: Girò), the daughter of a French barber and apparently born in Mantua, since she was frequently designated 'mantovana' on playbills. In his dealings with Goldoni, Vivaldi referred to her as his pupil, and since a thorough acquaintance with the technique of singing was one of the essential requisites for an Italian opera composer at this time it is quite possible that in Mantua he instructed Anna Giraud in song and dramatic performance, subsequently starting her on a career as an operatic singer. She first appeared in Venice in 1724 in the opera *Laodicea* by Tomaso Albinoni, and contemporary reports describe her as a skilful and intelligent actress with a pleasant, though rather small voice. From 1726 on she was constantly singing leading roles in Vivaldi operas, and in 1737 the composer explained, in the letter we have already cited, 'Far l'opera senza la Girò non è possibile, perchè non si può ritrovare simile prima donna' ('It is not possible to perform the opera without Giraud, because no comparable prima donna is to be found'). This artistic relationship was strengthened by a more personal one, for Paolina, a sister of the singer, became the composer's nurse, and both the sisters accompanied him on his travels. Vivaldi's close ties with the two Giraud sisters—who lived at his house in Venice—were, moreover, to give rise later to a reproach from the Church concerning his 'amicizia' with Anna, who in Venice was simply called 'l'amica del prete rosso' ('the friend of the red-haired priest'). There was thus quite a broad scope to the rumours circulated about the composer, of whom it was asserted, amongst other things, that he was a eunuch—a report apparently based on a travel journal by Edward Wright, who in 1720 said of the girls in the Ospedale della Pietà: 'They have a eunuch for their master, and he composes their music'.

It is probable that directly after his work in Mantua Vivaldi performed his opera *Ercole sul Termodonte* in Rome in January 1723, but he appears then to have felt the need to make Venice his permanent home once more. In a resolution of July 2, 1723, there is an evident attempt to make a fresh agreement with the master, the old one having somewhat fallen apart, and all the more so since it was obviously clear that the reputation of the institute very much depended on his presence there. Nevertheless further absences were tacitly taken into account. The informative document reads: 'In order to maintain the esteem the institution has hitherto gained, it is necessary to make provision for the instrumental concerts, and the administrators of the church and the seminary require . . . every month two of the well-known works of the Rev. Antonio Vivaldi, as he has written two for the present festival of this our own church'. An agreement is concluded 'with the afore-mentioned Vivaldi to deliver, as he proposes to do, two concertos every month for the time when he is himself in Venice, and during the time of his absence to send these by messenger if this can be done without any especial increase in the cost of transmission'. The board named a fee of one sequin for each work with the proviso that the composer should direct three or four rehearsals for each performance if he was in Venice. Assuming that Vivaldi actually abode by this contract, from this time on until his departure from the service of the Ospedale alone, he must have written about 400 concertos just for this institution!

In the following years Vivaldi's activities in great musical centres both in Italy and abroad covered a considerable area. In the 1724 carnival he performed two operas in Rome, one of which was heard by Quantz, who tells of the enormous impression the new experience of the composer's style made on the audience. On the occasion of his stay in Rome he also played before the Pope—probably Innocent XIII—and was most graciously received by him. A commission of 1725 to write a Gloria for the wedding of Louis XV of France is evidence of the master's far-reaching fame.

For the years 1725–35 there are again no references to Vivaldi entered in the records of the Ospedale, and the letter of 1737 provides us with the explanation: 'Sono quattordici anni che siamo andati [he is speaking of the Giraud sisters] in moltissime città d'Europa' ('Fourteen years ago we went together to a good many European cities'). Only a few of the stops he made on these travels are known, but Vivaldi himself recounted that he was in Vienna ('sono chiamato a Vienna'—'I have been called to Vienna'). The Emperor Charles VI, who in 1725 had the famous contrapuntal textbook *Gradus ad Parnassum* by his composition teacher, Johann Joseph Fux, printed at his own cost, was not simply a music-lover, but a real connoisseur of the art; indeed he himself directed operatic performances from the harpsichord. He apparently got to know Vivaldi in 1728 in Trieste, on an Italian journey. Despite the tremendous diplomatic tensions at the time, the upshot of which was the Treaty of Seville (1729) followed by the Second Treaty of Vienna (1731), the Emperor found time for lengthy conversations about music with the composer. It was even said in a letter by a contemporary that he spoke more with Vivaldi in two weeks than he did with his ministers in two years. On this occasion the master is said to have been given a large sum of money, a chain and a gold medal and to have been honoured with a knighthood, for which he then expressed his gratitude in the dedication of the twelve violin concertos, Op. IX. Handwritten parts of this work in the Vienna National Library bear the title: *La Cetra / Concerti / Consacrati alla Cesarae Cattolica Real Maestà / Di Carlo VI Imperatore / l'anno 1728*. The work appeared in print the same year in Amsterdam; in the dedicatory preface the composer speaks of the Emperor's 'magnanima protezzione' ('magnanimous protection'). The journey to Vienna must have taken place in the following year, for on September 30, 1729, Vivaldi's father, then seventy-four years old, submitted to the procurators of St. Mark's Cathedral an application for leave, in which we find: ' . . . di star lontano anno uno dal servitio della Ducal Cappella, passando in Germania ad accompagnare un suo figlio' ('to be absent from service in the Ducal Chapel for a year, so as to accompany one of his sons to Germany').

It is possible that on one occasion Vivaldi was also in Munich. An opera that was first performed in Venice in 1716, *La Costanza trionfante degli amori e degli odii*, was in fact dedicated to the court at Munich, and was given there repeatedly in 1718. The Bavarian Elector Charles Albert must certainly have been an especial admirer of Italian music. During three days in January 1725 he heard no less than four operas in Venice, on a further Italian journey he was present on March 26, 1737, at a performance in Verona of Vivaldi's *Catone in Utica*, and in June of the same year he attended a concert at the Ospedale della Pietà.

Entries in orchestral part books to be found in Naples point to a stay in this city too, perhaps in the years 1727–8. After his period in Mantua, Vivaldi must also have obtained other stable positions of service inside Italy from time to time. In the libretto of the opera *Adelaide*, which was performed in Verona at the 1735 carnival, we find the following observation: 'La musica è del signor Don Antonio Vivaldi, maestro di Cappella di S.A.S. il Duca di Lorena e di S.A.S. il Principe Filippo d'Assia Darmstadt' ('The music is by Don Antonio Vivaldi, *maestro di cappella* to His Highness the Duke of Lorraine and to His Highness Prince Philipp of Hessen-Darmstadt'). The Duke of Lorraine was resident in Florence, where Vivaldi's art was in great esteem; indeed in 1727 he had been given the opera commission for the festival production at the re-opening of the Teatro della Pergola.

It is not clear what his relationship was to Count Venceslav Morzin, the heir of the Prince of Hohenelbe, and the dedicatee of Op. VIII. The work appeared in print at the end of 1725; Vivaldi says in the foreword: 'Pensando frà me stesso al lungo corso dè gl'anni, nè quali godo il segnalatissimo onore di servire à V.S.Illma in qualità di Maestro di Musica in Italia . . .' ('When I think of the long succession of years in which I enjoyed the honourable distinction of serving His Highness as *maestro di musica* in Italy . . .'). Perhaps during his stay in Italy Count Morzin was Vivaldi's pupil, but it is also possible that, following a custom of the time, as his *maestro di cappella in absentia*, Vivaldi was furnishing him with compositions. In any case the Morzins were a very musical family, for another branch of it produced the Karl Josef Franz von Morzin who in 1759 appointed the young Haydn as his *Kapellmeister*.

However, that Vivaldi was meanwhile repeatedly in his native city is shown by the performances of no less than eleven operas in the years

1725 to 1735, four of them in the year 1726 alone. Quantz recounts of one of these performances: 'Vivaldi had set to music the operas of the S. Angelo Theatre, and was himself the leader of his orchestra.' We also have a report of a festival concert in Venice in the year 1727 with the performance of a Te Deum he had composed and which he conducted.

From 1735 on Vivaldi was again active at the Ospedale, and again the administrators tried to come to a workable arrangement. However, the tone of the documents changes and it appears that Vivaldi had not only caused much dissatisfaction but also no longer met with the same respect as he had commanded in a similar situation twelve years before. He was required to supply concertos and compositions for all sorts of instruments, but also to be present with 'dovuta frequenza' ('due frequency') in order to ensure a good performance of his works. He was reproachfully reminded of his many journeys during the previous years.

A short time afterwards Vivaldi encountered a fateful blow. While he was busy with preparations for the staging of an opera in Ferrara, he was called before the Papal Nuncio on November 16, 1737, and by order of Cardinal Ruffo was forbidden to be artistically active in Ferrara, which at that time was in Papal territory, 'e ciò stante essere io religioso che non dice messa, e perchè ho l'amicizia con la Girò cantatrice' ('and this because I am a priest who does not say mass, and because I have the friendship of the singer Giraud'. Letter of November 16, 1737). In the first place, the ban hit Vivaldi hard in respect of his finances, for as an impresario he was bound by his signed contracts; but he must frankly have found this decree a crushing blow in a personal sense, quite irrespective of the nature of his connection with Anna Giraud. It is possible that it was a case of one of those professional intrigues so common in theatrical life having taken on a guise of moral concern and having somehow come to the attention of high ecclesiastical dignitaries. In any case the ban was an eloquent witness to Vivaldi's declining repute as a musician, for he was now no longer excused for certain peculiarities of his way of life which, even according to the notions of the eighteenth century, were hardly compatible with holy orders. On the same day Vivaldi wrote from Venice to his patron in Ferrara, described his plight, explained himself eloquently and asked him to use his influence in getting the ban lifted. However, since the performance did not take place, the Church authorities must have stood firm by their decision, though without subjecting Vivaldi to an investigation and without in any way restricting his future activities; for shortly afterwards he travelled to Amsterdam, his publisher's city, where he had been invited to direct theatrical performances when the

Stadtschouwburg celebrated the centenary of its existence. On this occasion Vivaldi conducted a festival programme on January 7, 1738, with an opera and a cantata of homage by other composers, and opening with a large-scale work given in the programme as 'C. gr. à 10 stromenti del sign. Vivaldi'. Again in the year 1738 there were two performances of Vivaldi's operas in Venice; and it is probable that in 1739 Ferdinand of Bavaria, a brother of the Elector, heard in Venice the scenic cantata *Mopso*, described in the sub-title as 'egloga pescatoria' ('fisherman's idyll'). On this occasion the brilliant playing of the orchestra was admired and Vivaldi was fittingly honoured.

In the years 1738–40 there was also the visit of the Elector Friedrich Christian of Saxony to Venice, where on March 21, 1740, he graced the Ospedale della Pietà with his presence. A volume in the Saxon National Library in Dresden, containing three concertos and a sinfonia, bears witness to this event. The title reads: *Concerti con molti Istrumenti Suonati dalle Figlie del Pio Ospitale della Pietà avanti Sua Altezza Reale Il Serenissimo Federico Christiano Principe Reale di Polonia et Elettorale di Sassonia. Musica di D. Antonio Vivaldi Maestro de Concerti dell'Ospitale Sudetto. In Venezia nell'anno 1740* ('Concertos with many instruments played by the girls of the merciful Ospedale della Pietà in the presence of His Royal Highness the most serene Friedrich Christian, the Royal Prince of Poland and Elector of Saxony. Music by D. Antonio Vivaldi, conductor at the above-mentioned hospital. Venice, 1740'). However, his relationship with the institution seems to have gradually become so poor that it did not appear desirable to remain there any longer. In addition to the master's frequent absences, stylistic considerations must also have played their part in the decision. Charles de Brosses, who in 1739 became a close friend of Vivaldi, wrote from Venice about him on August 29: 'To my great surprise I found that he is not so highly regarded as he deserves to be in this country, where everything follows the fashions, where his works have been heard for too long a time, and where last year's music is no longer box-office.' In the Ospedale the works of more recent masters were cultivated too, and Vivaldi was constantly held up for comparison with the younger generation in his own house, as it were, which is shown by entries in the account books: one dated January 16, 1735, concerns a payment made to Tartini for his sonatas, Op. I, and on October 10, 1741, 72 lire were paid to one Alfonso di Franza 'for music from Paris'.

At any rate, Vivaldi took his leave of the Ospedale in 1740, and his name appears for the last time in the *notatorio* on August 29. His financial situation must have already been in a sorry state at this time, for on leaving he sold a series of concertos, receiving 15 ducats and 13 lire for 3 concertos and 1 sinfonia on April 27, 70 ducats and 23 lire for 20 concertos on May 12 and 1 ducat per concerto on selling 'a great number of concertos' on August 29.

These were really mean prices in view of the fact that the terms of the 1723 agreement had stipulated he should receive 1 sequin per concerto. If he had not urgently needed the money for his travel preparations he would surely never have agreed to such a fee.

It is not known when Vivaldi left Venice or what route he took. It is probable that he turned immediately to Vienna, where his old patron Charles VI lived. But circumstances were clearly not propitious. The Emperor's death in October led to the War of Austrian Succession, which immediately claimed all the country's forces. There was not the remotest possibility of developing any kind of lucrative artistic activity, nor even of a post. Then Vivaldi was probably prevented by illness from possibly making another journey to Dresden and trying his luck at the court of Saxony. Only since 1938 has it been known that the composer died in Vienna in 1741. The following passage is from the manuscript *Memoirs* of Gradenigo: 'The *abbate* D. Antonio Vivaldi, the incomparable violinist, known as the red-haired priest, highly esteemed for his concertos and other compositions, earned at one time more than 50,000 ducats, but because of his immoderate prodigality died a pauper in Vienna'.* Taking a lead from this, Rudolfo Gallo did some on-the-spot research and found entries in the necrology and account books of St. Stephen's relative to Vivaldi's death and obsequies:

28th ditto (= July 1741)
The Very Reverend Mr. Antonj Vivaldi, Secular Priest, in Satler's house by the Karner gate, in the Hospital Burial Ground, *Kleingleuth* (poor-bells) (Vienna, Cathedral and Metropolitan Parish of St. Stephen, necrology, Vol. 23, fol. 63)

Vivaldi's funeral train | the 28th July
The Very Reverend Mr. Antonj Vivaldi, Secular Priest, died, according

---

* In the supplement to the large edition of his book (p. 292 f.) Pincherle has dealt with the question of Vivaldi's income in different currency denominations and in the context of unsteady market-values. Even if Gradenigo's figure is certainly extremely approximate, careful reckoning of Vivaldi's income from his employment and from his works shows a sum which, if translated into a monthly figure, represents about fifty times as much as his father's pay as a violinist in the Cathedral orchestra.

to the coroner's verdict, of an internal inflammation in Satler's house
by the Karner gate, aged 60 years, in the Hospital Burial Ground.*

Kleingleuth	2.36
Curates	3.—
Pall	2.15
Parish emblem	−.30
Burial site	2.—
Gravedigger and Sexton	1.15
Sacristan	−.30
6 Pallbearers	4.30
6 Storm lanterns	2.—
6 Choirboys	−.54
Bier	−.15
	19.45

Pelican

(Vienna, Cathedral and Metropolitan Parish of St. Stephen, necrology,
Vol. 23, fol. 63)

In the context of the times, this could only have been a pauper's burial.
According to eighteenth-century Viennese burial customs we may take
the date of his death to have been the 26th or 27th of July. The house
in which Vivaldi died no longer exists. Its site was in the space between
Ring, Kärntnerstrasse, Krügerstrasse and Walfischgasse and was de-
molished in 1858 when work was started on Ringstrasse. The Hospital
Burial Ground too was taken over on this occasion.

* Der Wohl Ehrwürdige Herr Antonj Vivaldi, Weltl. Priester, ist im Satlerisch Haus
beym Karner thor an Innrem Brand bschaut worden, alt 60 Jahr, im Spitaller gottsacker.

IN MEMORIA DI MAVRO FOÀ
I GENITORI

IN MEMORIA DI RENZO GIORDANO
I GENITORI

II. Vignettes from the Foà and Giordano collections in the Turin National Library
showing Mauro Foà and Renzo Giordano.

III. Vincenzo Coronelli (d. 1718), Veduta della Riva degli Schiavoni con la regata (Venice, Museo Correr). The second identified building from the left was Vivaldi's place of work; the 'Chiesa della Pietà e della Visitazione' to be found there today is the work of Giorgio Massari (1745). It was consecrated in 1760.

BACKGROUND AND
PERSONALITY

Anyone who has seen the palaces of the old Venetian aristocratic families in the evening light on the Grand Canal, anyone who has stood on the church tower of the Isola S. Giorgio and taken in the view over the Riva dei Schiavoni, the Cathedral and St. Mark's Square and beyond, as far as the wide ramifications of the system of canals; anyone, finally, who has known the simply immeasurable artistic riches of the Doge's Palace, can have an idea of how strong must have been the formative influence of a city like Venice, at the height of its truly glorious history, on the spiritually and artistically receptive mind of a maturing composer. But the wealth of splendid works of architecture, painting, sculpture and the very different branches of artistically formative handicrafts, all crowded together into such a small space as if by a miracle, was no gift from Heaven; over a thousand years of extremely hard, tenacious work was necessary to create it all. When in 453 Attila led his Huns down from the Friulian plateau towards the alluring South, the wretched fishing settlements on the not very accessible islands of Veneto were hardly a target for bold conquerors. It was to there that inhabitants of the mainland withdrew again and again to seek sanctuary in the turmoil of mass migration, and finally became settlers, founding small townships that were under the leadership of maritime tribunals, as a protectorate first of the Lombards, then of the Byzantine rulers of Ravenna. After their amalgamation, a 'duca'—called in the Venetian idiom a Doge—was chosen for the first time in 697; after the experience of hard-fought struggles for power between the Franks and Byzantium the site of the young community was transferred to the 'Rivo alto', later to become the Rialto, and there, with pile-construction of great technical accomplishment, the first houses of the new town were built.

Its constitution as a republic of noblemen with a Doge who was elected for life, and with strong supervising corporations, was a masterstroke of political shrewdness, on the one hand offering to capable offspring of trustworthy families the highest governmental positions and on the other hand minimizing the danger of unsettling state affairs through the incompetence of any individual in power by virtue of descent, or through irresponsible ambitiousness. The inner strength it had thus gained repeatedly served it in good stead in later conflicts with pirates, Turks, rival cities and popes. Besides the dogate a second stabilizing pillar in the political and cultural development of the city was the bishopric whose see was the state church of San Marco; the effect of this was particularly beneficial to musical life, rescuing it from the whims and caprices of absolutist political thought, to which it was often enough enslaved in France, Germany and England. The office of *maestro di cappella* at St. Mark's was soon one of the leading positions in European musical life; the greatest organists presided over the organ in Venice; the Cathedral's choir and orchestra provided a large number of good musicians, with the opportunity for artistic activity; the city became a centre for the making of extremely valuable musical instruments and was for centuries the home of important music printers and publishers. Names like those of Adrian Willaert, the Netherlander engaged in 1527 as *maestro di cappella* of St. Mark's Cathedral, of his successors, of the famous theoretician Gioseffo Zarlino and the operatic composer Claudio Monteverdi, of the organist-composers Claudio Merulo, Andrea and Giovanni Gabrieli, of the printers Petrucci, Gardano, Vincenti, Amadino, Magni, Sala, of the violin makers of Vivaldi's time, Matteo Gofriller (1670–1742), Domenico Montagnana (1683–1756), Francesco Gobetti (1690–1749), Petrus Guarnerius (1695–1762) and Santo Seraphin (1699–1744): all these bear witness to the wealth of the city's musical life.

Soon, alongside fishing, shipping and trade became a main preoccupation of the inhabitants of the city that, since its establishment as a community of settlements, had been named Venegia, or Venezia; this was a result of its situation by the sea—at the same time open and sheltered.

The treasures of the Orient had indeed been prized in all Europe, particularly since the crusades, and presented very profitable trading opportunities. For centuries Venice was the chief port of reshipment for commercial trade with the cities of the Eastern Mediterranean. The history of the second Crusade shows how they looked after their interests in a way that was coolly calculating and completely untroubled by ideological considerations. When they were asked to put their fleet at the disposal of the crusaders as a means of transport across the sea, the latter had first to pay their fare, as it were, by conquering for the fleet's owners the town of Zara in Dalmatia, an old rival for their maritime trade. Then, while the army of crusading knights was fighting in the Holy Land, the Venetians made use of the intervening time to settle trade agreements and to extend their business relations. The space left on board ship by the heavy casualties of the Crusade was filled with cargo, and they returned home after their enterprise having taken possession of Corfu, Crete and part of Peloponnesus as additional bases for their extensive commerce. Their possessions in the Mediterranean and in the East were then complemented by a further expansion on the mainland towards the Alps so as to secure a route to the Central European trade area. However, all these footholds, and above all those in the East, could only be conquered and maintained with great difficulty and constant struggles. Victories at sea, like that of Lepanto in 1571—celebrated in St. Mark's with great splendour and with music by Andrea Gabrieli written to a government commission—repeatedly safeguarded Venetian possessions for some time. However, gradually their powers of self-assertion began to wane proportionately as the onslaught of younger nations increased. After the Peace of Passarowitz in 1737, Venice lost the best part of her East Mediterranean possessions despite a successful war record; and during the altercations over the Spanish succession, which brought the French, the Germans and the Spaniards to Italy, the Republic of the Doges was no more than a powerless bystander. Apparently Vivaldi followed the political developments with deep concern and he reveals to us his thinking as a Venetian patriot in a dedication, that of his opera *Adelaide* (1735) to the 'Capitano' and 'Vice Podestà' of Verona, Antonio Grimani. Here we read: 'It was really fitting to dedicate this drama to a Patrician of Venice, since the period of history in which the action is set could only give great displeasure to a good Italian—one who, unlike so many today, is not an enemy of his nation. It will remind him of how, after the expulsion of the last Italian kings, poor Italy went to ruin, no longer able, under foreign domination, to free herself of this most deplorable misfortune. Our only relative consolation for this was the renowned Republic of Venice, in which the freedom of Italy has been maintained from its founding up to the present day, and may God uphold it till the end of time . . .' The urgent, flowing language of this dedication makes quite a contrast with the style of those addressed to dynasts! Vivaldi's ardent wish was indeed only to be fulfilled more than a hundred years later with the Risorgimento, in which Verdi was to play such an important role. In the decades of Italian political powerlessness that followed Vivaldi's death, Venice too led only an unreal existence, losing her political independence in somewhat infamous circumstances when Napoleon entered Northern Italy, and becoming a part first of the Cisalpine Republic and then of the Austro-Hungarian Dual Monarchy.

Vivaldi's work still falls into the last great period of the city's splendour, whose especial artistic glorification was expressed by the architecture of Massari and the paintings of Tiepolo and Canaletto, all of whom received commissions, some from the government, but some also from wealthy families of noblemen, merchants and shipowners. Besides Legrenzi and Pollaroli, the musical directors at St. Mark's, the composers Lotti and Gasparini worked at the Cathedral. Venetian theatrical life was just as important as the cultivation of *musica sacra* and the extensive concert activities of the orphanages where music was practised. The theatre of San Cassiano, erected in 1637 and in fact one of the first opera houses open to the public, was soon followed by others, mostly named after the neighbouring churches, according to which parish they were situated in. At the end of the seventeenth century there were no less than fourteen theatres in existence, of which seven mounted operas exclusively and a further three occasionally. There was fierce artistic competition between them and they could only successfully hold their own if they continuously offered the public new works by the leading composers.

Antonio Vivaldi, at an early age, was introduced by his father to this world whose musical culture in the Church, in theatres, in concerts and in private circles was so abundant. After his tonsure, which could be received at the age of fourteen in Italy at that time, the training of a young priest certainly cannot have prevented Antonio too much from pursuing intensive musical studies and also taking part in the manifold musical life of Venice. In any case, before his ordination as a priest, Vivaldi must have already had a good reputation as a violinist, for otherwise his engagement at the Ospedale della Pietà would be inexplicable. His first published concertos, Op. III, contain many whose antiphonal conception and layout suggest that prior to this engagement, and perhaps even afterwards too, he had worked as a composer for the orchestra of St. Mark's and had been creatively stimulated by the artistic potentialities of this fine ensemble as well as by constant familiarity with its members.

After a few years of peaceful and concentrated work in the musical seminary, public success as a musical director and far-reaching recognition as a composer were quick to follow. But then, just at the time when Vivaldi's music was creating a stir abroad and Roger's offers were coming in, the young master turned to opera and soon became highly rated and sought after in this field too, particularly in his native Venice. In this diversification of his activities Vivaldi began to show certain traits of character that were to be emphatically remarked upon by many visitors to Venice. Thus de Brosses wrote in 1739: 'Vivaldi became my intimate friend so as to sell me some concertos at a very high price. In part he succeeded; but I too got what I wanted, which was to hear him and to have frequent hours of good musical recreation . . .' But as early as 1715 Herr von Uffenbach recorded in his journal: 'After dinner Vivaldi, the famous composer and violinist, came to my home, as I had sent him frequent invitations, and I spoke to him about some concerti grossi that I would like to have from him, and ordered the same from him, also having him sent a few bottles of wine because he was one of the Cantores.' Already three days later Vivaldi went to see Uffenbach again, bringing with him ten concertos, and explaining that he had composed them expressly for him (in three days!), and offering his services as violin teacher so as to introduce his client to the style of the works. This business acumen and this ability to keep one's ear to the ground were pronounced characteristics of many eighteenth-century composers, and can be explained by the particular conditions affecting the musical market. In fact the music-publishing trade, which was beginning to be really big business just around 1700, relied heavily on composers' lack of legal rights over their own works. For example, the pieces of Vivaldi's that the important English publishing house of Walsh and Hare in London had brought out were certainly no more than pirated editions, and the composer got nothing from them. Once he had let a work out of his hands he had to contend, unprotected by law, with all kinds of misappropriation of his creative property—a concept, however, which still meant nothing in those days. It is more than once recorded that copyists were bribed in order to get works cheaply, indeed that rival publishers even did this in order to bring out an edition in advance of the rightful first edition. In such a situation a composer had to discover how to assure his material existence by means of his creations, and no less a man than Beethoven had a masterly understanding of how to solve this problem at a time when the foundations of appropriate legislation were gradually beginning to be laid. Thus when Vivaldi tried to sell his works directly to foreign visitors at the highest possible prices, we can understand only too well that he was adapting himself to circumstances and taking the obvious advantage of possibilities presented to him. Then, when the composer had moved into the milieu of operatic impresarios, prima donnas and ballerinas and finally himself became, to use Uffenbach's term, an 'entrepreneur', his skill in dealing with money matters seems to have become much greater. He once turned down an opera commission for the San Cassiano theatre in Venice because he would have received only ninety sequins instead of a hundred. However it was also probably a question of prestige: a composer could not afford to be compared unfavourably with colleagues who were well remunerated. From his letter about the Ferrara affair we know what sort of sums were involved when Vivaldi himself was the contractor. For the performance which did not take place he had incurred contractual liabilities in the region of 6,000 sequins—enough to pay a composer for sixty operas! From a modern point of view it seems incomprehensible that a priest, working as a composer, could become so deeply involved in the often very shady world of the impresario. However, as we know from the life of Handel, in the long run it was apparently the only possible thing for an opera composer to take the business into his own hands, not only to guarantee the quality of the performance to a certain extent, but also to protect himself against all sorts of exploitation. 'I cannot perform the opera without being there myself, because I do not wish to entrust to anyone else so great a sum'; this is what Vivaldi himself said on the subject. If a composer or a virtuoso neglected to look after his economic interests in good years, or if he lacked the necessary skill to do this, then he could be sure of a fate such as Mozart's!

For all his talent in financial affairs Vivaldi was in no way miserly; on the contrary he had a certain inclination for the grand style of living, though even with his high level of income he could not indulge in it for ever. Gradenigo has alluded to 'sproporzionata prodigalità' (immoderate prodigality) and Vivaldi himself stated that journeys were expensive for him because, on account of his illness, he always had to be accompanied by four or five people, two of whom, for the whole of fourteen years, were the Giraud sisters.

It was just this relationship—both artistically and personally intimate—of the composer with the leading interpreter of his stage works that then unleashed the catastrophe which must have struck at the roots of the ageing master's existence. 'After such a heavy blow Your Excellency can imagine my situation,' Vivaldi complained in his letter of November 16, 1737. Then he went on to explain how he had been absolved from saying mass because of his illness, and had not again taken up his duty. In fact this same part of the letter, in which he defended himself against the reproaches of the Papal Nuncio, does not read very convincingly. The composer's ecclesiastical superiors, certainly inclined to generosity of mind as was appropriate to eighteenth-century Venetian mores, had apparently noticed for a long time already that the master, allegedly so ill, was giving concerts as a violinist, that he was active as an impresario and that not only did he prepare his operatic performances down to the last detail but he also even directed them from the leader's desk or the harpsichord. Here we find a distinct discrepancy which has appeared to both posterity and his contemporaries as a very dark stain on the composer's character. On the other hand, however, the fact that Vivaldi's work at the Ospedale was markedly a work of charity as well as of education must be taken into account. It may be supposed that at least in the first place he was in complete agreement with the Church authorities, when his interests turned more and more to music. At a time when instrumental music played a part much larger than is imaginable today in church worship, not only the master's liturgical music but also his concertos are to be largely regarded as artistic contributions to the divine service.

In contrast with many features of a very mundane way of life, Carlo Goldoni in his memoirs, with great literary charm and point, ascribed to Vivaldi a piety which is also corroborated by Gerber. The latter goes so far as to say that the ageing composer was extraordinarily bigoted and that his rosary was only out of his hands when he was composing. The meeting between the twenty-eight-year-old Goldoni and Vivaldi is interesting for several reasons. He had been commissioned to arrange Apostolo Zeno's libretto for the opera *Griselda* in accordance with the composer's wishes, and went to see the latter at his home.

'I found him surrounded by scores, his breviary in his hand. He rose, made the sign of the cross with broad gestures, put his breviary down and made me the usual compliments: "To what do I owe the pleasure of seeing you, Signore?"—"His Excellency Grimani has commissioned me to make the alterations in the opera for next season. I have come, Signore, to acquaint myself with your intentions."—"Ah! Ah! You, Signore, have been entrusted with the alterations in the opera *Griselda*? Is Signor Lalli no longer associated with Signor Grimani's productions?" —"Signor Lalli, who is already very old, will still enjoy the profits from the dedicatory letters and the sales of the libretto, which I do not trouble myself with. I shall have the pleasure of an enjoyable job and the honour of starting out under the directives of Signor Vivaldi." (The *abbate* took up his breviary again, once more made the sign of the cross and did not answer.) "Signore," I said to him, "I should not like to disturb your religious observances; I had better come back some other time."—"I well know, my dear sir, that you have a talent for poetry; I have read your *Belisario*, and it gave me a great deal of pleasure; but this is something quite different; one may be quite capable of writing a tragedy, or if you like an epic poem, and still not be able to compose a musical quatrain."—"Do me the honour of showing me your drama." —"Yes, with pleasure . . . where has that *Griselda* got to, it was here . . . Deus in adiutorium meum intende, Domine . . . Domine . . . Domine . . . it was here just now. Domine ad adiuvandum . . . Ah, there it is. You see here, Sir, this scene between Gualtiero and Griselda; it is an interesting and moving scene. The author has put a pathetic aria at the end; but Madamigella Giraud does not like such languid songs and would like an expressive, agitated piece, an aria which expresses passions in different ways, with disconnected words, for example, and with sighs, with action, with movement; I don't know if you understand me."—"Yes, Signore, I understand very well; but I have had the honour of hearing Madamigella Giraud, and know that her voice is not very strong . . ."—"What, Sir, you insult my pupil? She is good at everything and sings everything."—"Yes, Sir, you are right; let me have the libretto and I can get to work on it."—"No, Sir, I cannot let it go, I need it, I am extremely pressed."—"Very well, Sir, if you are pressed lend it to me for a moment and I shall do what you want right away."—"Right away?"—"Yes, Sir, right away."

The *abbate* laughed at me, handed me the drama, gave me paper and ink. Then he took his breviary again, walked up and down and recited his hymns and psalms. I read the scene again, for I already knew it, made a résumé of what the composer wanted, and in less than a quarter of an hour worked out on the paper an aria of eight lines divided into two parts. I called the priest and showed him my work. Vivaldi read it, wrinkled his brow, read it again, uttered cries of joy, threw his breviary to the floor and called Madamigella Giraud. She came: "Ah!" he said, "here is a rare man; he is an excellent poet: read this aria: and this gentleman has composed it, here on the spot, in less than a quarter of an hour." And turning to me, he said: "Ah! I beg your forgiveness"; and he embraced me and swore to me that he would never henceforth avail himself of any other poet. He entrusted me with the drama and commissioned me to make other alterations. He remained satisfied with me, and the work succeeded in a marvellous way. It was thus that I was introduced to opera, to comedy and to intermezzi that were the precursors of the Italian *opera buffa*.'

The famous poet of the Italian comic theatre has here given us a living portrait of the composer just as we encounter him also in his works:

lively, impulsive, sparkling with ideas, and always surrendering himself to the moment and its demands. In Goldoni's report, the music, the breviary, the opera libretto and Anna Giraud form an inner unity which appears just as essential to the composer's personality as it is to his compositions.

The far-reaching effect of his works, being printed in Amsterdam, Paris and London, the cultivation of his music in the most important cities of Italy and abroad, the numerous proofs of the highest recognition, all these things instilled in Vivaldi a great degree of self-esteem, all the more so since he had sprung from modest circumstances and owed his success simply and solely to intensive work centred around the Ospedale. When in his 1737 letter he adduces all the grounds he has for his exoneration, he can proudly say 'These truths are known in almost all of Europe' and declare without any presumption: ' . . . I have the honour to be in correspondence with nine high princes, and my letters travel throughout all Europe'. It says much for the inner resilience of a man who for all his life had been in poor health that, dealt such a heavy blow by fate at the age of sixty, he took the decision to abandon his ungrateful homeland and once more try his luck abroad.

THE WORK

SYNOPSIS AND TABULATION

In the broadest circles of connoisseurs and amateurs Antonio Vivaldi is known only as a composer of concertos. Yet his work embraces all the musical genres, extending from sonatas for melodic instruments with figured bass to oratorios and operas. As a first approach to the authenticated complete works, which run to about 825 compositions, we shall be best served by a numerical categorization according to large groups, more precise details being discussed in the chapters which deal with individual musical genres.

In the case of Vivaldi's works several reasons make it impossible to give precise figures, because the individual musical genres are not always exactly defined or definable, so that their designation too may vary. Thus there are works in two or more copies bearing different titles, for example two sinfonias in the Dresden collection, one of which is entitled 'Concerto' in Turin and the other in Schwerin. A concerto in the Turin collection (P. 360) has the title 'Sonata' in Dresden. We have other works in several versions, many of which, however, differ so much from each other that they should really be regarded and counted as independent compositions, and particularly so when they have only one movement in common. We must also distinguish between authenticated works and those that have been preserved. In fact we know of the existence of a whole series of Vivaldi works from various sources, without having the works themselves. Thus five sinfonias are known only from a list of manuscript scores that were put up for sale in 1762 by the publishers Breitkopf and Härtel in Leipzig. Moreover the thematic catalogues of the important collector Aloys Fuchs, drawn up in the first half of the last century, include works of Vivaldi which have since disappeared. We can name most of the operas only from the librettos or from mentions of performances.

THE WORK

The present state of research yields the following figures, some of which, however, may only be taken as approximate:

	Authenticated	Preserved in their entirety
Sonatas	78	76
Sinfonias	21*	16
Concertos	456	445
Other instrumental works	1	1
Stage works	48	14
Separate arias	c.100	c.100
Secular cantatas	59	58
Oratorios	2	1
Other sacred vocal works	60	57

The tabulation of Vivaldi's works presents a very special problem. For the period before the discovery of the Durazzo collection the *Thematic Catalogue of the Printed Works of Antonio Vivaldi* prepared by Wilhelm Altmann was sufficient, and could only be complemented by the library catalogues of Dresden, Paris, Schwerin, and other depositories of Vivaldi's works. The first inventory of the Turin findings was drawn up in 1936 by Olga Rudge, the secretary of the Accademia Chigiana in Siena. In spite of many errors, this catalogue is still valuable today, because it contains the opening of each movement. A further attempt by Mario Rinaldi can be described as a complete write-off, for which the difficulties of wartime conditions can only partly be held responsible, for they cannot explain the number of works not included, nor those which have two entries. Moreover Rinaldi continued the numbering of the works in the manner of those printed in the composer's lifetime, in this way reaching Opus 319— leaving space in the middle for works yet to be discovered—and thus gave rise to the impression of a chronological ordering. Antonio Fanna, director of the 'Istituto Italiano Antonio Vivaldi' then undertook for the complete edition published by Ricordi a numbering by types of ensemble, designating them by roman numerals. The individual works within such a group were numbered in arabic figures (Survey of Group Ordering in 'Antonio Vivaldi', Indice tematico . . ., Ricordi).

Finally, as the second part of his great work on the composer, Marc Pincherle prepared a thematic catalogue of the instrumental works (*Inventaire thématique*), which for the first time grouped these into sonatas, sinfonias and concertos. The concertos were listed according to tonality, major keys always being linked with their relative minor. Since the works

* Excluding sinfonias used in operas as overtures, entr'actes or other interludes.

printed before Vivaldi's death are also treated separately, and comparative tables are appended, Pincherle's catalogue, in which only slight errors and a relatively small number of inaccuracies remain, provides an excellent survey. Above all his numbering has also established itself extensively in the recording industry, and it guarantees an unexceptionable means of identification for the works. Since no less than 220 violin concertos by Vivaldi have been preserved and 95 of these are in C major and A minor, an exact form of designation is absolutely necessary.

THE DEVELOPMENT OF INSTRUMENTAL MUSIC IN THE SEVENTEENTH CENTURY

In musical history, the seventeenth century was not only the first century of the development of opera, but beyond that owed its special lustre to a hitherto inconceivable flowering of instrumental music, which in its further development formed the basis of the classical symphony. It is symptomatic that neither of the two great masters of the beginning of the century, Monteverdi and Schütz, left a single purely instrumental work, whilst at the end of the century it is possible to find composers like Torelli and Corelli, who left hardly any vocal works. The consequence of this marked shift from vocal to instrumental music was a profusion of radical changes. At the time of the two Gabrielis instrumental ensemble-playing was very dependent on the practice of vocal music, pieces were taken over from the sphere of the madrigal and the chanson, and the orchestral canzone and ricercar were developed, forms which pointed the way to the later fugue. With the gradually increasing independence of the singing voice, the text lost its importance as a form-generating element. From then on a continually more concentrated language of motifs established itself, and more and more pronounced attempts were made to articulate form from harmonic principles. Only in this way was it possible to give an autonomous existence to the 'Sonada', which had originally been rather a curiosity, presented alongside vocal music.

Completely new tasks of dramatic portrayal and presentation of the most diversified spiritual moods were then given to instruments in the opera, which in 1600 was coming into existence. In its early years this form was entirely at the service of court theatres; in Mantua, Monteverdi could draw on the richest resources and develop an orchestra which had a magnificent range of colours. However, when in the 1630s operatic performances became accessible to the public and impresarios put the theatre onto a primarily commercial basis, a certain standardization of means proved essential. The string orchestra with first and second violins, violas and basso (= violoncello, double bass and harpsichord) became the nucleus of the orchestra, expanded by two oboes (or flutes) and bassoon, and for hunting, martial or ceremonial scenes by horns, trumpets and kettledrums. In these decades the series of dance movements which was already common in lute music was also taken over gradually by wind and string ensembles, at first in such groupings as contingencies permitted, and then more and more by the string orchestra.

The reduction of Monteverdi's orchestra to an only slightly enlarged string band was certainly an acoustical impoverishment, but it benefited the development of instrumental genres and forms to an enormous extent. Out of the canzone, so rich in contrasts, and in liturgical usage performed in excerpts, grew the church sonata, by a gradual process in which its parts became autonomous; these sonatas were cultivated in all the different groupings of instruments, from solo violin with figured bass to the full orchestra: a solemn introductory movement was followed by an Allegro—generally in fugato style—and a similar pair of movements formed the conclusion. The secular counterpart of this 'Sonata da chiesa' was the 'Sonata da camera', or Suite, whose basic type was mostly in four movements, but which could be expanded at will. The combination of dances changed with the fashion, for which the French court soon became the model. If at first the two types of sonata were carefully differentiated from each other, there gradually came about an assimilation and intermingling. In chamber works, striving for a more opulent shaping of the music, composers took over the fugato style and arioso melody, whereas in instrumental compositions for the Church, short dance movements were occasionally smuggled in, though usually without being designated as such.

With advances in the field of playing technique, however, the soloistic element in musical types and forms became more and more prominent. The interest of composers, at first engaged above all with the trumpet, very soon turned to the violin, which, after initial deprecation as an itinerant musician's instrument, had become the prima donna of the string orchestra. Since the creative musicians were themselves for the most part violinists, their style of writing, which had originally been derived from vocal style, became more and more permeated with figurations that came naturally to them from the violin. They developed a genuinely instrumental style whose motifs were largely determined by the technical possibilities of string instruments. When, at the great religious and secular festivals, where orchestral music was played, the 'professori' (professional musicians) performed in their capacity as permanently appointed virtuosos of their instrument alongside amateur musicians who had been called on to augment the performing forces, the practice was soon evolved of letting only soloists play technically difficult passages, and even echo-like repetitions of formal sections. Thus a small ensemble, the 'concertino', was juxtaposed with the main part of the orchestra, and the 'concerto grosso' was born. This was not a form, but rather a musical practice or a mode of instrumentation, and was used in church compositions as well as in suites. Corelli's much-played twelve concerti grossi, Op. VI, first printed in 1714 but already heard singly by Muffat more than thirty years previously in Rome, were models for a whole generation of composers.

However, it was not enough for the 'Maestro de' concerti' to play as a soloist in the context of the concertino—usually consisting of two violins and figured bass (violoncello and harpsichord). Probably stimulated by the example of the operatic aria, the Bologna church viola player and later *Konzertmeister* at Ansbach, Giuseppe Torelli, wrote works for one soloist and string orchestra, and in so doing made use of a formal framework that had already proved itself in the operatic aria: an orchestral part formed the introduction and returned after the solo sections as an interlude and postlude; it was called a ritornello, after the Italian word *ritornare* (= return). Torelli's Op. VI, printed in Augsburg in 1698, already shows rather tentative probings in this direction, but his Op. VIII, published after the composer's death by his brother Felice in 1709, consists of six fully developed solo concertos and six concertos for two violins, all of which are laid out in accordance with this formal scheme.

These extremely interesting years at the close of a century that had produced so many new forms, while still more were being elaborated, were the years of Vivaldi's youth. With alert intelligence, he took up the influences that were crowding in on him and by the strength of his originality, developed them beyond Corelli and Torelli.

THE SONATAS

If in the sixteenth and early seventeenth century a young composer wished to make a successful professional début, he had to write a book of madrigals which would be to a certain extent a prentice work. Monteverdi and many composers of his generation did this, and Heinrich Schütz, who in Italy called himself Enrico Sagittarius because the Italians found his name unpronounceable, had a 'primo libro de Madrigali' printed in Venice in 1611 as his Op. I, thus honouring the tradition of his hosts. However, at the end of the seventeenth century a composer who wished to make a name for himself had to show his craftsmanship in a dozen trio sonatas. It was in this way that Torelli, Corelli, Albinoni and many others recommended their future works to professional colleagues as well as to music lovers, and Vivaldi too chose this path to present himself in the company of the masters. As his Op. I he brought out twelve 'Sonate da Camera a tre' with Giuseppe Sala of Venice in 1705. It was with these and with his Op. II, the twelve 'Sonate a Violino e Basso per il Cembalo' of 1709, that Vivaldi first became known locally as a composer of sonatas.

The works preserved include 76 sonatas (all with figured bass), which fall into the following categories:

30 violin
10 violoncello
 6 musette (or other instrument)
 2 recorder
 2 oboe
 1 flute
19 2 violins
 2 lute and violin
 1 violin and flute
 1 violin and cello
 1 violin, flute and bassoon
 1 recorder and bassoon

Two further works are known only from their opening bars in catalogues. One sonata classed by Pincherle from the Dresden collection (Qu 9) is designated in the Turin collection as a concerto; the particular problem of works of this kind will be dealt with in the chapter on the chamber concertos. Pincherle's catalogue should also be augmented by a trio sonata, a violin sonata and two cello sonatas of which the Schlossbibliothek at Wiesentheid possesses the only copies, as well as a flute sonata in the Cambridge University Library. P. 441, given as a 'Sonata à quatro' in the manuscript, should probably rather be an orchestral work.

However, the 76 sonatas figure alongside no less than 446 concertos in the Pincherle catalogue, so that the sonatas only occupy a relatively small place in the composer's output. Of these sonatas, 42 appeared in print during Vivaldi's lifetime, and indeed were given opus numbers:

Op. I   12 trio sonatas
Op. II   12 sonatas for violin and continuo

Op. V	4 sonatas for violin and continuo
	2 trio sonatas
Op. XIII	6 sonatas for musette (vielle, flute, oboe, violin)

In addition, Le Clerc of Paris brought out in 1740 six sonatas for cello and continuo without opus number, which perhaps constitute the frequently mentioned Op. XIV, of which no copy has been traced. Of the sonatas not printed in Vivaldi's lifetime there are 16 in Dresden, 8 in Turin, 2 in Naples, and 1 each in Cambridge, Uppsala and Venice as well as the 4 already mentioned in Wiesentheid.

What is striking about the printed sonatas is the large gap between Opp. I/II/V and Opp. XIII/XIV. One's first reaction is to conclude that after a copious production of sonatas during the first period of his career Vivaldi renounced the genre, to take it up again later. However, with Vivaldi one must guard against the assumption that the printed works were composed immediately before their publication. It is much more likely that the sonatas that were not published until towards the end of his life originated from a much earlier date, perhaps even as early as the years in which Opp. I and II were composed. Such a supposition is well backed up by the fact that a manuscript of one of the cello sonatas published in 1740 has been preserved in the castle at Wiesentheid. On the basis of the sources it would not be possible to attempt to present Vivaldi's sonatas in order of composition so as to show his development in that field from the early Op. I up to his mature style.

THE TRIO SONATAS

In the years 1712–13 Vivaldi's Op. I appeared in Amsterdam under the title: *Suonate da Camera / a tre / Due Violini e Violone o Cembalo / di / D. Antonio Vivaldi / Musico di Violino. Professore Veneto / Opera Prima / A Amsterdam / chez Estienne Roger Marchand libraire / no 363.*

In the foreword to his concertos Op. III, printed a short while previously, the composer had said that this work was the first to have the privilege 'of being engraved under the famous hand of Monsieur Estienne Roger', whilst his earlier works had suffered from 'poor printing'. Clearly it follows that Op. I had already appeared in Italy and that it had only been republished by Roger. But it was not until a few years ago that the composer Gian Francesco Malipiero, whose researches and publication of the work of Vivaldi have been of great worth, succeeded in discovering at least a first violin part in the Library of the Venice Conservatoire, and thus in throwing some light on the edition. The composer's comments on

IV. Francesco de' Guardi (1712–1793), gala concert in honour of the Grand Duke Paul and the Grand Duchess Maria Feodorovna in the Sala dei Filarmonici Venice, 1782 (Munich, Pinakothek).

Di D. Antonio Vivaldi Opera Seconda.   C

V. Page 19 of the Italian edition of the Violin Sonatas Op. II (Antonio Bortoli, Venice 1709).

the poor quality of the Italian edition are understandable when we compare a Venetian publication of this time with one of Roger's (see Plates V and VI). The Italians still assembled the staves from single printing stamps and each note with a tail had its own block, separated from the preceding and following ones. Such a procedure was possibly still good enough for older vocal music, but not so for groups of semiquavers and demisemiquavers in instrumental works. Roger was one of the first to join the shorter notes of a basic rhythmical value together with a single beam, and thus, simply by a graphic division of the sequence of notes, made it easier to get a quick idea of the music, facilitating sight-reading. His great commercial successes were not least dependent on these modern printing methods, and allowed him a wide range of activity as a publisher, especially of Italian orchestral and chamber music. Besides this he was the inventor of numbered publications for the convenience of listing and ordering works, for previously the numbers had only served to keep stored printing blocks in order.

Vivaldi's Op. I is generally underestimated, or seen as showing a supposedly marked debt to Corelli's Op. V, the violin sonatas and suites that had appeared in 1700, coming out in the same year in Rome, Amsterdam and London, and certainly well known to Vivaldi. The main pointer to Corelli's influence is the fact that Vivaldi, like the Roman master, included at the end of his dozen works variations on 'Folies d'Espagne', a saraband-like dance that had already enjoyed great popularity in sixteenth-century lute and keyboard music and was in 1700 once more being taken up by various composers. Indeed certain points in Vivaldi's work do seem to show a certain dependence on Corelli, but it is important to point also to the many features having a strongly individual imprint. Whilst Corelli's construction is relatively loose and he attaches little importance to the motivic cohesion between the upper voice and the bass, Vivaldi generally brings into play a concentrated motivic unification, and consequently a concentration of the music's course which marks off the whole of the composer's Op. I from similar compositions of this time. Thus in Variation 3 the two violins are treated as complementary and in contrary motion, and in Variation 4 a truly instrumental leaping motif passes through the voices in the closest sequence (Exx. 1 and 2). This tendency towards motivic technique and combinative methods can also be found in the structure of whole movements; in this respect Vivaldi goes a long way beyond Corelli. Thus for example the Allemanda from the third sonata is divided into eight structural groups, clearly defined by harmonic cadences, and showing abundant motivic interrelations between them.

However, what is important is not these combinative methods themselves, but the musical flow which results from them in a seemingly natural way, never giving the listener the impression of compositional 'working-out'. The high quality of these works as regards their constructive thought and their delight in light, dance-like movement admits of the conclusion that this technique—already highly developed and very thoughtfully handled—was the fruit of long and even extremely productive studies and that Op. I was perhaps a selection from a large number of sonatas written during the composer's youth. Even if one allows for the influence of Corelli's violin sonatas, the way in which the young composer selects from the possibilities offered him and develops them further is extremely characteristic of his musical thought. In retrospect it is quite possible that Vivaldi got to know Corelli's work from copies even before it was printed in 1700.

Furthermore, Vivaldi's Op. I sonatas, with regard to their sequence of movements, occupy an interesting position in the development of the reciprocal influences of the church and chamber sonatas. Here are some examples:

Sonata III	Adagio	Allemanda	Adagio	Sarabanda
		Allegro		Allegro
Sonata IV	Preludio	Corrente	Adagio	Allemanda
	Grave	Allegro		Allegro
Sonata VIII	Preludio	Corrente	Grave	Giga
	Largo	Allegro		Allegro

Whilst in most of the sonatas three dance movements follow the solemn introductory movement, here church and dance movements alternate, and imitative passages in the faster movements further underline the amalgamation of the two types.

THE VIOLIN SONATAS

The twelve sonatas for violin and continuo, Op. II, were dedicated 'a Sua Maestà il Re Federico Quarto di Danimarka e Norvegia' (to His Majesty King Frederick IV of Denmark and Norway) in 1709 on the occasion of his visit to Venice. Unfortunately the foreword tells us nothing about the work or the manner in which it was to be played, but it is a model of that attitude of extreme submissiveness with which such writings were composed. 'Di Vostra Maestà Umilissimo Devotissimo Ossequissimo Servitore Antonio Vivaldi' (Your Majesty's most humble, most devoted, most submissive servant A.V.), the signature reads. The sonatas of Opp. II and V are partly in three movements, and partly in groups of movements similar to those of Op. I:

Sonata III	Preludio	Corrente	Adagio	Giga
	Andante	Allegro		Allegro
Sonata XII	Preludio	Capriccio	Grave	Allemanda
	Largo	Presto		Allegro

The great demands on performing technique, still unusual in works in sonata form of about·1700, are striking in the twelve sonatas of Op. II. It may be supposed that Vivaldi wrote this work in the first place for his own use and gave brilliant concert performances of it in the presence of its dedicatee. A certain kinship with Corelli, for instance between the capriccio-like opening of the latter's first sonata and Vivaldi's second, is unmistakable. But what is also striking about many movements of the Op. II sonatas is the close motivic linking of the upper voice to the bass, which in Corelli one finds only sporadically in the fugato movements. The first movement of Sonata III is an astonishing example of such dovetailing (Ex. 3). This is no longer a 'sonata for solo violin and figured bass', but a genuine duo with two equally important voices, which can very well be given also without any inner harmonic filling-out. The feeling for motivic working and combinative methods evinced in such movements was perhaps a decisive criterion for the formation of the composer's style. Later, in his concertos, Vivaldi seldom bound together the outer voices in such (one might almost say) studious intensity. But once such a technique had been developed, and was constantly present to a certain extent in his musical subconscious, the composer was saved from falling into an excessively slipshod style even at times when he was most hard pressed by commissions.

Vivaldi designated his Op. V as the second part of Op. II ('O Vero Parte Seconda del Opera Seconda'—Or also the second part of Op. II). It contains six sonatas that are numbered 13–18 in conjunction with the twelve sonatas of Op. II. Nos. 13–16 are sonatas for one violin, and Nos. 17 and 18 for two violins and figured bass. Again the following layout of movements is typical:

Sonata 13	Preludio	Corrente	Sarabanda	Giga
	Largo	Presto	Andante	Allegro
Sonata 14	Preludio	Corrente	Gavotte	
	Largo	Presto	Allegro	
Sonata 18	Preludio	Allemanda	Air	Menuetto
	Largo	Allegro		Allegro

Thus they are short suites with a church-sonata-like introductory movement.

It is interesting to find in the thirteenth sonata a melodic type which recurs again and again in Vivaldi's sonatas as in his concertos and which is familiar above all from Corelli's famous Gavotte from his Sonata Op. V, No. 10 on which Tartini wrote his variations *L'Arte del arco* ('The Art of Bowing') (Ex. 4). It is above all in such melodic parallels that Corelli's influence has been thought to be detected. The melodic/harmonic formula $\frac{1}{I} \quad \frac{2}{V_{(6)}} \quad \frac{3}{I}$ was, however, a commonplace of musical vocabulary in around 1700, persisting in many composers' language up to the classical and romantic periods and in no way providing a clue to any particular influence.

THE CELLO SONATAS

As the composer's many cello concertos show, Vivaldi had a particular liking for this instrument. Of the ten sonatas for cello and continuo that have been preserved, six appeared in print in Paris in 1740, two can be found in manuscript in the Naples Conservatoire Library, and two more in that of Schloss Wiesentheid. These works represent the cream of the best cello works of the time and are laid out similarly to the Opp. I, II and V sonatas, with the predominating sequence Largo—Allegro—Largo—Allegro. The Allegro movements of the Paris sonatas have a markedly dance-like character, and in the last sonata the composer has even given them the headings Allemanda/Allegro and Corrente/Allegro. From the formal point of view, too, the fast movements are built like baroque dance-movements: two repeated sections, the first of which modulates into the dominant, whereas the second is itself split up into two parts with a short development-like group and a kind of reprise. The slow movements of the sonatas are distinguished by a far-flung cantabile melodic style, whilst the Allegros contain ideas which proceed with a sort of virtuosity and show an elegant melodic line profusely spiced with syncopations (Exx. 5 and 6). Since nonetheless the cello sonatas are not too demanding from the technical point of view, they represent an admirable introduction for students and amateurs to the baroque concert repertoire and have enjoyed great popularity with cellists since 1916, when they were edited by Chaigneau and Rummel. In 1922 the composer Vincent d'Indy had the unfortunate idea of bringing out an edition of the sonatas 'mises en concert' (made into concertos) for cello and string orchestra, in other words, realizing the basso continuo in an orchestral version. Paul Bazelaire, the distinguished cellist and professor at the Paris Conservatoire, then undertook to do this with the fifth sonata, publishing it as 'Concerto en mi mineur' (Concerto in E minor). To a certain extent, both could be excused at a time when the many original cello concertos of the Turin collection were not yet known. But a whole generation of French cellists, eternally faithful to their teacher, still play the work publicly in Bazelaire's stylistically spurious edition; indeed, Bazelaire and d'Indy have even acquired a posthumous collaborator: a Decca recording (F—128 Hi Fi!) by Pierre Fournier and the Stuttgart Chamber Orchestra under Karl Münchinger is announced on the record sleeve as follows: Concerto in E minor: 1. Largo (Arr. Paul Bazelaire), 2. Allegro (Arr. Vincent d'Indy), 3. Largo (Alla Siciliana), (Arr. Siegfried Barchet), 4. Allegro (Arr. Paul Bazelaire). Neither did the Italian composer Luigi Dallapiccola resist the temptation to arrange the work for soloist and string orchestra. In his edition of the six sonatas, which first appeared in 1955 with the International Music Company, New York City, the fifth carries the annotation: 'The orchestral accompaniment by L.D. for this Sonata is available on rental (Naturally!) from the Publisher.'

Moreover, Dallapiccola's edition for cello and piano is notable for a fundamentally mistaken conception of the realization of the figured bass. In order—as he says in his foreword—to loosen up the texture of the material, the editor has added imitative passages almost throughout, or at the least has laid out the material in three parts with a middle voice having the most independent line possible. However, as a result of the fixing of the harmony by figuring the bass, the bass of a work dating from the era of the basso continuo has a predominantly harmonic function, even compared with its melodic function. A sonata for a melody instrument and figured bass is primarily a two-part piece (Hindemith's 'superposition of two parts'), and in principle the occasional baroque practice of improvised imitation ought not to upset the two-part layout. If a baroque composer wanted to have a three-part work, then he would write a trio sonata! However, the Vivaldi trio sonatas show quite clearly what the composer's conception of a three-part piece was. And if, besides, he laid out his trio sonatas with very little imitative movement except in fugato passages, this was by no means because of any lack of technical accomplishment on his part! As is shown by Ex. 6, Vivaldi kept the bass particularly simple in his cello sonatas' fast movements, so that at many points it acted simply as a rhythmic support. However, rather than being loosened, the material is overburdened by the middle voice, in itself naturally a skilful invention by a composer of Dallapiccola's distinction, and it misses the mark completely in that it detracts from the principal voices (Ex. 7). For the same reasons any arrangement for string orchestra is bound to be a misrepresentation of the composer's conception, even if the arrangement is technically accomplished. The peculiar fate of the six cello sonatas, and particularly of the fifth, in our time, shows how little certain famous composers, virtuosos, conductors and record producers still know of quite elementary basic concepts in the technique of composition and the practice of performance of baroque music. A little bit of true High Fidelity would really be good for the old masters!

THE CONCERTOS

SYNOPSIS

In his thematic catalogue of Vivaldi's instrumental music, Pincherle includes altogether 447 works as concertos. Subsequently he himself was able to identify one of these (P. 447) as a work of Giovanni Battista Sammartini, and another (P. 355) must be based on a confusion with P. 414, and in any case was never in Dresden. Pincherle omits: a Concerto in E♭ major for violin and strings, 'Il Ritiro', in the Conservatoire Library at Naples, and edited by Szabolcsi/Ephrikian; also eight cello concertos and an incomplete oboe concerto, manuscripts of which are in the possession of the Wiesentheid Schlossbibliothek. The total thus becomes 455, a number which might, on account of duplicated designations or versions, be subject to slight variations. Of these works, one can only be verified by reference to an old catalogue; of a further seven, we have only the first movement; and in four others the middle or final movements are lacking, so that in all we have 443 complete concertos by Vivaldi.

After having once ascertained the total number of concertos, it is even more difficult to decide on a system of categorization within these groups according to instrumentation. For example, the Concerto P. 259 is a violin concerto with the proviso: 'Questo Concerto si puo fare ancora cor (= con) l'Hautbois' (This Concerto may also be played on the oboe), and P. 8 is likewise an oboe concerto *ad libitum*. Again in other concertos, orchestral wind instruments are occasionally treated as solo instruments, though they are given too modest a role for the works to be classified as real 'Concerti con molti Istrumenti', whilst in other, similar cases, one might perhaps choose this type of classification. And in those works which exist in a second version for a different solo instrument, it is a matter of opinion whether they should only be classified under the instrument of their original version, or whether they should be listed in the second version as well. A Flute Concerto from Op. X, which is preserved in Turin in an older version for recorder, is here counted under both instruments. Finally the indication 'con Violoncello obligato' may mean the cello as the only solo instrument, but occasionally means that the cello is only used as a supporting bass, appearing in the context of a solo group of higher instruments in the old manner of the concerto grosso. Here there are borderline cases in which a clear decision is scarcely possible. Thus, many of the following numbers should be regarded as only approximate, and should be compared with those given by Pincherle on p. 62 of the larger edition of his book:

	Authenticated	Lost	Incomplete
Concertos without solo instrument	49	—	—
Concertos for solo instrument:			
violin	220	6	2
cello	27	—	—
viola d'amore	6	—	—
mandoline	1	—	—
flautino	3	—	—
recorder	3	—	—
flute	10	—	3
oboe	11	—	1
bassoon	37	—	1
Concertos for two solo instruments:			
2 violins	25	—	—
violin and cello	3	1	—
2 cellos	1	—	—
viola d'amore and lute	1	—	—
2 mandolines	1	—	—
2 flutes	1	—	—
2 oboes	3	—	—
oboe and bassoon	1	—	—
2 trumpets	1	—	—
2 horns	2	—	—
Concertos for three and more solo instruments	32	—	—
Chamber concertos	15	—	—

THE ELEMENTS OF VIVALDI'S CONCERTO STYLE

In 'The Life of Mr. Johann Joachim Quantz, described by himself' which in 1755 appeared in Marpurg's *Historical and Critical Essays on Music* in Berlin, Frederick the Great's flute teacher tells how in his youth he modelled himself as a violinist and composer on works by Telemann, Heinichen, Biber, Albicastro and Corelli. In 1714, when he was seventeen, he stopped at Pirna on his journey to Dresden, because in that town's musical union 'a fellow was taken ill', and it was while working with the town band that he first got to know works by Vivaldi. He says: 'At that time in Pirna I first saw violin concertos by Vivaldi. As a then completely new species of musical pieces, they made more than a slight impression on me. I did not fail to collect a considerable assortment of them. In later times the splendid ritornellos of Vivaldi provided me with good models.' At the age of almost sixty, Quantz recaptured from his memory what all professional and amateur musicians had felt on first coming into contact with the new style of Italian instrumental music, particularly as it was embodied in Vivaldi's works. This newness can be seen by a comparison on the one hand with the music of Corelli, whose concerti grossi, even though not printed until 1714, represented a style that had spread throughout all Europe for some time already, and on the other hand with the production of suites that were influenced by Lully and had achieved a great effect, notably in Germany itself. Its most conspicuous manifestations were in the possibility of deploying soloists on a large scale, and at the same time in constructing forms from large sections, in a harmonic style clearly founded on the functions of basic tonic, dominant and subdominant, and in rhythmical accentuations which, in their strength and variety, were a complete revelation to listeners of the time. In the concerto grosso of Corelli, the solo trio formed a self-contained unit, the material was often laid out in the manner of a trio sonata, and the solo voices only rarely broke out from this texture. The solo parts were correspondingly treated in shorter sections, frequently consisting of two-, four- and eight-bar groups which were juxtaposed with the orchestra by alternation. In the Torelli/Vivaldi type of solo concerto the individual personality was allowed to develop freely. The unrestrained play of the imagination, and the improvisation coming from the playing of a virtuoso, led to solo sections that were for the most part built in wider spans than in works of the earlier period. If the total form was to remain well-balanced, the orchestral sections had to be made correspondingly large. The first works of this kind must have impressed the public as a revelation of a new human freedom, and their long stretches of development must have had quite a breathtaking effect. One of the technical means composers brought into play in presenting such formal constructions was functional tonality, or the technique of clearly linking all the formal sections to a tonal centre and to those keys most closely related to it. When in 1722 Jean Philippe Rameau explained this technique in his *Traité de l'harmonie*, it had long been a compositional reality in the works of Vivaldi and his contemporaries. However, the new harmonic thought took effect just as much in the construction of motifs and the development of small formal sections as in the overall form. At first, in contrast to the modal thought which was still strongly felt up to about 1700, and its variety of harmonic steps over a restricted range, this produced a certain impoverishment of harmony. In Vivaldi movements generally begin with a broad statement of the tonic key (Ex. 8). The triad of the basic tonality however is broken up rhythmically and melodically most imaginatively (Exx. 9 and 10). Often the upper voice consists of just a single note, the keynote. But the wealth of possibilities Vivaldi uses to vary it seems almost inexhaustible (Ex. 11). The three distinct chords which frequently open the orchestral introductions in the concertos, and which clearly and unambiguously determine the rhythmic and harmonic structure, must have been especially striking to Vivaldi's public, and a contemporary even spoke of the 'Hammerstrokes of Vivaldi' (Ex. 12).

All these characteristics occurred only occasionally with Corelli and his generation, but in Vivaldi they were already much admired as stylistic traits. Their chief characteristic is the effect of highlighting the basic harmonies and, on the one hand producing a marked impression of a symmetrical formal layout, on the other a rhythmical accentuation emphasizing these highlights, such as can be found in music prior to Vivaldi mostly in the late works of Torelli. In this way is created a unity of harmony and rhythm, reflected in all the other features of the composition, such as construction of motifs, motivic working, melodic line and formal structure; these are developed extensively, even in comparison with Corelli's music. So close a relation between all the elements of this stylistic revolution makes it almost impossible to consider these elements severally. If this is to be attempted in the interests of learning, the unity of style must be constantly borne in mind, so that the single elements do not become scattered about on the dissecting table of musical analysis.

Rhythm

Music before 1600 was basically vocal music. Over a verbal foundation, in which the text was organized into greater unities of sense, a broadly flowing melody developed, borne on human breath, such as may typically be found in the music of a Josquin des Prés or a Palestrina. In the early attempts to create opera this 'prima prattica', in which the word was subservient to the music, was soon ousted by the 'seconda prattica', in which the signification of even a single word was given exalted importance, and thus the word ruled supreme over music. Perhaps it was most markedly the accenting of important words and phrases in the sentences of the recitatives that led to rhythmic accentuation in music as well, which, by means of strong and weak beats, had to conform completely to the practice of speech. If a composer linked groups of notes in a recitative, supporting them with a single chord, the change of harmony that generally followed on a strong or auxiliary beat underlined this accentuation of speech. In this way a new rhythmic order was established, having particular divisions of accent, but also being influenced by the dance, the dance-song, the madrigal (the basis of whose composition was the pointing of verbal expression) and the chanson. When the chanson, taken over by instruments, became the model for the canzona, the new instrumental language of motifs developed from the textual accentuations and small rhythmical groups such as ♩♩♩♩♩ became current usage. While much of the old, flowing melodic style was still preserved in the bel canto aria, this tendency to rhythmic accentuation became increasingly strong in instrumental music—above all on the leading solo instrument of the baroque orchestra, the trumpet, whose tonguing, extensively used in music of the seventeenth century, facilitated rhythmic precision, and whose natural affinities with march-melodies—a result of its military exploitation—led to a certain symmetry of construction that was expressive of a new corporate feeling. Typical of this is a passage from a trumpet sinfonia by Torelli (Ex. 13). With the leap from tonic to dominant on the auxiliary beat and the clear harmonic subdivision into half-bars in the next bar, the point of development had been reached which Bukofzer describes as 'fully established tonality which regulated chord progressions, dissonance treatment, and the formal structure', and which is typical of the period around 1680. It is in fact the music for strings of this time that shows how much the trumpet, whether consciously or otherwise, had become the principal model; indeed in several of his concertos Vivaldi even designated the solo instrument 'Violino in trombe' (violin, in the manner of a trumpet): in other words, the violin was treated as a trumpet in the motivic invention, and often in the choice of notes themselves (P. 117, 138 and 179 = Ex. 10). The light *détaché* style of bowing that was so characteristic of baroque music is very reminiscent of the tonguing technique of the trumpet, and it is in connection with the elastic rhythmical verve of this type of bowing that are to be understood themes such as the following, which is expounded in the manner of a fugue (Ex. 14). Here the bowing method transforms the apparent poverty of invention, and is to a certain extent written into it; in analysis it must be heard too if a correct value judgment is to be reached. To this type also belong phrases such as are evident in the opening bars of concertos which follow (Exx. 15 and 16). If trumpet-like motifs are to be heard in practically every work for strings by Vivaldi, it was certainly not only the bright, radiant sound that he was subconsciously striving to emulate. The instrument's symbolic power, too, must have been very strong, embodying as it did particularly in the baroque era, and had from ancient times, nobility and divine glory; nor should it be forgotten that the trumpet was one of the official symbols of the Venetian Doge. Such a theme as the following must surely have brought the sound of trumpets to the eighteenth-century listener's mind (Ex. 17).

Moreover, the three strokes (Ex. 12) so characteristic of Vivaldi retained their effectiveness up to the classical period, and in works like Mozart's *Jupiter* Symphony remained an expression of a magnificently radiant opening. Vivaldi introduced harmonic modifications of these, harmonizing them perhaps as I–I–I, I–V–I or I–V–VI, but also he varied them rhythmically, and above all continued his melodic line directly from the three chords, thus admirably combining the effect of rhythmic accentuation with the melodic driving force (Ex. 18).

As was already evident in the sonatas (Ex. 6), syncopation was one of the composer's basic means of producing rhythmic effects. It gives his melodies that elegance which we can admire in the best works of Telemann, and often also a somewhat audacious touch, which probably came to Italian art-music from folk-music by way of the villanelle and similar genres (Ex. 19). But syncopation can also be a means of working up exciting tension (Ex. 20). It is often used in this way in the composer's dramatic music. Syncopation in the upper melodic line is usually found in conjunction with a rhythmically unequivocal bass, falling on strong beats; in this way the complementary material forms a strongly concentrated unity (Ex. 57). These too were progressive features in music after 1700, and made the rhythmical refinement of Vivaldi's works appear modern in contrast to the concerto grosso type that bore the imprint of Corelli and had originated in the older church sonatas. Another type of syncopation, making use of bowing articulation, became typical of rococo melodic style shortly after Vivaldi's death. If it appears in Vivaldi, it is tempting to see in it a feature of his late style where the composer already anticipated elements of a development which did not really set in until the 1760s (Exx. 21 and 22).

Finally, one more rhythmic/melodic element remains to be mentioned, which roused the public to transports of enthusiasm when Vivaldi went to Rome. Quantz records the following events of 1724: 'I was immediately eager to hear some music; this I could easily manage to do by way of the many churches and monasteries which I visited as much as possible. The most recent which reached my ears was in the so-called Lombardic style, as yet totally unknown to me, which Vivaldi had introduced to Rome shortly beforehand in one of his operas, and subsequently the local people had taken to it to such an extent that they would hardly listen to anything that was not similar to this style. Meanwhile I at first had great difficulty to find anything pleasing in it and to accustom myself to it; then finally I too found it expedient to conform to the fashion.' Vivaldi was by no means the inventor of the Lombardic rhythm, which was a slurred figure on the strong beat of the bar; but it was admirably suited to the reinforcement of accentuation effects, and thus became an organic part of the composer's style (Ex. 23).

Melodic style

Vivaldi's melodic style, too, is best approached by an understanding of its rhythmic driving forces. It is built up of motifs of differing lengths which either receive their tension from movement towards a strong beat, or move on from an accent (Exx. 24–27). Scalic and chordal formations are the means of further progression most favoured by Vivaldi after the strong beat of the bars (Exx. 28 and 29). All these examples show the operation of small motifs in the development of the smallest of formal units. Such motifs are further built up in sequences, but they are also recast—diminished and augmented—in the course of a movement, and the direction of their impetus may be reversed: in short, they may be varied in all the possible ways which were intrinsic to classical motivic working. In Vivaldi this motivic technique became an extremely important element of melodic construction—if, indeed, one can refer by this term in general to all his procedures of development. In fact there is a clear fundamental difference between the types of invention in movements whose tempo is fast and those in the slow central movements. In the quicker outer movements of the concertos the kinetic nuclei are generally rhythmically concise motifs. Once the composer felt that the power of such a motif had spent itself in respect of its effectiveness for the listener, then he would introduce another one to replace it and to bear the brunt of further development. Thus in Vivaldi's fast movements, it is hardly a question of constructing what musicians would normally call a melody, or perhaps a theme. Rather, in the outer movements of his concertos, the composer strung together motivic groups in the orchestral parts—a procedure which will be examined in greater detail in connection with formal construction. It is relatively rarely that one encounters a theme, inasmuch as a theme is understood to be a formally clearly defined structure of melodic independence that may be the basis for a lengthier formal development.

Vivaldi's way of developing the melodic line in middle movements contrasts with this construction of movements by motivic working and juxtaposition of motivic groups that is characteristic of his fast movements. Naturally here too motifs bear the weight of the development, but they hardly lead a formal life of their own, and it is less their rhythmic strength than rather their melodic power that is put to effect; it is the melodic arch, with its great striving towards a point of repose, that is the prime mover, and the motifs are simply building bricks in the melodic line (Ex. 30). In its span of exactly eight bars, with the dominant prepared in modulation and entering in bar 4, a melody such as this can already to a great extent be considered under the head of classical symmetry.

However, like almost all composers between about 1600 and the time of Beethoven, Vivaldi was 'bilingual'; in other words, besides the most advanced means of expression, he was a master of the 'stilus gravis', the old, solemn style whose sound immediately brings to mind church interiors. It is no accident that thematic complexes from this stylistic sphere appear above all in the introductory movements of the sonatas, and there they have a markedly chiesa-like effect (Ex. 31). But in fast concerto movements, too, fugue themes and themes that are presented fugally are often constructed in the church style. Suchlike features of archaic thematic construction can also occasionally be found in Bach's concerto style, as for instance in the final movement of the Fourth Brandenburg Concerto. To use these as points of reference in an attempt to date stylistic developments would be quite misguided in view of the period in question. The fact that again and again Vivaldi made use of such older stylistic methods shows that he included them quite consciously for specific effects.

The harmonic formula I–V$_{(6)}$–I, which served as a basis for invention for two hundred years after about 1700, either used consciously or present in the subconscious, has already been alluded to in connection with the question of Corelli's stylistic influence on Vivaldi. This formula also necessarily gives rise to specific melodic formulae, which—precisely because of this—appear particularly often in Vivaldi, giving a clear presentation of the harmony at the beginning of ritornellos in conjunction with the basic tonic–dominant harmonies. One of these stereotyped melodic turns of phrase is the sequence 1–2–3, already evinced in the sonatas (Ex. 4). In the concertos it appears on practically every page, but so diversely modified that we can see how essential a source of invention the delights of variation were to the baroque composer. In a Concerto for recorder, violin and bassoon (without orchestra!) the third movement begins with a similar formula (Ex. 32). Another harmonic formula that is often found in Vivaldi is the sequence (Ex. 33) that yields the note-structure 1–5–8 in the melody, such as in the first movement of an orchestral Concerto in D major, an overture in the French style (Ex. 34). The continuation of a bass line such as this leads to a diatonically falling bass, which was in fact so widespread and common to baroque composers that it can hardly be regarded as characteristic of Vivaldi. However, the composer's individuality shows itself in his use of such everyday creative principles in variation as well as in the shaping of the upper voice (Ex. 35). Where there was an ostinato repetition of melodic phrases in the upper voice with an effect similar to that of the organ point, harsh chordal clashes often arose (Ex. 36). It was relatively seldom that Vivaldi used the chromatically falling 'Lamento Bass', which had been so familiar to masters of opera as well as of sacred music since the early seventeenth century. The single note with its abundant possibilities of modification (Exx. 11, 15 and 16) should be included with the types dealt with here as being the most elementary; we should also include cadential melodies spanning a restricted range, such as melodies enclosed by a third or a fifth, which are particularly evident in the bass line of the fast movements of the concertos.

A survey of Vivaldi's repertoire of melodic formulae, both of the most limited and of more extended range, shows a relatively small number of basic types, but these are varied with virtually inexhaustible fantasy. Such a highly developed variation of types favoured rapid creation as well as producing a large number of works which essentially do not make use of melodic material already exploited.

Harmonic Style

Major and minor tonalities, with a conspicuous presentation of basic harmonies, are an essential characteristic of musical development after about 1680. In Vivaldi this had become consolidated and its effects reached the most subtle of formal constituents so that even in this respect his music was felt to be new and progressive. It has already been shown that the openings of movements, and particularly of introductory movements, are defined by very clear and broad presentations of the basic tonality combined with rhythms susceptible to variation (Exx. 10–12, 14–26, 28 and 29). These tonic areas generally stand in symmetrical relation to dominant areas. Since the bass was now to a great extent determined by chords fulfilling a primary tonal function, it largely lost its melodic independence in Vivaldi, in complete contrast to the bass lines encountered especially in the slow movements of the sonatas. There arose what Bukofzer has referred to as continuo homophony: in other words, the technique of figured bass was still retained, but the movement had largely become homophonic. In place of real melodic movement, short motifs were exploited in the bass, mostly centred round the root or its third. They became stereotyped formulae, and their function was harmonic and rhythmic, but now hardly melodic (Exx. 37 and 38). However, such formulae arose from the practice of diminution, as is shown in particular by the second example, and were common knowledge. Indeed, Quantz drew up an exhaustive classification and description of them.

The melodic curtailment of the bass in favour of its becoming purely functional went much further still and reached a point which was to become typical of the early works of Haydn and even of Mozart (Ex. 39). Just how strong the effect of the dominant had become at this time is shown in a passage from a Flute Concerto in D major, in which the upper voice ventures as far as a chord of the dominant eleventh (Ex. 40). It was from just such pedal-point-like bass lines that harsh clashes frequently arose (Ex. 41). The cadential tension of dominant, subdominant and tonic chords had become so essential at this stage in the development of musical style that not only was it used to build final cadences in the larger and smaller formal sections, but it also acted on the smallest constituents and thus became the real agent of melodic construction (Exx. 42 and 43). Indeed, even intervallically adventurous melodic lines can be explained by a cadential bass (Ex. 44).

The development of Vivaldi's harmonic style shows a characteristic that is typical of all periods of revolution: every step forward towards the evolutionary goal can only be achieved at the expense of certain past acquisitions—a loss is the necessary concomitant of a gain. In harmonic writing of the decades after 1700 this loss was a gradual relinquishment of the harmonies built on modes which were still a basic stylistic characteristic of such masters as Legrenzi, Vivaldi's teacher. The 'bilingualism' we have already mentioned saved Vivaldi from losing these harmonic possibilities altogether; he compensated for the loss with a new means of creating tensions over dominant-based harmonies. Especially in his church music, Vivaldi wrote in a harmonic style which shows a striking contrast with that hitherto apparent. When such works stood in close relation to the liturgy of Holy Week, the expression of the world of feeling evoked by the Passion story led to a harmonic technique which was of unusual audacity for the years 1710–20 (Ex. 45). However, similar harmonic tensions can be found in the concertos too, and there above all in the middle movements (Ex. 46).

With regard to tonality it is interesting to find a very wide compass in the few cadenzas in Vivaldi's hand that we possess. In an A major Violin Concerto, one of the Dresden Pisendel concertos, eight bars before the closing ritornello of the final movement there is a cadenza which for 31 bars pursues a strictly diatonic course. Then follow some bars that are harmonically unusually adventurous (Ex. 47), leading directly to the final trill.

Solo Concerto Form

Wilhelm Fischer has described the form of the baroque solo concerto as 'the most influential form of instrumental music in the High Baroque'. After Torelli had apparently been the first to turn to it wholeheartedly, it was Vivaldi who gave it its special imprint; and, like Quantz, many composers all over Europe collected a fair supply of works composed and structured in this new way immediately after 1710 so as to adopt them as models for their own works. With few exceptions, the solo concerto had a rigid sequence of movements, distinguishing it from the church sonata (which had more movements) and from the freely expansible suite; practically every composer deployed these in the following sequence:

1st movement   Allegro
2nd movement   Andante (Largo)—occasionally just a few bridging bars
3rd movement   Allegro (Presto)

This succession was obviously derived from the Italian operatic sinfonia, which was primarily used as an overture and which was so current that often enough composers found it superfluous to include any tempo indications at all. The practice of occasionally introducing a minuet—possibly with variations—in place of the last movement was also taken over from the operatic sinfonia, and the equally occasional appearance of a gigue-like last movement was probably a legacy of the suite.

Just as in the classical sonata the first movement provided the whole work with an individual formal imprint, and its form was rightly designated 'sonata form', the formal layout of the first movement of a solo concerto is also typical for the genre, and has likewise been dubbed 'solo concerto form'. The orchestra's playing of the ritornello, which appears as a rule four, often five times, acts as a sort of backdrop for the entry of the soloist. For such a formal construction too there was already an established operatic precedent, the ritornello aria. It seems that

Monteverdi was the first to write out clearly refrain-like recurring orchestral sinfonias and also to call them ritornellos. Around the middle of the seventeenth century masters like Carissimi, Rossi, Cavalli, Stradella and others used the prelude for strings before an aria as an interlude between the stanzas and as a postlude, and this type of aria, soon to become the most important element of operatic forms besides the ground bass, was later also taken over in cantatas and oratorios. In operas the ritornello normally remained in the same key. Above all this was very practical, since by giving the indication 'segue il ritornello' (the ritornello follows) repeated writing-out in the score as well as in the orchestral parts could be obviated. But the real musical reason for this restriction was the constraint imposed by modes which did not permit of modulation in the modern sense. With the freedom of modulation gained in about 1680, and the tempered scale that was its inevitable consequence, it was possible to bring in the ritornello on different harmonic degrees in accordance with a scheme planned on the basis of a large form. This scheme was already present in Torelli, but then Vivaldi developed it in such a way that it became one of the essential formal acquisitions of his time, being taken over together with concerto form in the works of nearly every other composer of the period.

The sequence of tonalities which occurs most frequently in the ritornello is: for major keys, I–V–VI–I; for minor keys, I–V($\flat$)–III–I. In their instrumentation and sonority, the intervening solo sections provide a strong contrast to these ritornellos, and in the basic type of this form were accompanied by only a basso continuo (generally, cello and harpsichord or double bass and harpsichord, similarly organ). Harmonically too the solo sections were freer and more varied; above all, their task was to modulate into the tonality of the next ritornello. The general layout for a major tonality was normally as follows:

Ritornello I   (I) Orchestra
    Solo I   (Modulation I–V) Soloist and basso continuo
Ritornello II   (V) Orchestra
    Solo II   (Modulation V–VI) Soloist and basso continuo
Ritornello III   (VI) Orchestra
    Solo III   (Modulation VI–I) Soloist and basso continuo
Ritornello IV   (I) Orchestra (generally identical with Ritornello I, and
        hence indicated simply by D.C.—da capo)

A glance at the layout of Bach's fugues will show how enormously formal thought during the High Baroque was influenced by this structural scheme. One has only to substitute the fugal working-out for the ritornellos and the episodes for the solo sections, and the basic type of the Bach fugue, with the same harmonic layout, remains.

In the 450 or so concertos we know of Vivaldi's, but also in most of the sinfonias, he almost invariably writes the first movement—and generally the last movement too—in this form, so that we have about 900 movements in solo concerto form from his pen. However, the formal scheme is rarely repeated mechanically, but rather it is usually modified most ingeniously and imaginatively to suit the musical ideas. Above all, in the recapitulation the ritornello is hardly ever repeated note for note. That would soon have led to a relaxation of tension and would have wearied the listener. Generally Vivaldi curtails ritornellos II and III considerably, and at the most places the entire ritornello once again at the end, to a certain extent as an end-pillar to support the form. This curtailment and remodelling is facilitated by the fact that the ritornello is rarely dominated by a theme and its development, but its construction is rather an assemblage of small groups, each built up from a motif (Ex. 48). Single motif groups can be omitted without jeopardizing the ritornello's coherence, and the manner and means by which Vivaldi proceeds bring to mind a sort of composition with motivic building blocks. In the Concerto P. 24 the ritornello is varied as follows in its four repetitions:

Ritornello I	A minor	A	B	C	D	E	C_1	E
Ritornello II	C major	A	B	C				E
Ritornello III	E minor	A	B		D			E
Ritornello IV	D minor—A minor	A	B	C	D			
Ritornello V	A minor		B				C_1	E

In ritornello II the D group, in ritornello III the C group and in ritornello IV even the final E group is omitted. Since in this movement the ritornello appears five times, once more than usual, Vivaldi even abbreviates the closing ritornello V, indeed even more so than the previous ones, for it consists only of the groups B and C as well as the closing group E, which is important for the ending. Such a procedure allows the greatest variety within a unity that is preserved in its essentials.

It was above all necessary to extensively vary and abbreviate the ritornello when it was laid out as a fugue, as in P. 351 (the seven-bar theme has already been given as Ex. 14). The sequence of entries: 1st violin (and 1st oboe), 2nd violin (and 2nd oboe), viola, cello (and double bass), together with an eight-bar continuation using a motif group and a two-bar cadential formula produces a ritornello of unusual length (34 bars).

Ritornello II is cut by exactly a half (17 bars), and the theme appears only a single time complete, being expounded polyphonically in contrast to ritornello I. Ritornello III is only 13 bars long, and the idea of imitation is again taken up from ritornello I, except that only the head motif is imitated, and that at an interval of one bar, in other words there is a significant thickening of texture compared with the opening. The normally favoured possibility of a d.c. (da capo) could not be used for the closing ritornello IV, since a long-winded fugal exposition appearing at the end of the movement would have robbed it of all effect. Vivaldi contents himself with a 19-bar postlude with motifs from the theme and an echo group; the theme itself appears no more, having yielded its last drop and fulfilled its responsibilities.

How Vivaldi continues his construction in a coherent exposition and develops the motivic substance of a fugue theme in the first solo section is plainly shown by the last movement of P. 312, from which 34 bars are given as an example by Pincherle (p. 183).

Often Vivaldi begins a ritornello in the manner of a trio sonata: one of the two violins begins with a figure of thematic character, and the other answers at the dominant or—less frequently—in unison. To link up with this the composer continues to develop further in the usual way with a series of motif groups (Ex. 49).

The relationship of the solo to the ritornello can also be designed with extreme variability as regards motivic coherence. The following possibilities present themselves, and appear in Vivaldi: (1) The soloist takes up the opening of the ritornello unaltered and continues to develop its motifs as if in a free improvisation (Ex. 50); (2) The solo and ritornello are motivically completely independent of each other (Ex. 50); (3) The soloist opens with entirely new material, but later returns to the ritornello motifs, subjecting them to a developmental working-out. Quite often all these possibilities appear in the same movement, and the change of procedure continually provides new tensions in Vivaldi's concerto form.

In the form's basic type the soloist and the orchestra are juxtaposed in a clearly contrasting instrumentation, for the solo sections are accompanied by only the basso continuo. This too had its practical advantages in the everyday life of the busy composer and orchestral musician: the time involved in composition was reduced to a minimum, and a play-through of the ritornello sufficed for the preparation of a performance. With a skilled *maestro di capella* at the harpsichord, the solo sections could be 'fitted in' without rehearsal. Only in this way can we understand an occasion related by Dittersdorf on which one evening twelve new violin concertos arrived by messenger, and six were performed at sight before dinner, six afterwards!

All the same, Vivaldi copiously modified the simple opposition of types of instrumentation and in his works there is a wealth of possibilities by which these types interpenetrate, so that for example the solo instrument may be taken over into the ritornello (Ex. 51). It is much more often the case that the secco accompaniment of the bass (that is, the accompaniment for only the basso continuo) is transformed into an accompagnato (in other words the orchestra takes over the accompaniment of the solo), in the same way as was already customary in opera and oratorio when richly expressive content demanded an equally rich means of expression. However, in Vivaldi it rarely comes about that the orchestra has a purely accompanimental function somewhat as if the basso continuo had been written out for orchestra. When he includes the orchestra in the solo sections it generally involves motivic participation, as in the Concerto P. 351 we have already referred to several times (Ex. 52). The orchestra is handled particularly sumptuously as regards motifs when the solo instrument is indulging in virtuoso figurations which contain either only a small part or no part at all of the work's motivic substance. In the concertos for wind instruments too, where the soloist has a much smaller range of technical possibilities compared with those of the string player, the orchestra joins noticeably whole-heartedly in the solo sections, though perhaps this can be attributed to the fact that with the acoustical opposition of a solo wind instrument to a string accompaniment there is hardly any danger that the soloist will be 'swamped'. In many Vivaldi movements the soloist and the orchestra combine in such a concentrated unity of material that the result is worthy of the best techniques of classical development (this is true especially of the Concertos P. 69, 89 and 77*). Ignorance of such works has led to Bach alone being credited with developmental motivic working in the baroque concerto; certainly Bach's tendency towards motivic concentration was far more marked than Vivaldi's. Of course it is hard to determine to what extent Bach knew works of this kind by the Venetian composer and could have been stimulated in this direction by them. But among the works of Vivaldi that Bach arranged there is one in which the essential features of this kind of working-out technique were already very much in evidence. This is the Concerto Op. III, No. 12, P. 240, in E major, which in his arrangement Bach transposed into C major. Already in the first ritornello of the final movement there is imitation between the 3rd and 4th violins (Ex. 53). A passage of virtuoso writing

* See Kolneder, *Solokonzertform*, pp. 62–9.

for the solo violin in the first solo section is accompanied by the orchestra (Ex. 54). In the second solo the orchestral violins engage with the soloist's arpeggio in playing alternating motifs (Ex. 55). Motivic treatment of the orchestra could very well be learnt from such a work, which Vivaldi published as early as 1712! Bach developed further this kind of concerto dialogue which came closer to his musical thought than the type of concerto planned in contrasting sections, and certain movements from his violin concertos as well as from the Brandenburg concertos mark the highest attainments of the baroque concerto.

Middle and Final Movements

Vivaldi's final movements are generally laid out in solo concerto form. Occasionally there is a tendency—probably taken over from the operatic sinfonia and the suite—to conceive the last movement as a dance movement, whether simply in its rhythm or gigue-like material, or in its form, with two reprise sections, as in the Recorder Concerto in A minor P. 77. However the middle movement turns away fundamentally from all these possibilities of formal construction in the outer movements—again in the interests of a contrasting effect. Here the orchestra is frequently silent, and the Andante or Largo is unfolded in the three sections of straightforward Lied form, A–B–A, or may be slightly varied at the return of the A section; it is generally played by only the soloist and the basso continuo group. A movement designed in this way is, however, occasionally framed by a short orchestral prelude which returns again as a postlude.

Relatively seldom did Vivaldi try out the ritornello layout of the outer movements in the middle movement. In relation to the tempo it produced too long-winded a formal conception, unless the single sections of the form were to be extensively truncated. Middle movements in ritornello form, such as that of the Cello Concerto in C minor, P. 434, may be regarded as formal experiments with which the composer was not satisfied, and which therefore he did not adopt as part of his repertoire of forms (see p. 125).

On the other hand, the ground bass recommended itself very well for the construction of a middle movement. Indeed the composer often designated such a movement as a 'Chaconne' (P. 19), and in other cases did not indicate the form. Probably the most interesting chaconne movement is in the B♭ major Violin Concerto 'in due cori', P. 368. Vivaldi begins with a two-part exposition of a much used eight-bar ostinato bass (Ex. 56). Here the violas double the bass while varying it. Furthermore the eight-bar bass is reduced to seven bars by a displacement of the Segno so that the two appearances of the tonic—at the beginning and at the end—are combined in one bar; this yields an asymmetry which is laden with tension. After the eight bars given as our example is written 'Segue Sempre l'Istesso Rit: Mentre Suona il Prinzipale' (The same ritornello always follows, while the solo violin is playing), and then follow the 52 bars (plus final chord) of the solo written out in one part. At the end, a direction reads 'Segue Subito ambi li Cori Ut sopra' (Both orchestras follow immediately as above), whereupon the last statement of the ostinato bass, written out completely in four parts and explicitly marked Forte, closes the movement.

We also find the chromatically falling bass, as for example in a Concerto ripieno in G minor, P. 361 (Ex. 57). The composer's manuscript shows an interesting correction: the first violin's semiquavers in bars 3–5 were already present in the first bars on the second violin, but were then heavily crossed out. Evidently Vivaldi soon saw that in this it was better to have a three-part exposition and to introduce the counterpoint later as a means of enhancing the interest.

The Solo Concerto as a Three-movement Form

In many respects Vivaldi seems to have been very preoccupied with the problem of designing a complete work over and above the mere sequential ordering of three movements. In some of his manuscripts we find the total number of bars given at different points in a movement, and occasionally at the end of the score the totals of the individual movements are listed one under another. Such instances point to the fact that the composer worked to quite definite proportions, in other words, he had scrutinized his experiences of artistic construction in a rational way and found there certain rules which, if followed, would evidently facilitate working at speed. Quantz, the theoretician of the baroque epoch of the solo concerto, who was certainly much indebted to Vivaldi's example, recorded in his famous book on playing the flute the essentials of concertante works of his time in some detail and, indeed, in the form of formulae. These are corroborated down to the last detail by investigation of Vivaldi works, and as a contemporary description they are wholly authentic, even though Quantz was a convinced advocate of eclecticism and introduced French taste into his considerations, having become intimately acquainted with it during his stay in Paris in 1726-7.

In the XVIIIth chapter, 'How a Musician and a Musical Composition Are to Be Judged', he says of the concerto in general: 'A timepiece may be consulted to ensure suitable length in a concerto. If the first movement takes five minutes, the Adagio five to six minutes, and the last movement three to four minutes, the entire concerto will have the requisite length. In general it is more advantageous if the listeners find a piece too short rather than too long.' (§ 40) Quantz says of the first movement that it must have a 'majestic ritornello carefully elaborated in all the parts' (§ 33, fig. 1): 'The ritornello must be of suitable length. It must have at least two principal sections. The second, since it is repeated at the end of the movement, and concludes it, must be provided with the most beautiful and majestic ideas.' (§ 33, fig. 8) Quantz says of the solo and its relationship to the ritornello: 'At times the solo sections must be singing, and at times these beguiling sections must be interspersed with brilliant melodic and harmonic passage-work appropriate to the instrument; these sections must also alternate with short, lively and majestic tutti sections, in order to sustain the fire [of the piece] from beginning to end.' (§ 33, fig. 10) 'The concertante or solo sections must not be too short, and the tutti sections between them must not be too long.' (§ 33, fig. 11) 'The accompaniment during the solo sections must not have progressions that might obscure the concertante part; it must consist alternately of many parts at one time and few at another, so that the principal part now and then has a chance to distinguish itself with greater freedom. In general, light and shadow must be maintained at all times. If it is possible, a good effect is produced if the passage-work is invented in such a way that the accompanying parts are able to introduce a recognizable portion of the ritornello simultaneously.' (§ 33, fig. 12).

In his remarks about the middle movement he touches on key relationships: 'In general the Adagio must be distinguished from the first Allegro by its rhythmic structure, metre and tonality. If the Allegro is written in a major tonality, for example, in C major, the Adagio may be set, at one's discretion, in C minor, E minor, A minor, F major, G major, or G minor. If, however, the first Allegro is written in a minor key, for example, C minor, the Adagio may be set in E♭ major, F minor, G minor, or A♭ major. These sequences of keys are the most natural ones. The ear will never be offended by them . . .' (§ 35) 'The Adagio furnishes more opportunities than the Allegro to excite the passions and to still them again.' (§ 36) 'This melody must be just as moving and expressive as if it were accompanied by words.' (§ 37, fig. 5).

Quantz's remarks about the final movement, above all in its relationship to and its many fundamental differences from the first movement, are most interesting: 'The final Allegro of a concerto must be quite different from the first in the style and nature of its ideas as well as in its metre. If the first movement is to be serious, the last must be jocular and gay. Metres such as two-four, three-four, three-eight, six-eight, nine-eight, and twelve-eight may be serviceable in it. All three movements of a concerto must never be set in the same metre. If the first two movements are in duple time, the last must be set in triple. Although the last movement must be written in the same tonality as the first, care must be taken to modulate to successive tonalities in a different order than in the first movement, so that excessive likeness is avoided.' (§ 38).

Finally Quantz remarks further about the genre's origins and history: 'The concerto owes its origin to the Italians. Torelli is supposed to have made the first.'

In our consideration of the contemporary aesthetics of large formal design, which are in such close agreement with Vivaldi's works that they appear as a distillation of them, the question arises whether the composer did not attempt, by means of a motivic and thematic basis common to different movements, to bring into play what is today fashionably called 'thematic unity'. Investigations along these lines must be restricted to those cases which come to the fore so conspicuously that the listener becomes conscious of the relationship as a structural element intended by the composer. In this sense there are only isolated cases of the thematic linkage of movements in Vivaldi. In the G major Flute Concerto, Op. X, No. 6, P. 105, Vivaldi wrote a melody in Lied form ($\|$: 8 :$\|$: 8 :$\|$) in the Largo (in the minor of the same key), having a very colourfully conceived orchestral accompaniment (without harpsichord!) which, transformed into the major mode, is varied in the subsequent final Allegro movement. The two movements form a unity as a theme with variations, and in a thoughtful interpretation will be played without a real break.

If, however, we include by thematic unity everything that was produced by typical affinities in the style of that time, then in Vivaldi almost every movement of a work, and indeed almost every work, shows 'thematic unity' with the others. However, we may be certain that the eighteenth-century listener did not notice some recognizable sequence in the structural framework, such as $\begin{smallmatrix} 1 & 2 & 3 \\ I & V & I \end{smallmatrix}$, but rather what was being played in the foreground, so to speak, namely rhythmic and melodic motifs which in spite of typical affinities were different enough for their structural relationship to be audible, and not just verifiable after the event. Meanwhile Vivaldi's works offer the visual analyst a fruitful field of activity in this respect.

Dynamics

The organ of the Renaissance, and to a large extent of the Baroque period as well, having no swell-box, could not produce fine gradations of dynamics, and dynamic differentiations could only be achieved unevenly by the addition of stops and the use of intensities that were relatively widely spaced. In the same way, the harpsichord could only yield the dynamics permitted by its stops, and the possibilities of using compositional means to thicken or thin out the texture, or to compose in a higher or lower register so as to provide gradations of dynamic colouring, were relatively few. The concept of 'terrassed dynamics'—a term probably coined by Hugo Riemann—is a consequence of these two instruments. Since, as has been inferred, the organ and the harpsichord were the chief progenitors of the baroque sound, musicians before about 1750, a few late exceptions apart, were only familiar with terrassed dynamics. Then, when Riemann first discovered, so to speak, the Mannheim masters, whose accomplishments in the art of dynamics evoked the delight of all their hearers in about 1760–70, the official dogma became what Burney had already said in 1773 about Mannheim in his travel journals: 'It was here that the Crescendo and Diminuendo had birth; and the Piano, which was before chiefly used as an echo, with which it was generally synonymous, as well as the Forte, were found to be musical colours which had their shades, as much as red or blue in painting.' As a relatively well-informed historian, the most excellent Burney ought surely to have known something of the history of musical dynamics. And he must have known that as early as the beginning of the sixteenth century pains were taken to transfer the expressive capabilities of the human voice to instruments. In 1535 Sylvestro Ganassi said in his textbook on the flute, *Opera intitulata Fontegara*: '. . . just as a really skilful painter will reproduce everything created in Nature by varying his colours, so you can imitate the expression of the human voice with a wind or stringed instrument' (Chapter 1). 'As regards the breath, one can learn from what the human voice teaches, namely that it must be used at a moderate strength . . . so that at any given time one can increase and decrease its intensity' (Chapter 2). In the first operatic performances, the singers moved their hearers to tears by the power of their individual emotional expression; terrassed dynamics could hardly have done this much. At this time as an integral part of the technique of bel canto there arose manners of singing such as 'esclamazione' and 'messa di voce', that is, crescendi and decrescendi on long notes. Already in 1638 the famous trumpeter Girolamo Fantini demanded in his work on trumpet technique the ability to imitate these vocal dynamics on his instrument. Violinists had certainly established this imitation long before; indeed Monteverdi was already asking for a dying-away manner of bowing. Then Torelli was soon putting into practice such refined dynamic string effects as playing 'sopra il manico' (on the fingerboard). By about 1700, copious dynamics had become so natural, not only in singing but in instrumental playing too, that the harpsichord and the organ, with their humble stepwise dynamics, were felt to be no longer adequate. It was then that was born the piano, of which four examples existed in Florence by 1709. In 1712, in England, Abraham Jordan invented the organ swell-box which soon enjoyed great popularity. In the same year, with the publication of his violin sonatas Op. I, G. T. Piani introduced the hairpin signs: < > and thus made it possible to give an exact indication of dynamics over a small range such as had already been in common usage for a long time previously.

However, in Vivaldi's manuscript scores—less so in the printed works—we find a range of dynamics that exceeds anything that can be found in the music of his contemporaries. In its refinement and its range of hitherto almost unknown shades of colouring, not only is it the expression of a refined sensibility, but also it reflects a high level of accomplishment in the art of performance, which can be explained by the special environment in which Vivaldi was able to work, and which far transcended the level of music-making as it was more generally practised in the early eighteenth century.

In the times of the absolutist régime good music was a real necessity for the upper classes, because of cultural standards which, even taking a cross-section of society, were very high; but it had to fulfil a pronouncedly social function, and it could only rarely press a claim to spiritual autonomy which would be recognized by society. Court musicians who played dance music, *Tafelmusik* and chamber music while men were sitting at the card-table nearby had most likely to be content as a rule with trying to drown the conversation and the clatter of plates with mighty bow strokes. In such circumstances the many small ensembles, reinforced with secretaries, valets and caterers, would hardly have evolved ambitious dynamic gradations, for only personalities who commanded outstanding recognition such as Handel could dare to 'shout down' the Princess if she were indulging in conversation during the chamber music. It was not much better in the opera, visits to which constituted a part of society life, and indeed a very prominent part. Dinner was taken in the boxes, visits were paid on all sides, and these generally stopped only for an aria by a prima donna.

THE WORK

There was no incentive for the operatic musician to refine his performing style. Bach, who in the *Sketch for a well-appointed Church Music; also some impartial considerations of the decline of the same* gives us a drastic picture of the scanty forces that were placed at his disposal for the liturgy, was certainly pleased enough to have composed his cantata for every Sunday, to have copied out the parts and to have kept together his singers and musicians during performance. There was rarely enough time in rehearsals, or indeed at all, to polish up the dynamics. Rektor Gesner has vividly described how Bach 'imposed the rhythm and the beat, signalling to one performer, stamping his foot at another, and threatening a third with his finger, as he would give the required note to one in the upper register, another in the lower and a third in the middle; and despite the loudest sound the ensemble could make, and although he himself was performing the most difficult part, he alone would immediately notice when and where something did not sound right, and would hold everything together in order, evening out occasional discrepancies . . .'

Vivaldi worked in the music department of an orphanage, and could pick the most talented from a large number of girls, whom as violin teacher he would then train. Even though the oldest and best of his pupils were constantly leaving, they were available for individual practice and orchestral rehearsal for several hours a day through all of ten or twelve years. In this way a level of accomplishment was attained which stood comparison with the best orchestras in Europe. Vivaldi's performances took place in church, and therefore in complete silence, for even applause was strictly forbidden. Dynamic subtleties were really heard by the public, and were savoured as special delicacies. The enthusiastic contemporary descriptions of Vivaldi performances resulted from the profound impression that this peculiar style of execution evoked.

The most astonishing evidence of these dynamic refinements can be found in the scores which Vivaldi used for his concerts over a long period of time. The dynamic scale encompassed no less than thirteen different gradations: pianissimo, piano molto, piano assai, mezzo p, pp, p, quasi p, mezzo forte, un poco forte, f, f molto, più f, ff. It should be noted here that in the early eighteenth century pp meant più piano, and not pianissimo!

Often the composer gives all these dynamic values in rapid succession, and then their effect is almost that of a crescendo or decrescendo. However, often also widely differentiated values are juxtaposed in the interests of a strongly contrasting effect, as in the first movement of a Concerto 'con 2 violini obligati' P. 436, with the characteristic tempo and performance direction 'All° ma poco e cantabile' (Ex. 58). Simultaneous

65

contrasting dynamics occasionally appear in descriptive music, as in the second movement of the Spring Concerto, which is based on the text: 'E quindi sul fiorito ameno prato/Al caro mormorio di fronde e piante/ Dorme'l Caprar col fido can'a lato.' (In the flowers of the meadow, amongst the rustling of the leaves, the goatherd sleeps, his faithful dog by his side.) To the 'pianissimo sempre' of the three upper parts, representing the sleeping goatherd, are opposed the 'molto forte' and 'strappato' (snatched) of the barking dog, whose depiction Vivaldi has entrusted to the viola (Ex. 59).

However, in general the simultaneous use of different dynamic gradations is aimed at bringing out the solo violin strongly from the accompanying string instruments. How far the composer went in this direction can be seen from the final movement of a D major Violin Concerto (Ex. 60): from the orchestra's three dynamic values p, pp and pianissimo, the sound of the solo violin is differentiated by dynamic indications always one degree louder; but, furthermore, the point of entry of each value is displaced by a quaver, because the soloist and the orchestra are given differently constituted motifs. (Anyone daring to edit an unmarked work of the composer in this way—à la Vivaldi—and to publish it may be sure of the censure of all the so-called Baroque specialists!)

Perhaps the most forceful case of a simultaneous dynamic contrast appears in the E minor Violin Concerto P. 126 (Plate VII): a ppp chord on the upper strings is contrasted with a bass line which is particularly forcibly articulated with octave leaps, hammering quavers and syncopations, and which bears the dynamic marking 'Forte molto'. On its return this ritornello opening is given the same markings.

In Vivaldi, as in baroque music in general, one has to play f if nothing else is prescribed; this dynamic gradation is particularly usual at the beginnings of movements. The third movement of a Violin Concerto in E minor, P. 125, presents an attractive exception: it begins with a 12-bar 'Piano molto'.

No doubt Vivaldi's emotion-laden dynamic writing had a lesser influence in his time than his rhythm, harmony and concerto form. In the first place this was due to the fact that the composer, conscious that his performing style was a personal hallmark and inseparable from his orchestra, was apparently reluctant to transfer too much of it into printed editions. But another factor was that all the northern musicians who had the opportunity of hearing Vivaldi's performances in Venice were faced with the impossibility of realizing the master's dynamic marvels in all their range when they returned home. It was only towards the end of the

Baroque period that the much-travelled Quantz set down in didactic form something of what he had heard and learnt in Rome and in Venice. Quantz says of the German singers: 'They are better versed in note-reading than many *galant* singers of other nations, but they hardly know how to manage the voice at all. Thus as a rule they sing with a uniform volume of tone, without light and shade . . . They have little feeling for Italian flattery, which is effected by slurred notes and by diminishing and strengthening the tone.' (XVIIIth Chapter, § 80)

The instrumentalist could learn little from this. Quantz recommends the imitation of Italian manners of singing: 'If you must hold a long note for either a whole or a half bar, which the Italians call *messa di voce*, you must first tip it gently with the tongue, scarcely exhaling; then you begin pianissimo, allow the strength of the tone to swell to the middle of the note, and from there diminish it to the end of the note in the same fashion, making a vibrato with the finger on the nearest open hole.' (XIVth Chapter, §10) 'The singing notes that follow a long note may be played a little more prominently. Yet each note, whether it is a crotchet, quaver or semiquaver, must have its own Piano and Forte, to the extent that the time permits. If, however, several notes are found in succession where, in strengthening the tone, the time does not permit you to swell each note individually, you can still swell and diminish the tone during notes like this so that some sound louder and others softer.' (XIVth Chapter, §11) 'The effect produced is good, however, if the upper part draws out and concludes the last note with a diminuendo, and then begins the following notes with renewed force, continuing in the manner described above until another caesura or conclusion of an idea occurs.' (XIVth Chapter, §12)

However, Quantz can also give exact technical directions for the playing of dynamics on stringed instruments, and he was well acquainted with the problem of the point of attack: 'If you wish to increase the strength of your tone, you may, during the stroke, press the bow more firmly against the strings and guide it a little closer to the bridge; this makes the tone stronger and more piercing. When playing Piano, however, the bow may be guided even a little farther from the bridge on each instrument than stated above, in order to set the strings in motion more easily with a moderate bow.' (XVIIth Chapter, Section II, §28)

Quantz's directions for unmarked or little-marked works are of some importance. He says: '. . . it may be inferred that to observe the Piano and Forte only at those places where they are indicated is far from sufficient, and that each accompanist must also know how to introduce them with discernment at many places where they are not marked. Thus, to achieve success in this regard, good instruction and much experience are necessary.' (XVIIth Chapter, Section VII, §30)

With regard to the significance and aims of copiously graded dynamics in music-making, Quantz's unequivocal pronouncements show him to have been in line with his Italian and French precursors: 'If, on the contrary, you express the Forte and Piano by turns, in accordance with the nature of the ideas, and employ them properly in those notes that require them, you will achieve the goal you seek, namely, to maintain the constant attention of the listener, and guide him from one passion into another.' (XVIIth Chapter, Section VII, §25)

In the musical examples (Tables IX–XVII), Quantz enlarged on his descriptions by giving examples of the most subtle melodic interplay of dynamics, such as for obvious reasons are not to be found in Vivaldi scores. These examples are important contemporary documents and form a valuable complement to what we know of Vivaldi's dynamics from his works.

Tempo and Agogics

Medieval musical practice recognized a basic value of tempo, the *integer valor notarum*—to a certain extent the pulse rate of music, to which all variations of tempo stood in a rational proportional relationship. The first repudiation of these measured relationships that had been imposed on music followed quickly from the madrigal, but more especially through the opera, where tempi and their variations were determined by the psychological tensions being acted out on the stage. However, in music that was predominantly linked to the church the old basic pulse certainly left its mark for some time to come; only recently, an attempt was made to relate all Bach's music to a basic tempo of 72 beats per minute, corresponding to an average human pulse. But it was precisely during Bach's youth that a second jolt was given to this unity of tempo by the Italians; already in Torelli, but much more in Vivaldi, there are tempo indications which imply a great degree of differentiation in the concept of tempo. Indeed, this differentiation corresponds to the refinement of dynamics, and it may be assumed that particularly listeners from the North would have found Vivaldi's Venetian performances all the more exciting as a result of their refinements of tempo as opposed to the familiar basic tempo that was their native heritage, though admittedly they would not have been able to say precisely what it was that excited them.

Of course, Vivaldi was certainly still familiar with the basic tempi Allegro, Andante, Largo etc., but he furnished them with an abundant

68

range of graded auxiliaries. Thus arose many possible ways of 'emphasizing the dominating principle effect' (Quantz). For the Allegro alone no less than eighteen gradations and indications can be found in Vivaldi: Allegro assai, A. molto, A. molto e spirituoso, A. con moto, A. non molto, A. mà non molto, A. mà cantabile, A. poco, A. mà poco, A. mà poco e cantabile, A. mà molto amabile, A. poco poco, A. mà poco poco, A. non troppo, A. mà non troppo, A. mà d'un mezzo tempo, A. A. molto più che si può, A. più ch'è possibile. There also appears the indication 'Andante molto e quasi allegro'. Some of these indications seem to define the tempo rather according to the expression. But it must be remembered that allegro (= cheerful) is still used in everyday Italian speech, and it is more in other countries than in Italy itself that it has become a real tempo indication.

Vivaldi certainly gave a lot of thought to the function of the tempo; again and again we find in his scores later corrections. Particularly in his printed works the tempo indications do not always tally with those in the manuscript copies. The composer evidently basically reconsidered every detail in the event of publication.

For instance, in the G major Violin Concerto, P. 122, the first movement was marked 'All. molto', and the 'molto' was later deleted, since the music demanded a somewhat more moderate tempo.

In several works we find the striking indication 'spiritoso' (= spirited, witty), which generally follows a cantabile or a dolce. This of course was in the first place an indication of expression; but it was also probably intended as a slight modification of the tempo. The third movement of the Bassoon Concerto in C major, P. 46, justifies such an assumption, for the articulation itself could have been adequately guaranteed by means of legato bowing and other markings (Ex. 61). Moreover all cadenza-like passages were played freely with regard to tempo. In the Flute Concerto *Il Gardellino*, P. 155, the solo flute's imitation of the goldfinch is marked 'à piacimento' (ad libitum). The last sections of cadenzas, which are generally harmonically adventurous, but sometimes even only the final trills, as a rule bear tempo indications such as Adagio or Andante. In many cases in his stage works, Vivaldi fitted the choice of tempo entirely to the dramatic situation, and juxtaposed small structural sections in often very contrasting tempi. There is a characteristic example of this in the opera *Ottone in Villa* (see p. 175).

Articulation

The term 'articulation' can cover a number of things: scansion, jointing, formation of sounds, clear enunciation. In music it means the clear

(= articulate) reproduction of the internal divisions of the components of a phrase; its task is at the same time to link and to divide, and the most important means eighteenth-century composers had of presenting it were slurs, dots and wedge-heads.

Vivaldi's articulation is completely derived from violin-playing, which had been his first musical training and was his foremost means of musical expression. When he writes a connecting slur, this slur is in fact identical with the violin bow with which he joins the notes together; when he writes a dot or a wedge-head, for him such a sign is immediately obvious as a symbol for a detached stroke, or a way of attacking the string with the bow. But the innate Italian affinity with the voice meant that for him the violinist's bowing would also be a symbol of human breath. Just as Monteverdi, Mozart, Verdi and other great masters received an essential stimulus towards musical design from the singer's intake and expulsion of breath, the systole and diastole, Vivaldi's music too, even though it may be realized on instruments having apparently infinite breath, takes its breath just as much from the basic provisions of the human body, and from them receives its internal divisions.

The marking of articulation signs was still a relatively recent practice in Vivaldi's time. Vocal music, depending on speech and its articulation, did not need such markings. For the same reasons, early instrumental music too remained without marks, since it was either transcribed vocal music such as the tablatures of choral settings, or else it was derived from such models as the chanson and the madrigal, as were the canzone and the ricercar. With the gradual development of an instrumental music which had its own laws and the formation of a motivic language based on the properties of instruments, there was more and more necessity for a clear playing articulation. At first, and also even at a later date, it was admittedly not considered necessary to write out such articulation, and expect the player to follow it. It was very much the case with musical practice that direct tradition was sufficient to guarantee approximate conformity of performance in relatively uncomplicated music. During the middle period of Torelli's (d. 1709) and Corelli's (d. 1713) activity, composers still basically made do with slurs over a few notes. The refinement of musical language during Vivaldi's youth also brought with it, in the field of articulation, a hitherto undreamt-of wealth of nuances, which the composers could now hardly leave to the discretion of performers to reproduce. Vivaldi's combined activity as a violin teacher and a conductor at the Ospedale, in daily contact with an orchestra whose best talents were constantly departing and having to be replaced by

VI. First page of the solo violin part of the *Spring* Concerto, Op. VIII, No. 1, P. 241, in Michele Carlo le Cène's edition, Amsterdam 1725.

VII. Violin concerto in E minor, P. 126, page 1.

novices, was probably one of the chief reasons for his particularly precise marking of articulation in his works. But only some of his scores show this precision. When he was in a particularly great hurry—and that must often have been the case with him—he wrote down music which showed no articulation marks at all, and in such cases could probably count on the Pietà orchestra's familiarity with his style. However, in general he expressed his requirements on the subject of articulation very exactly, and many of his manuscript pages resemble a modern score in their minute indications.

For example, in performing crotchets in a moderate Allegro tempo, Vivaldi demands, besides the slightly detached stroke usual at the time, a stroke with clinging bow-change, in other words, with the single notes closely joined. This bowing must have been unusual, for it is often specifically indicated with instructions such as 'con arco attaccato' (P. 439), 'attaccata alla corda' (P. 428, Ex. in Kolneder, *Aufführungspraxis* p. 39), 'con l'arco attaccato alle corda' (with closely succeeding—attached, adhering—bow strokes) (P. 419) or 'arcate lunghe anco le violette' (long strokes, also the viola) (opera: *L'Olimpiade*).

Even in his bowing marks Vivaldi shows peculiarities which are found rarely, or hardly at all, in the practice of the time. In order to draw the player's attention to the unusualness of such articulation he even marks it 'guardate la ligatura' (note the ligature) (P. 171). Very capricious bowing marks can be found in many of Vivaldi's works (Exx. 62–64). In editing an unmarked work, who would dare to proceed as the composer did? Above all Vivaldi seldom writes out the bowings schematically, and through an apparent lack of logical organization achieves a very individual presentation of each part in many works (see Ex. in Kolneder, *Aufführungspraxis* p. 43). Triplets too are not always mechanically phrased in groups of three notes (Ex. 65). Frequently Vivaldi's bowing marks seem to have traits of the Rococo, such as when in the Concerto ripieno P. 231 he slurs together the second and third notes of each half-bar and thus obtains a kind of very attractive syncopation (Exx. 21 and 22). Do such clues provide sufficient evidence to list a concerto of this nature as a late work? In the chapter on programme music we shall consider, with the help of examples, the fact that Vivaldi used legato as a means of programmatic representation.

Vivaldi indicates the clearly detached bow stroke, in which the note's value is shortened, with wedge-heads and dots. The problem of defining these signs was once again raised a few years ago in connection with Mozart during work on the new Complete Edition, and became the subject of a competition, though none of the extremely interesting studies that were submitted succeeded in finally solving the problem with any certitude (see Bibliography under Keller). Many passages in Vivaldi's manuscripts permit one to suppose that this composer, too, did not always precisely differentiate between the two signs. Clearly it was not easy, when writing hastily with the quill pens of the time and perhaps sometimes with very viscid ink, to make dots on coarse-grained paper. In such conditions, the wedge-head would be the more convenient sign. On this point it is interesting to refer to the letter of December 29, 1736, that Pincherle has reproduced in facsimile (large edition, p. 280). For the dot—when writing i, a colon or a full stop—he there uses the following forms: thin and thick point (the main forms), stroke leading slightly to the lower right like the grave accent (in shorter and longer forms), short transverse stroke, small hook (<), shorter or longer stroke leading slightly to the upper right, signs like ∪ ∩, and even wedge-head strokes made from the top downwards, and also diagonally. Often there are different forms used in the same word; for example, Vivaldi often writes a colon with a dot on top and a diagonal stroke in no particular direction underneath. Here the connection with the duct becomes evident: after the upper dot, the hand remained in the same position, whereas after the lower one it moved on! Furthermore, for the grave accent, Vivaldi used, besides the correct sign, strokes and wedge-heads in all directions, and even the comma-like apostrophe. Is it not presumptuous, in view of such graphic multiplicity for a sign that is in itself so simple and completely unequivocal, to expect of the composer as precise a differentiation between wedge-heads and dots as modern musicologists would wish for?!

However, the majority of Vivaldi scores show a conscious distinction between the two signs. An E minor Violin Concerto, P. 125, has in the Largo three signs in the space of two bars (Plate VIII, top): the staccato dot, then the wedge-heads, here placed over the slurs, and a diagonal stroke over the B before the cadenza trill, exactly like the linguistic grave accent. On a later page of the score of the same work, from the third movement, Allegro (Plate VIII, bottom), dots and wedge-heads are likewise differentiated. It follows from these examples, that the dot was used only as a staccato sign, in other words that the bow remained on the string at this point and only its movement was interrupted. Whether this was to be a sharp staccato or more of a portato movement of the bow depended not a little on the tempo. However, it must be remembered that with the old bow and its convex curvature it was in any case impossible to play with a modern staccato such as relies on the elasticity of

72

the inward-curving bow. Thus in the example, Plate VIII top (Largo!), a relatively gentle, expressive portato is intended, and the wedge-head bowing which introduces the cadenza must have indicated a threefold abrupt lifting of the bow. Leopold Mozart has given an exact description of both manners of bowing: 'Often a composer writes some notes which he wishes to be performed staccato, each having its own stroke and isolated from the next. In this case he indicates his intention by small strokes, which he places above or underneath the notes: e.g.' (there follows an example with isolated wedge-heads).

In §17 an example is described in which each group of four notes with dots above or underneath is linked by a slur: 'This indicates that the notes appearing under the connecting sign must be played not only in one stroke, but should be differentiated from each other by a slight stress applied to each note.'

'If however instead of the dots, small strokes are written, then the bow is lifted at each note; consequently all the notes appearing under a connecting sign must indeed be played in one stroke, yet completely isolated from each other, e.g.' (there follows an example in which a slur connects every four notes, of which the first is unmarked and the three others provided with strokes). 'The first note of this example comes on a down bow; the other three, however, should be played with an up bow, lifting the bow each time and separating them from each other by a strong stress.'

The isolated diagonal stroke over the B in the example (from P. 125 Plate VIII, top right) is interesting and is probably a musical use of the *accento grave*, indicating the turning-point of the cadenza with a forceful attack. The example from the third movement provides clear evidence that the wedge-head, when used without a slur in quicker tempo, requires a *jeté* bowing, and the dots and slurs need to be played once more with a portato bowing (note the subsequent Legato!). A necessary premise for accepting this indication as meaning *jeté* is the rejection of the notion— as false as it is widespread—that in the Baroque period, the bow was always kept on the string (see Kolneder, *Aufführungspraxis*, pp. 45 ff.).

In a kind of 'imitatio violistica' these articulation marks, which had arisen from the playing of the violin, were taken over by the wind instruments; for instance, portato dots with slurs appear in a Bassoon Concerto P. 72 (Ex. 66). The Concerto P. 155, *Il Gardellino*, is of interest: its first version—a concerto with chamber orchestra—in many places has the marking ⌢⎮⎮⌢, but in the printed edition the slurs are omitted and the wedge-heads only appear at the start of such a sequence; often the wedge-heads too are omitted. Thus it probably happened that Vivaldi, from his instincts as a violinist, wrote out violin-type articulation for the wind instruments without thinking, but then omitted the superfluous slurs when it came to preparing the work for printing. However, in both cases a comparatively violent staccato is required. A peculiar example from the secular cantata *La Sena festeggiante* (The festive Seine) shows typically string-like articulation transferred to vocal music (Ex. 67). In the same work there are also different means of articulation where the first violin's line is in unison with the singing voice (Ex. 68).

The rapidity of the composer's hand often gives the impression of a marked differentiation over a short time, as in the last movement of a Concerto for Violin, Organ and Oboe in C major, P. 36 (Ex. 69); however, it is clear from similar passages that all the first six notes should have wedge-heads.

Often a passage is given a very characteristic imprint by isolated wedge-heads alternating with slurs (Ex. 70). It is not easy to explain a passage in the first movement of a Cello Concerto in C major, P. 30 (Ex. 71). In an Allegro it can no longer be performed in the way indicated by Leopold Mozart, and here it can only be a case of a kind of flying staccato. Many string players who have been inhibited by false representations of the Baroque style, will find it hard to accept this, occurring at such an early date. To sum up, it can be said of dots and wedge-heads that Vivaldi in general used them in the same way as that described by Leopold Mozart, and made a precise distinction between them. Only in hastily written scores do the wedge-heads gradually become dots. However, a clear distinction can always be made in the light of the context.

Vivaldi had a surprisingly abundant repertoire of bowing techniques, and consequently of methods of articulation. Besides the possibilities already mentioned, there is the 'sciolto', ties on the same note with a change of position, and even in certain cases bowed phrasing. Only a precise performance of the articulation, which is often so exactly indicated, will give to his music that internal division which corresponds to its rhythmic and dynamic refinements.

The Performance of the Figured Bass

So-called figured bass, or basso continuo, is a basic compositional hall-mark of the entire Baroque period. The composer thought essentially in two parts, with the main part at any given time having a leading line, and a bass which had not only a melodic function, but also supported the harmony. In the composer's conception of sound, the melodic and harmonic tendencies thus come into a special relationship, and only a few works of this time, such as for instance Bach's Inventions and Sinfonias, can be considered as standing outside this creative conception; and even here, in any case, harmonic thought is not excluded, though the harmonic writing is subordinate to the primarily polyphonic layout.

Vivaldi's basses are always 'figured' basses, no matter whether they bear figures or not. However, the composer was very sparing in writing out figures, and in many of the manuscript scores of his that we possess the bass is completely without them. If such pieces have been edited without filled-out harpsichord part, then this shows a fundamental misunderstanding. There are many reasons for Vivaldi's 'unfigured figured basses'. The first of these is the chronic lack of time the overworked maestro had; but then there is also the fact that, particularly in the fast movements, the harmonies are so much reduced to tonic, dominant, etc., that for long stretches figures were hardly necessary. Finally too, figuring would often have been superfluous because either Vivaldi himself would be at the harpsichord, or he could count on some colleague well versed in matters of basso continuo, or perhaps on a well-trained pupil, such as Maestra Luciana Organista.

The Dresden manuscript of the A major Violin Concerto, P. 228, dedicated to his pupil and friend, shows what the master himself thought about the necessity of figuring the bass. The whole work is unfigured except for one passage. In the foreword to the Peters Edition (No. 4206) Ludwig Landshoff says of this: 'Only in bars 61–66 of the last movement does he make an exception and indicate to the continuo player by the warning sign 7 6, four times repeated, that here a sequence is in progress in which on the first crotchet of each of the bars indicated a seventh should be allowed for, and it should be resolved onto the sixth on the next crotchet. He writes "Per li Coglioni" in capitals over the figures to shame ignoramuses and at the same time to explain to Pisendel that he did not mean the instruction to be intended for him, the connoisseur.' Vivaldi's marginal annotation is ambiguous and very acid; the milder sense might be translated as 'for blockheads'.

In the slow movements, which with their chromatic tensions over a short space of time were laid out harmonically very differently from the fast movements, Vivaldi occasionally left very exact indications, above all in his sonatas and church works. Moreover the printed editions as well as the manuscripts contain many wrong figuring marks. These are probably in the first place errors made in haste, as for example when in the central movement of the 'Con^{to} in due Cori P. la S. S^{ma} Assontione di M. V.' (Concerto for double orchestra for the Assumption of the Blessed

Virgin Mary) in C major, P. 14, a suspension of the ninth is marked 4 3 in the bass. Fair warning against fidelity in the realization of the bass! We possess a few examples for the realization of figured bass Vivaldi wanted that are remarkable in many respects (see Kolneder, *Aufführungs-praxis*, pp. 85–88). They contrast strikingly with what we are told by contemporary textbooks on the figured bass. The chords on the keyboard's upper stave are generally very highly pitched, sometimes in the same register as the melodic line, and sometimes even higher. Thus the composer's intention was not to fill up the space between the melody and the bass, somewhat after the general practice of linking the chords closely with the melody; rather they were for him a coloration of the sound which he juxtaposed with that of the melody instrument. This will be particularly evident from a 'Con^to con molti Istrom^ti ', P. 87, in which he calls for two harpsichords on account of the size of the ensemble (see p. 142). In the middle movement the orchestra is silent, and only the solo violin plays with the two harpsichords; in executing the continuous quaver bass, these relieve each other at half-bar intervals (see Kolneder, *Aufführungspraxis*, p. 87). The accompanying chords are filled out with demisemiquaver figuration which in this case also lies in the melody register, the appealing mixture of sound being the real purpose of a realization of the continuo bass. A peculiarity of the few bass realizations by Vivaldi that have survived is the occurrence of unrestricted parallel octaves between the bass and the upper voices. They show that a comfortable playing position of the right hand and the sound colour of high-lying chords were more important to the composer than technical immaculacy.

It is interesting to come across many of Vivaldi's directions such as 'Senza Cembalo', 'Senza Organi ò Cembali' and 'Senza Cembali sempre'. One may be sure to find them whenever, for programmatic reasons, the expressive sound of strings or winds must not be disturbed by the brittle edge of accompanying chords on the harpsichord; such a place is the third movement of the Bassoon Concerto *La notte* (Night), P. 401, which bears the superscription *Il Sonno* (Sleep). However, similar instrumentation can also be found in non-programmatic works. In the middle movement of the Violin Concerto in A minor, Op. III No. 6, P. 1—a work which has been popular with violin teachers ever since Küchler's edition appeared—the basses have a break, three orchestral violins and a viola weave a four-part carpet of sound upon which the solo violin then unfolds its melody (Ex. 72). Here too the orchestra is dynamically differentiated from the soloist and the upper voice of the four-part accompaniment lies above the solo melody. The parallel unisons in bars 4–6 and above all the doublings of the leading note in the cadence show that here too considerations of sound-colour took priority over purity of technique and that a genuine five-part polyphony was not intended.

In this movement the bass part is pitched an octave higher than usual and given to the viola. This high bass register, and its performance by the upper group of the string orchestra, are often to be found in Vivaldi; in the absence of middle parts, they produce a thin, tightly coordinated style and can indeed be regarded as a characteristic of the composer which then appeared to a more marked extent in Tartini, and can still be found in Mozart's violin concertos. So as to indicate to the orchestral players that at such places they no longer had to play a middle part of subordinate importance but an important bass part, in spite of its high register, such as was called a 'Bassetchen' (Quantz, Leopold Mozart), a bass clef was usually written at such points, though the part had to be played an octave higher. A direction such as this was not necessary if a complete movement was written without a bass instrument, as for instance in the two-part middle movement of a G major Violin Concerto, Op. IX, No. 10 (= P. 103). The two orchestral violins and the viola play a pizzicato line which proceeds in broken chords (Ex. 73). The question now arises whether or not in such cases a keyboard instrument would be incorporated to fill out the harmonies. Fortunately the orchestral material used by the composer himself for some of his own works has survived; we also possess the harpsichord part of the E minor Violin Concerto, P. 126, and this is notated only as a figured bass. In the first movement, the harpsichord is silent with the basses for 48 out of 93 bars. From this it is obvious that the keyboard instruments should be omitted not only when instructions are expressly given to this effect, but also in places where the bass is given to alto or violins and the bass instruments (cello and double bass) have rests. This means in fact that almost half of Vivaldi's music should be performed without an instrument to fill out the harmony. The harpsichord was certainly still regarded by Vivaldi as a traditional orchestral instrument, but it gradually became superfluous when his ideal became that of sparse writing with bass parts which often lay in a high register (a style which then became so typical of early Classical music) and when, as in many places, the harpsichord would have been detrimental to the orchestral sound.

The cello and double bass were a matter of course in performing the bass line of ritornellos; when wind instruments were included in the orchestra, the bass line was generally reinforced by bassoons, even if the instrument was not specifically asked for. Quantz (XVIIth Chapter, Section I, §16) recommended the use of a bassoon with as few as 9 stringed instruments; with only 14 strings, 2 oboes and 2 flutes, 2 bassoons; and with 21 strings, 4(!) oboes and 4(!) flutes, 3 bassoons. When accompanying a solo, the bass line is occasionally given to a solo double bass with the direction 'Violone solo', as for example in an A minor Bassoon Concerto, P. 47, as well as in an aria with obbligato cello in the opera *Ottone in Villa*. In general the solo sections of the violin concertos are accompanied by only one cello (with keyboard instrument). However, if the cello is joined by the double bass, Vivaldi has in several places eased the rather thick sonority by using pizzicato. In an aria from the opera *Tito Manlio* there is the indication 'Violone pizzicato—Bassi con l'arco', where Bassi means cellos. The score of a sumptuously orchestrated church festival Concerto in C major 'per la solennità di San Lorenzo' (for the Feast Day of St. Lawrence), P. 84, indicates the use of the bassoon as a bass accompanying the solo. The string orchestra is augmented by two recorders, two oboes and two clarinets, and the bass line bears the heading 'Bassi e Fagotto'. Whenever the wind instruments in the upper parts are given prominence as a solo group, the indication 'Fagotto solo' almost invariably appears in the bass. Thus it may be taken as the rule that with a solo wind instrument the bassoon took the bass, so that when there was a duet in the upper voices the result would be what Georg Muffat so charmingly called the *dreistimmig besetzte Tertzl*.

Numerous entries in Vivaldi's scores—sometimes in different ink or in different script—point to the fact that the composer even altered his continuo bass instrumentation from one performance to another. This may be connected with having to use a different ensemble, or different players whom he would use according to their abilities, or perhaps too it had to do with the acoustical properties of different places of performance. But extremely variable instrumentation can also be found in one and the same work, as for instance in a 'Con^{to} à 10 obligati' in the Dresden collection (P. 359), which in the Turin manuscript bears the title 'Concerto p S.A.R. di Sas^a del Sig. D. Antonio Vivaldi' (Concerto for His Royal Highness the King of Saxony . . .). The work is scored for oboe principale, violino principale, two recorders, two oboes, two bassoons, two violins, viola, cello, double bass and two harpsichords (the bassoons, cello, double bass and harpsichords all being counted as one part!). At the beginning, the head of the bass stave reads 'Tutti li Bassi', but further on, to match the different solo instruments in the spotlight, the bass line is instrumentated as follows: 'Grande Bassone solo', 'Tutti', 'Bassone solo', 'Tutti li Bassi del Concertino', 'Basso dà fiato', '1 solo Bassone' etc. However, not only did Vivaldi give different sound colorations to the bass line episodically, but he even did so over a very short space of time. In another Dresden concerto à 10, the Concerto in G minor, P. 383, for solo violin, two recorders, two oboes, bassoon, two violins, viola and bass (cello and double basses with harpsichord) there are half-bar alternations similar to those in P. 87.

The furthest Vivaldi went in this concern for a variegated instrumentation of the bass line was in an unfortunately unfinished sketch of thirteen bars for the central movement of the Violin Concerto in B♭ major, P. 349 (given in Kolneder, *Aufführungspraxis*, p. 115). The chromatically falling bass with six equal quavers per bar is split up into crotchets on violins, violas and basses. In fact Schoenberg's much discussed melody of tone colours had here been anticipated two hundred years beforehand.

THE CREATIVE PROCESS

As a creative personality, Vivaldi belonged to the precocious and prodigious type of artist, together with Pergolesi, Mozart, Schubert and Mendelssohn. At a time when the printing of music and the distribution of printed music were in their infancy, and consequently the resident *maestro di cappella* had to satisfy the enormous demand for music largely from his own pen, rapid production was almost a professional precondition for a bandmaster and was quite common among the composer's contemporaries. If Vivaldi's work-rate constantly astounded his contemporaries, then it must have been so extraordinary that even a generation professionally given to fast and copious writing found it striking. Vivaldi himself seems to have enjoyed the smooth functioning of his workmanship, and boasted of it. On August 29, 1739, Charles de Brosses wrote to his friend M. de Blancey: 'He is an old fellow who has a prodigious passion for composition. I have heard him boast of composing a concerto with all its parts in less time than it would take a copyist to copy it.'

The rapid work and therefore great number of compositions of the Baroque composers have very various reasons. As opposed to listeners of today, who will accept music written within a period of at least 300 or 400 years, Vivaldi's listeners were entirely geared to 'first performances'. That Bach wrote several complete yearly cycles of cantatas because his public wanted to hear 'new music' every Sunday and Feast Day is a reflection of a situation that would be quite unthinkable today. This unceasing productivity weighed heavily on the composers, however. We know that Monteverdi was once drawn to the brink of physical collapse, and the Darmstadt court *Kapellmeister* Christoph Graupner, by whom 1,418 church cantatas have survived, once complained: 'My work burdens me to such an extent that I am almost unable to do anything else at all; I can only make sure that I am on time with my composition, and as if Sundays were not enough, there are Feast Days and—oftener still, even—other events coming between whiles.' Such circumstances furnish the explanation for many a feebler composition of Vivaldi, many a routine work whose main aim was to meet a performance or production date. The Baroque solo concerto form, in which Vivaldi was such a proficient craftsman, presented itself as a convenient frame for rapid production. In its simplest form, the ritornello, constructed according to the principle of juxtaposition, was shortened by omitting certain of its sections on its numerous transposed returns, and the last ritornello was indicated by D.C. (da capo). The solo sections were accompanied only by the figured bass, and the orchestra was generally silent altogether in the middle movement. Vivaldi had a reliable method for cases in which especial haste was necessary: the ritornello was partly or completely laid out in one part, and played by the whole orchestra in unison; in other words, the composer notated only one part, and in the other staves of the score wrote a type of shorthand sign that meant 'ut sopra'. Suchlike abbreviations, which were also usual at the time in Italian handwriting, are common in Vivaldi. A particularly attractive one is the sign ♯ for the key signature of D major or B minor.

Above all the ability to write quickly was a necessity also in the operatic life of the seventeenth and eighteenth centuries. Certainly the impresario would plan his season long in advance and would commission so many works that, given an average number of performances, the seasonal programme would be well filled. If, however, an opera was unexpectedly a failure—and this happened often enough, simply as a result of the intrigues of rivals—then a substitute had to be concocted at a moment's notice, as it were. Allotting the acts to different composers and plundering freely from one's own (or even other composers') earlier works were common, and in the circumstances inevitable methods; but above all one needed at one's disposal an inexhaustible flow of ideas and a skilled hand. In such situations Vivaldi was probably many times the saviour in the hour of greatest need. On the manuscript score of the opera *Tito Manlio* is written 'Musica del Vivaldi fatta in 5 giorni' ('Music by Vivaldi, composed in five days')!

Many manuscripts of the master betray their rapid origins. Ludwig Landshoff, in the foreword to his edition of P. 228, has described his impression on studying the score, of Vivaldi's creative frenzy: 'With the creator's mounting agitation the vivacious handwriting becomes more cursory from page to page. Evidently the hastening pen was scarcely able to keep up with the cataract of thoughts flowing from a mind that was inexhaustible in its ideas. The signs at the beginnings of staves take on larger and larger dimensions, the baroque verve of the accolades and of the treble clefs whose flourishes extend into the lower stave take on a more and more powerful sweep. Many accidentals that had been overlooked in the rush are only restored at a second glance, and because of lack of space *between* the notes are written *over* them. And at the slightest opportunity Vivaldi uses a form of shorthand.'

This rapid and seemingly unrestrained production in fact ran contrary to the critical opinion of many contemporaries. Admittedly without mentioning Vivaldi by name, Johann Joachim Quantz sharply attacked the master to whom he owed the decisive stimuli of his youth. In the XVIIIth Chapter, §58, of his book on the flute, he has Vivaldi and Tartini in mind in connection with the decline of musical taste in Italy: 'Two celebrated Lombardic violinists who began to be known about thirty or more years ago, one not long after the other, have independently contributed much to this state of affairs. The first was lively and rich in invention, and supplied almost half the world with his concertos. Although Torelli, and after him Corelli, had made a start in this genre of music, this violinist, together with Albinoni, gave it a better form, and produced good models in it. And in this way he also achieved general credit, just as Corelli had with his twelve solos. But finally, as a result of excessive daily composing, and especially after he had begun to write theatrical vocal pieces, he sank into frivolity and eccentricity both in composition and performances; in consequence his last concertos did not gain as much approbation as his first . . . Whatever the case may be, because of his character this change in his manner of thinking in his last years almost completely deprived the above-mentioned celebrated violinist of good taste in both performance and composition.'

Apparently Quantz was not alone in thinking this. Above all in Venice itself, as can be seen from a letter of de Brosses (see p. 20), Vivaldi's works came by degrees to be received very critically. Did he really compose unrestrainedly and uncritically, and after once having come upon and retained the concerto form, simply make as many routine copies of it as he needed? Doubtless he could have done that, and also did not hesitate to do so when time pressed him. Yet examination of the Turin autographs, of which a good many are working manuscripts, thus not fair copies made after composition, shows that Vivaldi corrected much and was by no means uncritical towards his own works. An extremely interesting case of such a correction occurs in a 'Con^to in due Cori P la S. S^ma assontione di M.V.' (Concerto for double orchestra for the Assumption of the B.V.M.), P. 14. In the final movement the violin cadenza (given in Kolneder, *Aufführungspraxis*, p. 70) is preceded by a 40-bar solo episode over a pedal-point. This is laid out in such a way that the harmonic course is built up of four-bar groups which are then curtailed to two-bar and then to one-bar groups. Vivaldi accelerated the transition to one-bar groups by crossing out a bar in each of two places. Such corrections in the interests of abbreviation, and thus of concentration, are often to be found, as for instance in a Concerto ripieno P. 231. In this type of concerto, in which the sustaining opposition between soloist and orchestra is lacking, the danger of a loss in tension was to a large extent concomitant with too extensive a formal plan. If it had not been achieved in the first draft, a shorter construction had to be produced by deletions (Plate IX). In the Concerto ripieno P. 230 too, Vivaldi deleted much in the outer movements, though for the Largo he crossed out a three-bar opening and, beginning again, stretched it out over twice the length. Similar corrections made in the course of work are shown by the score of a Concerto for two violins in D major, P. 190, as well: the ritornello was shortened before he had even written out the bass. A different case is the Concerto P. 165: here the composer introduced corrections when the parts were already written out. It may be supposed that the alterations were the result of the aural experience of a rehearsal or a performance. The Concerto P. 35 is important for an understanding of the creative process in the early eighteenth century: Vivaldi wrote out the harmonic sequence in the upper stave of the organ before he composed the leading melodic voice, an interesting illustration of Rameau's proposition 'La mélodie naît de l'harmonie' (The melody is born of the harmony)!

Besides compressing and concentrating by crossing out superfluous bars, there are other corrections which concern the total conception. Thus in a Bassoon Concerto in C major, P. 46, Vivaldi began the third movement in 4/4, but apparently remembered after three bars that both the previous movements were in the same metre. He then discarded the opening and chose 3/4 time for the final movement. In another instance, in the Violin Concerto in C major Op. IX, No. 1 (= P. 9), the composer actually changed his modulation. In his creative absorption he seems to have forgotten his initial key, modulated to B minor and also written a tutti entry in this key. But a tonality two steps away in the circle of fifths was beyond the bounds of harmonic possibility according to the aesthetics of Vivaldi's times. Hence the modulation to B minor was crossed out and replaced by one to E minor, so that the sequence of tonalities for the ritornello became I–V–III–VI–I. The concerto is also worthy of note in that Vivaldi abandoned the last movement of the Turin manuscript and composed an entirely new one for printing. In fact in works that have survived in several versions, single movements were often changed. Thus the difference between the concertos P. 164 and P. 349 (there is a copy of each of them in Dresden and Turin) is their different central movements, whilst P. 282 exists in Turin in a version each for cello and bassoon, though here only the first movements are the same.

Double versions of this kind for two different instruments exist of several works, and provide a good insight into the composer's working methods. In the first place Vivaldi was influenced by the older ad libitum practice which rested on the fact that a specific playing technique for any particular instrument was only in its earliest stages of development and thus scarcely influenced the composer's thought. Whereas older composers had written in an all-embracing melodic style permeated with toccata-like figurations pitched in the middle register of the commoner instruments, works were produced such as Vivaldi's Op. XIII, *Il Pastor Fido*, 'Sonates, pour la Musette, Vielle, Flûte, Violon avec la Basse Continue . . .'—in spite of its high opus number, presumably not a late work! In preparing Op. VIII for publication, two works that were both originally intended for the oboe were taken over into a series of twelve violin concertos. In the published edition these are given as violin concertos, for oboe ad libitum. This meant renouncing specifically violinistic figurations, as well as double-stopping, the use of chords, and the register of the G string. But perhaps this itself won the gratitude of violinists in amateur circles—and also not least that of the publishers—for a work, which also contained the technically difficult *Seasons* concertos.

However, Vivaldi himself advanced the development and individuation of violin technique and invented and used characteristic figurations for other instruments too, such as the bassoon and the cello in particular, so that the ad libitum way of thinking was already superseded in his time. If for some reason or other he undertook a new version of a work—generally a transcription for a different instrument—he consequently had to tackle a new composition. Naturally this was not always the case. Thus between the already mentioned ad libitum possibilities and completely new composition, there were a number of intermediate steps. In contrast with the classical concerto, the baroque form to a large extent facilitated such a procedure. Since a motivic connection between the ritornello and the solo sections was not unconditionally essential, in extreme cases new solo sections could simply be interposed in the context of the ritornello framework. But even when the composer sought after motivic relationships, inserting new solo sections posed no problems. In many cases the essential shape of the solo section was retained, and simply adapted by the composer, who modified it wherever necessary while retaining the same basso continuo.

Generally in arranging a work Vivaldi started out from the properties of the instrument for which it was intended and thereby showed a highly developed sense of discrimination between instruments. In a Cello Concerto in G major in the Turin collection (P. 118) which he arranged for flute—still a new instrument to be chosen for solo playing at that time—the first solo section in the first movement is extensively remodelled though the motivic substance remains the same (Ex. 74). In the first place bars which have typically string-like broken chords and a widely leaping line are transformed into melodic lines for the wind instrument. From bar 22 on a sequentially repeated one-bar group is wittily varied and notably improved on by a very concise octave leap downwards. The threefold sequence in the cello version from bar 25 too is in a remarkable way virtually eliminated by variation and truncation; from bar 29 a further sequence is made inoperative by a simple device, and finally the bass cadence is metamorphosed into a closing melodic formation. The technique shown here of giving fresh tension to all-too-frequent repetition of motifs by variation is however one of the essential methods of baroque performing practice. If analysts and critics often speak of 'tiring rosalia chains', it is usually absolute fidelity of musical thought and performance that is at fault, leaving out of consideration an essential factor of eighteenth-century performance practice, namely improvised diminution.

If Vivaldi's works are compared in number with those of Bach, Telemann, Handel, Haydn and Mozart, it must be concluded that they remained entirely within the limits that were usual for his time, so that he was by no means excessively prolific. The masters of the eighteenth century composed for the most part without historical awareness, in other words the works of their predecessors had already disappeared from the repertoire or were by now regarded as outmoded, and were seldom played; the possibility of comparisons scarcely existed, either for the public or for the creator himself. Haydn and Mozart were the first composers whose works continued to be played when something like a repertoire with historical depth began to be established towards the end of the century.

Beethoven was the first composer of importance to work in consciousness of the works of his forbears and must thus have felt himself part of an evolutionary chain. Only in this way can his cautious and tentative approach to the symphony—for all his resoluteness—be understood, and also the sudden and marked decrease in the number of his works. Vivaldi, who had grown up in a time of enormously heightened musical consumption, found himself perfectly adapted both by his creative disposition and his compositional technique to the society around him, whose musical needs he satisfied with copious production. What is characteristic of him is not that he wrote so much but the high quality of some of those works which, when time and circumstances permitted, he indefatigably refined in a constant search for perfection. The Turin autographs provide evidence of this on almost every page.

VIVALDI'S PROGRAMME MUSIC

Many readers may be surprised to find at the beginning of our observations on the master's individual concertos a chapter on works of a programmatic kind; and all the more so since in many music-lovers' minds the eighteenth century is regarded as a period of absolute music, in other words of music whose origins are in no way determined by extra-musical stimuli. Since the last years of the fifteenth century, as a result of the close conjunction between words and music, which had been further strengthened by the Church's fundamental demands for the clear interpretation of words, certain rhythmic/melodic turns of phrase had been developed which directly served the communication of the words' meaning. Many of these imitate conceptions of movement or space, others arose from the expressive content of the dissonance. In Germany they were soon examined from the point of view of their aesthetic effect, and were classified and described in didactic works. Thus musical rhetoric became a branch of study and the most important part of the real science of musical composition, and it lost little of its significance when gradually an autonomous instrumental music was developed that was independent of the premises of the creation of vocal music. As a 'language of sounds' it found an important defender of its aesthetics in Mattheson.

We know of no textbooks dealing with musical rhetoric in the field of Italian musical practice, though in fact their abundant production of madrigals shows that Italian composers were thoroughly acquainted with musical formulae for the interpretation of words, used almost as tricks of the trade. Here a certain contrast between the musical character of the Germans and that of the Italians seems to become apparent: it seems that the Italian composer, with his direct sensuous responsiveness, had a direct approach to the possibilities of a music that was connected with or even portrayed the expression of emotions. The works of Monteverdi show how a master of madrigal composition could do justice to the new tasks set to the creative musician by opera. The far-reaching transformation of music in representing personal emotions, portraying martial and heroic situations, the pastoral realm and the underworld, and reproducing phenomena of nature such as the splashing of waves, storm and tempest, was finally effected in the country of opera, Italy, in the seventeenth century. It produced a new language of composition which was much less tied to words than that of the German musical rhetoricians, but rather made use of all the instrumental possibilities offered by the newly developing timbre-palette of the orchestra.

If we examine Vivaldi's works from the point of view of rhetorical figures, we shall be able to find relatively few examples of a conscious use of 'speaking' turns of phrase in the sense of interpretation of words, compared with the yield of a like examination of the music of Bach, for instance. But Vivaldi's instrumental music is rich in characteristic turns of phrase which are usually ascribed to the increased development of playing technique since Torelli and Corelli, but which are used in such a specific sense in his programmatic works that in them may be found keys to the interpretation of his complete œuvre. It is natural that a Venetian composer who had written one or two operas every year since his 36th year should have been so attached to descriptive music that he wrote instrumental music with programmatic titles. After all, in comparison with Torelli, Corelli, Albinoni, Marcello and other contemporary masters, programme music occupies such a sizable proportion of Vivaldi's entire output that one must conclude that he had a specific inclination and talent for this type of work. Already the general titles of his Op. III, *L'Estro Armonico* ('The Harmonic Inspiration'), Op. IV, *La Stravaganza* ('The Extraordinary'), Op. VIII, *Il Cimento dell'Armonia e dell'Inventione* ('The Contest between Harmony and Invention') and Op. IX, *La Cetra* ('The Lyre') point in this direction.

Altogether 28 of Vivaldi's works have individual titles:

P.	Opus	Title
7	VIII No. 6	Il piacere
86		Madrigalesco
106	XI No. 2	Il Favorito
112		Concerto o sia il Cornetto a Posta
143		Alla Rustica

VIII. Violin concerto in E minor, P. 125, excerpts from 2nd and 3rd movements.

IX. Facsimile from concerto ripieno in A major, P. 231, 1st movement.

THE WORK

That six of these works appear in Op. VIII (published in 1725) and three in Op. X (published in 1729)—thus in printed works whose appearance occurred within a short time of each other—perhaps points to a certain tendency of the time which Vivaldi subscribed to by adding his titles. In fact the *Seasons* concertos were soon among the master's most popular works, and after 1728 were repeatedly played in Paris where the publishers Le Clerc and Me Boivin had issued the entire Op. VIII soon after its appearance. In 1765 *Laudate Dominum de Coelis* by Corette was performed, bearing the subtitle 'Motet à Grand Chœur arrangé dans le Concerto de Printemps de Vivaldi'!

Many of the titles may have been intended as jests, and perhaps were not originated by the composer, as for example, the Violin Concerto P. 151, of whose four copies only one, that in Schwerin, has the title *Grosso Mogul*. Vivaldi's title to P. 308, *Il Proteo ò sia Il Mondo al rovescio* (Proteus, or The World Upturned), was also probably a joke. In the score the solo violin part is given in the tenor and bass clefs, and the cello part in the treble clef. The following direction is provided: 'Il Violino principale può suonare li soli del Violoncello et al rovescio il Violoncello può suonare li soli del Violino' (The solo violin can play the solos of the cello and conversely the cello those of the violin). In this way it could probably only be played on some occasion when a violinist could read in the tenor and bass clefs (and transpose up an octave). Cellists were accustomed to read in the treble clef (an octave lower) in any case, because in trio sonatas they often had to replace a missing second violin.

In the Flute Concerto *Il Gardellino* (The Goldfinch), P. 155, immediately after the introductory ritornello there is a solo cadenza with an ingeniously cheerful imitation of bird-song like that in Beethoven's Pastoral Symphony. Apart from this the work is constructed according to purely musical laws and only occasional trills in the solo part call to mind the programmatic design. In a similar way, in the violin concertos P. 338 *La Caccia* (The Hunt) and P. 112 *Concerto o sia il Cornetto a Posta* (Concerto or also The Posthorn), the titles only imposed horn- and trumpet-like motivic work on the musical invention, but otherwise in no way influenced the works' design. All those works in which the solo violin is treated 'alla tromba' also belong to this class, as indeed in a broader sense do all that are permeated with trumpet-like motif-work.

Four groups of concertos are especially important for the identification of the fundamentals of Vivaldi's musical thought and of the mental images which aroused his musical inventiveness: (1) works which, in keeping with their title, express states of mind; (2) the two *La Notte* concertos; (3) the two *La Tempesta di Mare* concertos; and (4) the *Seasons* concertos.

In the Violin Concerto *Il Riposo* (Repose), P. 248, the listener is reminded of the physical and spiritual circumstances indicated in the title in the first place by the legato melodic style of the ritornello (Ex. 75). The solo sections too are dominated by legato bowing (Ex. 76). The last movement is laid out in a similar way, with the exception of one solo, whilst the middle movement of only nine bars consists of a sequence of chords in long note-values. At the beginning of the work there is a direction in the bass stave: 'Senza Cembali sempre. Con tutti gli strumenti sempre sordini' (Always without harpsichords. All the instruments muted throughout), and everything points to the fact that this should be read as concerning the whole work. Correspondingly the orchestra is handled during the solo sections in such a way that all the harmony is present and the absence of a keyboard instrument is not felt as a deficiency. The programmatic intentions and full orchestral sound are maintained in the last movement too, though here a 16-bar solo is accompanied only by the basso continuo. Whereas already in the ritornello the viola has notes held over nine bars, the first solo section is built on held chords throughout (Ex. 77). Here the strings are used as the winds were in the classical orchestra, and the third solo section is instrumentated in the same fashion.

The concerto *Il Riposo* is probably the first orchestral work in the modern scoring for strings without a continuo bass; the repose was not to be disturbed by chords on the harpsichord.

The D major Violin Concerto *L'Inquietudine* (Unrest), P. 208, presents a contrast with this work. The first movement, which proceeds in Allegro molto tempo, is dominated by triplet movement and broken chords with wide leaps (Ex. 78). The triplets from the ritornello are also taken over in the solo sections (Ex. 78). This triplet movement is interrupted only for five bars in the whole 61 bars of the first movement, and is aimed at the most concentrated representation of the programmatic design; the canonic treatment of the two violins too—in which the old sense of the canon in hunting music can be felt, with one motif pursuing another—is a consciously applied effect.

In the Flute Concerto in G minor, Op. X, No. 2 (= P. 342) *La Notte* (Night), two movements bear special titles: the Presto section which links on to the Largo introduction is headed by the programmatic title *Fantasmi* (Spectres, phantoms), and preceding the final movement there is a Largo *Il Sonno* (Sleep). In the portrayal of ghosts, or rather in reproducing the spiritual unrest caused by the appearance of phantoms, semiquaver scales in thirds with canonic concentration, compressed alternation of short-breathed semiquaver motifs and a syncopated dactyl figure, enhanced by complementary rhythms, are used (Ex. 79).

The *Sonno* movement is naturally again scored 'Senza Cembalo' and 'Tutti gli stromenti sordini'. It is a small masterpiece of highly romantic tensions: from the bold unprepared suspension in bar 3 on, one dissonance leads straight to the next and in this way the tension is preserved over 27 bars (Ex. 80). The Bassoon Concerto in B♭ major *La Notte*, P. 401, is laid out similarly, though its last movement, with the title *Sorge L'Aurora* (Russet Dawn Rises) does not bear a very characteristic imprint.

For the special position of the two concertos *La Tempesta di Mare* (The Tempest at Sea) in Vivaldi's works it is significant that a similarly named movement appears in the composer's opera *La Fida Ninfa* (The Faithful Nymph). Storm music in opera was very popular in the eighteenth century and even up to Rossini's *The Barber of Seville*, and the French composer Marin Marais, in order to obtain the greatest possible effect by means of the orchestra for his opera *Alcyone* (1706[!]) even undertook studies on the Atlantic coast, and in this way became a master of orchestration. Tempest concertos were inserted into operas, either as interval music at the appropriate point, or else as actual operatic numbers, thus saving the composer the trouble of writing them in the short time the commission might allow him. Both of Vivaldi's works of this kind are relatively harmless pieces from the point of view of their subject, and their design follows exclusively musical laws, for the most part those of solo concerto form. In the Flute Concerto *La Tempesta di Mare* Op. X, No. 1, P. 261, the ritornello, like that of the 'ghost' movement in P. 342, is based on alternating semiquaver scales. Excited and exciting semiquaver movement is so predominant in the solo sections too that in the whole movement there are only a few bars in which somewhat calmer music appears. In spite of their programmatic titles, all these works still belong to the class of absolute music; in other words, the extra-musical presentation certainly influenced the material, but not—or scarcely—the manner of shaping the works, and their formal layout. But the material too remains completely within the bounds of the conventions based on the style of the epoch and the expression of personality. In order to understand such works, it is not absolutely essential to know their titles.

Only with the four *Seasons* concertos did Vivaldi venture into the realm of real programme music; these appeared in print as the first four numbers of Op. VIII. The composer dedicated the work the 'Illustrissimo Signor il Signor Venceslao Conte de Marzin, Signore Ereditario di Hohenelbe, Lomnitz, Tschista, Krzinetz, Kaunitz, Doubek, et Sowoluska, Cameriere Attuale, e Consigliere di S.M.C.C.' (Most Illustrious Mr. Venceslao, Count of Marzin, hereditary prince of . . . at present Chamberlain and Counsellor to His Majesty, the Catholic Emperor) and described himself as 'Maestro in Italia dell'Illustrissimo Signore Conte Sudetto . . .' (Music master to the aforesaid most illustrious Count in Italy). The dedicatory preface is interesting in many respects: 'Most Illustrious Sir, When I think of the long succession of years in which I enjoyed the honourable distinction of serving Your Highness as *Maestro di Musica* in Italy, I blush at the thought that I have not yet given any proof of my profound veneration. Therefore I have decided to have this volume printed, in order to lay it most humbly at Your Highness's feet. I beg of you not to be surprised if among these few and feeble concertos Your Highness should find the Four Seasons which, with your noble bounty, Your Highness has for so long regarded with indulgence. But may you believe that I have found them worthy of appearing in print, because with the sonnets not only are they enhanced by a completely clear interpretation, but so are all the things which are expressed in them. Therefore I am sure that, although they are the same concertos, they will seem to Your Highness as new.'

Thus Vivaldi wrote these four concertos some time before they were published and apparently often played them to the count. Whether the sonnets had already served as the theme of the composition or had only afterwards been composed for the publication is not really clear from this preface. The author of the sonnets is not known, and indeed the fact that he is not named makes it likely that Vivaldi himself was the poet. Before their publication Vivaldi fundamentally reworked the concertos, and this was certainly with a view to enhancing the presentation of the programmatic content.

The third of these concertos, *L'Autumno*, is particularly useful in studying the method and manner of their musical construction. It is headed by the 'Sonetto Dimostrativo' (Plate X), of which a free translation is given here:

A) 'With dances and singing the peasants celebrate
   the fine pleasure of a rich harvest,
B) inflamed by the potion of Bacchus;
C) then their rejoicing ends with sleep.
D) Thus everyone leaves off dancing and singing,
   the gentle air is pleasant,
   and the season invites all
   to the joyousness of a sweet sleep.
E) In the early morn the hunter sets off
   with horns, guns and dogs,
F) the wild beast flees, his scent is pursued;
G) frightened and wearied by the sound of guns
   and the howling of dogs, shot at and imperilled,
   too weak to escape, he perishes in the chase.'

The letters preceding some of the lines are to be found again in the score at the corresponding passages in the depiction; in addition the appropriate line of text is reproduced there, generally with a further programmatic subtitle as well.

Vivaldi begins the first movement of the *Autumn* Concerto with a peasant dance, probably a close rhythmical and melodic relative of a folk-dance of his time (Ex. 81). The solo violin takes it up in double stopping, and the orchestra concludes the first formal group. The real first solo section, corrresponding to the programmatic text marked B), is headed 'L'Ubriaco' (The Drunkard); under this appears the line 'E del liquor . . .'. Broken chords over almost three octaves, demisemiquaver movement, semiquaver triplets, a chain of trills and decorative quavers on the solo violin, these are the means of pictorial representation; the unorganic effect of their aggregation and their variegated succession is, of course, intentional. After this solo section has completed the modulation into the relative minor of the subdominant (G minor), the orchestra takes over again with the somewhat expanded peasant dance, which however is taken to the relative minor of the tonic (D minor). The solo section which then follows is also headed 'Ubriaco' and has a very characteristic melodic line (Ex. 82). In such solos the rather tricky problem is posed as to how far the soloist should go in depicting what is required by the programmatic plot. This decision also perhaps depends on the public. If a programme is provided, they will probably be ready to accept the soloist's somewhat 'drunken' playing. Berlioz's demand in the foreword to his *Symphonie fantastique* that each listener should have a printed programme in his hand, could also apply here!

After the solo section, the peasant dance, developed in syncopated motifs typical of Vivaldi, serves once again as an orchestral ritornello. There follows the third solo section (letter C), with the text 'Finiscono col Sonno . . .' Here the constant flow of a steady tempo that is characteristic of Vivaldi's fast movements is interrupted by the direction 'p e larghetto'; the solo violin's pace slows and there is a close on a fermata. In the Allegro molto (as opposed to the Allegro of the opening) the orchestra concludes the movement with the peasant dance ritornello. Here Vivaldi proceeded in the same way as did many masters of programme music in the nineteenth century, who used sonata or rondo form as their basic framework and identified the individual themes and formal sections with personages, ideas or the action of the given programme. In contrast to the programmatic sequence of the first verse of the sonnet, Vivaldi uses the peasant dance each time as a ritornello after the solo sections, thus conforming to the usual form of the solo concerto. The notion of giving the real descriptive passages to the solo violin in the solo sections resulted from the relationship between ritornello and solo section in solo concerto form: the ritornello provided the firm basis of the formal framework, and the solo sections were of a more improvisatory nature, being also less stable harmonically; these could accommodate the expression of any programmatic idea, without contradiction to the essential nature of the music's 'absolute' structure. In this way programme and form were to a large extent made compatible.

In the further course of the work the 'Ubriachi dormienti' (sleeping drunkards) are represented by a 'sleep' movement, whose design is very similar to that from the concerto *La Notte* (Ex. 80). The third movement *La Caccia* is based on the third and fourth verses of the sonnet. It is built in precisely the same way as the first movement, the orchestral ritornello being formed by a folk-dance-like melody of rude strength (Ex. 83) and fanfare-like motif-work, and at its first appearance it is conjoined to the two lines of text E). Then, with excited semiquaver triplets and demisemiquaver passages, the soloist depicts the actual hunt. But the orchestra too joins in this depiction in a very characteristic way, as for example at the passage 'Già Sbigottita' . . . (Ex. 84).

In the whole cycle of movements, Vivaldi strives in this way towards the well-tried formal scheme of the solo concerto. This can be most easily achieved in those places where the programme is adhered to in only a general way, as for instance in the final movement of the *Spring* Concerto, P. 241, a 'Danza Pastorale' (Shepherds' Dance) with a ritornello melody over bare bagpipe fifths (Ex. 85). In the first movement, too, the 'lieto canto' (happy song) on the arrival of Spring forms the ritornello frame for delightful concerts of bird-song on three solo violins, gentle rustling of zephyrs as well as contrasting thunder and lightning, whilst the sleeping shepherds are again the subject of the middle movement (Ex. 59).

The composer has to bring into play a freer structure when the programme contains very characteristic peculiarities which must be followed exactly by the music, as is the case particularly in the second movement of the *Summer* Concerto where there is a description of a weary man whose rest is disturbed by fear of thunder, lightning and swarms of angry flies. In the *Winter* Concerto, whose programme is likewise very detailed, the composer, in his efforts to make the music the servant of the description, has produced a fine early example of the representation of an extra-musical scheme. Right at the beginning the means of suggesting the sensation of chilling cold in sound are masterly (Ex. 86). In its further course the music has to portray a frightful wind, the chattering of teeth, raindrops, skating, a nervous skater who stumbles, cracking ice and the struggle between the sirocco and the north wind.

Those works of Vivaldi's which have programmatic titles, and his musical means of realizing the textual ground-plan, give rise to some fundamental considerations. The rise of instrumental music in the seventeenth century and the genesis of forms answering to purely instrumental conditions have frequently been shown in all too evolutionary a light, as a progression from the simpler technique of playing instruments to the more complex. According to this view, the violinists had perhaps become tired of playing only in the first position and had bit by bit ventured further into the unexplored regions of the fingerboard, and had likewise, in a sort of joyful spirit of scientific experimentation, discovered new possibilities of bowing technique; and in this way, progressing in stages from one discovery to the next, had created all the copious resources of figuration which the composers of about 1700 were able to draw on. Against such a view, which deduces the standard of playing technique from one work to the next without bothering about the reason for it, must be set the fact that it is far from fortuitous that one of the most important of early instrumental works, Biagio Marini's Op. I, written in Venice in 1617, bears the title *Affetti musicali*. And in his *Tractatus compositionis augmentatus* (c. 1660), Christoph Bernhard, a pupil of Schütz, makes a clear distinction between the older 'Stylus gravis' and the modern 'Stylus luxurians', 'which consists partly of fairly fast notes, occasional leaps such as are well able to sway the emotions, more use of dissonances and Figuris Melopoeticis . . .' Writers like Krüger and Giegling have repeatedly referred to the 'strong pathos, the agitation' that pulses through the instrumental music of post-Gabrieli times. It was this inner restlessness that continually burst the bounds of instrumental expression and hence also of contemporary playing technique, leading to a style that had already in the seventeenth century itself been termed the 'Stylus phantasticus'. The decades in which Torelli and Corelli were active represent the 'youthful *Sturm und Drang* period of absolute music' (Krüger), and everything that was achieved by way of instrumental accomplishments at that time—which then had to be taken up in new forms—can only be properly understood in the light of these extremely emotional forces. Such forces perhaps found their strongest expression in Vivaldi's music, and if his concertos, in the years after 1710, caused astonishment among his contemporaries and incited composers to intensive study, it was not because his use of positions surpassed that of Corelli or anything of that kind, but because of the tremendous inner impetus of the rhythmic and melodic driving forces that contemporary style underwent a revolution in all its aspects. His music must be interpreted in the light of this knowledge. Anyone who simply plays the scales, the broken chords, the double stopping and the different ways of bowing, will miss what is essential to this music. If the performer does not make the listener aware that in Vivaldi a scale or a broken chord can represent a man's inner disturbance (L'Inquietudine!) caused by his fear of ghosts (Fantasmi!) and of natural forces (Tempesta!), he himself cannot have felt the forces from which Vivaldi's notes arose.

THE CONCERTOS PRINTED IN THE COMPOSER'S LIFETIME

Those works that were printed before the composer's death comprise five series of sonatas and the following nine concerto opera:

Opus	Title	No. of concertos	Publisher	Publisher's number	Date of publication
III	*L'Estro Armonico*	12	Estienne Roger	50/51	1712–13
IV	*La Stravaganza*	12	Estienne Roger	399/400	1712–13
VI	—	6	Jeanne Roger	452	1716–17
VII	—	12	Jeanne Roger	470/471	1716–17
VIII	*Cimento dell'Armonia e dell'Inventione*	12	Michele Carlo Le Cène	520/521	c. 1725
IX	*La Cetra*	12	Le Cène	533/534	c. 1728
X	—	6	Le Cène	544	1729–30
XI	—	6	Le Cène	545	1729–30
XII	—	6	Le Cène	546	1729–30

Thirteen further concertos appeared in different collections, partly together with works by other composers; in fact, seven were brought out by Vivaldi's publisher in Amsterdam, three by Walsh and Hare of London, two by Gerhard Frederik Witvogel in Amsterdam and one by Boivin le Clerc in Paris (exact details in Pincherle, *Inventaire thématique*, pp. 23–25). Since in the series covered by opus numbers one work appears twice, this makes a total of 96 concertos. The fact that the Amsterdam publisher is given under different names is the result of the firm's history, having changed hands several times. It was founded by Estienne Roger, who had emigrated from Caen (Northern France) in 1686, first to work as an assistant and collaborator in two publishing houses, and then to set himself up independently in 1695. His name appears on early editions together with that of his assistant manager, and sometimes also with that of his wife. Occasionally Estienne's eldest daughter Jeanne was the publisher's signatory, and in 1716 Michel-Charles Le Cène, the second daughter's husband, entered the business, and managed it on his own after his father-in-law's death (1722).

There were many reissues of the Amsterdam edition: for example Op. III appeared as early as 1715 with Walsh and Hare of London, and again with the same publishers in 1723, besides being published in 1750 by Le Clerc le Cadet in Paris. It says much for Roger's own sales of the work that already in 1717—five years after the first printing—a second impression was needed. The following title of a printed selection is indicative of publishers' practices in the early eighteenth century: *Select Harmony being 12 Concertos in 6 parts, for violin and other instruments, collected from the works of Antonio Vivaldi, viz. his 6.7.8.9. operas, being a well chosen Collection, London Walsh and Hare.* Thus Walsh 'picked the plums' from Opp. VI–IX, which had been edited in Amsterdam by Roger Le Cène, and published them in one volume, naturally without the permission of or providing of financial compensation to either the composer or the original publisher. Such circumstances perhaps explain why only a relatively small number of concertos were printed compared with the total number. In certain cases higher receipts could come from direct dealings with music lovers, and demand might well have diminished if too many works were available in print. It is worthy of note that on the whole the printed concertos are of a lower standard of quality than those we only have in manuscript, and that in any case many of the particularly interesting works did not appear in print. Perhaps Vivaldi's concern was to retain for his own use the pieces which were especially demanding from the point of view of violin technique. We know of Paganini that he took great pains to prevent copies of his concertos, for he well knew that his unique position as a virtuoso was dependent on the fact that his rivals could not lay their hands on his works, and thus could appropriate neither his technique nor his style.

The peculiar relationship between the printed concertos and the un-printed ones in Vivaldi's output must be constantly borne in mind if we are not to arrive at false conclusions about the composer's development, since there are nonetheless clues about the dating of his works in the printed works which bear dates of publication. In his Op. III Vivaldi probably had the ambition to present his most splendid and most richly laid out—formally as well as instrumentally—works in order to establish his reputation as a composer of concertos. In Opp. IV, VI, VII, IX, XI and XII, possibly following the advice and wishes of his publisher, he was content to publish works from his repertoire that were relatively easy to perform. The six Flute Concertos Op. X occupy a special place with regard to the development of the flute as a solo instrument, and the twelve Op. VIII concertos, of which seven bear programmatic titles, are likewise exceptional.

THE TWELVE CONCERTOS OP. III

The highly gifted and equally enterprising publisher Estienne Roger must have had a pronounced flair for spotting young talents, as well as apparently wide-spread musical contacts, through whom he regularly received information about musical life in Italy. This is the only way to explain how, though being geographically a long way from Venice, he was the first to publish Vivaldi's concertos, as Op. III. Opinions as to the date of publication have been at variance for a long time, and Rinaldi, misled by the low publisher's number, took it as being 'around 1702'. But in those days, such numbers served first and foremost to assist the orderliness of storing printed stocks. If an earlier publication was withdrawn, a new work would be given the old number so as to save space. It was in this way that occasionally several works bore the same number, and often works which had appeared relatively late would be given low publishers' numbers. Thus other aids must be called upon to assist the exact dating. On the basis of publishers' catalogues and advertising material included in publications, Pincherle and Lesure have been able to throw light on the publication dates of the Roger firm and have given the date of printing of Vivaldi's Op. III as 1712–13. However, the composition of the concertos themselves must for several reasons be dated from the period beginning shortly after 1700; it seems likely that Vivaldi made a selection from a larger number of works that were already known and tested when Roger made the offer of a publication. It is striking that six manuscripts of concertos from Op. III have been found in widely scattered European towns: three in Dresden and one each in Vienna, Naples and Schwerin. Since it is hardly likely that these manuscripts would have yielded any profits after the music's publication, it follows that they were certainly known and widely distributed even before 1712.

The instrumental layout of several of the works in Op. III is unusual, as is the disposition of the whole edition according to the instruments featured:

Nos. 7 and 10	'con 4 violini e violoncello obligato'
Nos. 1 and 4	'con 4 violini obligati'
Nos. 2 and 11	'con 2 violini e violoncello obligato'
Nos. 5 and 8	'con 2 violini obligati'
Nos. 3, 6, 9 and 12	'con violino solo obligato'

Side by side with four distinct solo concertos there are four concertos with four solo violins, a type of work to which Vivaldi did not later return. However, it is striking that in the whole of Op. III, the printed edition remains in eight parts, namely: Violine I, II, III, IV; Alto viola I, II; Violoncello; Organo (in many editions indicated as 'Contrabasso e Cembalo').

In the concertos for one solo violin, the third and fourth violin parts are identical with that of the second, and violas I and II are identical throughout most of the concertos. Such a division of parts is only necessary when the orchestra is split—perhaps even spatially—into two distinct groups. Thus Op. III can only have been written for an 'antiphonal' type of performance, though certainly such a practice did not extensively affect the compositional techniques it displays. Analysis of individual movements from the Op. III concertos will confirm the composer's somewhat ambivalent attitude to the problems of layout and form. To facilitate this study, three works of differing instrumental layout have been chosen for analysis which appear as miniature scores in the Eulenburg edition, namely:

Op. III, No. 10   for four violins and cello obl.   Eulenburg No. 749
Op. III, No. 8   for two violins   Eulenburg No. 762
Op. III, No. 12   for one violin   Eulenburg No. 787

Concerto Op. III, No. 10 in B minor, first movement

B. 1–4 A trio of soloists, consisting of violins I and II and viola, begins with a four-beat group with characteristic motifs in the violins.

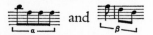

B. 5–8 The entire orchestra repeats this four-bar group which is embellished with an imitatively treated motif in violins II and IV. Violas I

and II have different parts, the texture is seven-part, those for cello and double bass being identical.

B. 9–12 Written in continuous semiquavers in the improvisatory manner of a cadenza, a line for the 3rd violin emerges from the tutti. It is accompanied by a continuo bass in which the double bass plays the fundamental notes of the cello in octaves.

B. 12–16 = 5–8, taken up again by the whole orchestra with a different disposition of parts.

B. 16–20 Similar to bars 9–12: now the 4th violin has a solo line.

B. 20–28 With new motifs in the 1st and 2nd violins (in a seven-part texture) and a fresh and untroubled closing group (only in 3–4 parts!) the orchestra concludes with a cadence. Up till now, the tonality of B minor has not been departed from, the six formal sections up to this point forming a unity maintained by the same tonality. A formal layout of this kind, with relatively short developments in an exchange between orchestra and soloists, is typical of Corelli, and shows Vivaldi to have been at first strongly influenced by that master.

B. 28–37 The 1st violin has a solo line, accompanied by 4th violin and cello, forming the typical Corelli solo trio of 2 violins and cello (with continuo bass). Modulation to D major, the relative major.

B. 37–40 Four-bar tutti in D major, identical with 5–8 and 12–16, but again with a different disposition of parts.

B. 40–53 The 2nd violin—not hitherto treated as a soloist—has a solo line, joined by 3rd violin and both violas (in unison). Modulation to F♯ minor, the dominant minor.

B. 53–59 Tutti in F♯ minor, in seven parts, developed from motifs ζ and β.

B. 59–68 Solo line of 1st violin. Modulation back to the home key, B minor, which will be retained till the end.

B. 68–72 Tutti, identical with 20–24.

B. 72–97 Solo section with all the solo instruments on a motif from the closing group, probably derived from the diminution of α.

B. 97–103 Final tutti, built from bars 5 and 6 and affirmative repetitions of the closing group, 26–29.

After the first 28 bars, the formal sections become longer and the solo sections are used for modulations, as in solo concerto form, giving rise to the harmonic ground-plan I–III–V♭–I. Furthermore, apart from the first four bars, the solo sections and orchestral tuttis are motivically quite distinct from each other. Seen in the light of solo concerto form, the movement could be considered to have in bars 5–8 (12–16) and 20–28 the elements of a ritornello, from which the later tuttis are developed by the technique of ritornello development. Yet the marked formal compartmentalization of the first 28 bars hardly gives the listener the impression of the sort of ritornello that will hold a movement together. In a peculiar way, the whole movement straddles the two formal tendencies hallmarked by Corelli and Torelli. However, this ambivalence did not prevent the composer from writing very inspired music of great motivic power. The possibilities to be found in the antiphonal placing of the orchestra are certainly not used in the sense of any pronouncedly antiphonal writing, but the seven-part texture of the tutti, which is contrasted with constantly changing spatial effects from the solo groups, shows that these rich possibilities were not entirely neglected.

Concerto Op. III, No. 8 in A minor, first movement

B. 1–16 Introductory ritornello. Despite the eight-part layout (4 violins, 2 violas, cello and double bass), the movement is only in 3 to 4 parts except for one bar. Throughout the whole concerto, violas I and II are in unison. The ritornello breaks down into 5 motivic groups:

a (1–4), b (4, 5), c (6–9), d (9–12), e (cadential formula, 13). Groups d (modified to d′) and e are repeated.

B. 16–22 1st violin has a solo whilst a ritornello motif is taken up (4, 5) from group b; 4th violin in unison with the two violas, and 3rd violin partly with this group, partly with the 2nd violin.

B. 23–25 Three-part tutti, d′ plus e.

B. 25–36 Solo of 2nd violin similar to 16–22, from 30 on the 1st violin takes over, accompanied by continuo bass. Modulation to relative major, C major.

B. 37–48 Tutti in C major with short solo interjections. It is built from a new two-bar idea, group c, and another new group, which, with an equally new cadential turn, leads to E minor (dominant minor), then D minor (subdominant).

B. 48–51 Two-part solo group with ritornello motif α.

B. 51–55 Tutti, ritornello group a, expanded by an upbeat.

B. 55–62 Two-part solo group with ritornello motif α, accompanied by 3rd and 4th violins with viola (written in the manner of a continuo bass). Modulation back to the tonic A minor, which is retained to the end.

B. 62–65 Tutti, ritornello group d plus e.

B. 65–67 Solo interjection as in 16, but abbreviated.

B. 68–71 Tutti, ritornello group a, expanded by a new upbeat.

B. 71–78 Two-part solo group with ritornello motif α, 3rd and 4th violins, together with unison violas, forming the orchestrally written-out continuo bass.

B. 78–86 Tutti, built on the ritornello groups b plus c plus d′ plus e.

B. 86–90 Two-part solo interjection, identical with 48–51 with exchange of parts and transposed to A minor.

B. 90–93 Final tutti, ritornello groups d′ plus e.

In contrast to the movement from the Concerto Op. III, No. 10, this one is dominated by a well-articulated ritornello, which is even expanded by new material in several places. Compared with the orchestral sections (totalling 52 bars), the soloists' portion is smaller (46 bars), and this is true not only in terms of bars but also of motivic material: nearly all the solo sections are developed from the ritornello motif α. In its harmonic aspect, the relatively small amount of the relative major tonality is striking, as is the early return of the home key. In this way no less than 62 bars are in A minor. The orchestral means which the printed edition shows to have been available are in no way made use of, the work being simply a concerto for two violins and four-part string orchestra. Only in a few bars is a five-part texture attained, and the tutti writing is mostly in three to four parts. By the strength of its ideas and the concentration of its structure this concerto too is one of the composer's best works. From the point of view of solo concerto form, it represents a step forward from No. 10, above all in its treatment of the ritornello. Certainly the harmonic ground-plan is not evenly balanced, and in later works Vivaldi broke up the harmonic continuity more successfully, thereby avoiding a too marked reliance on the home key.

Concerto Op. III, No. 12 in E major, first movement

B. 1–8 A three-part ritornello of fairly sparse motivic substance: a one-bar motif α is repeated in echo fashion and continued in the dominant; then the first two-bar group appears in the dominant, followed by a cadence in that key.

B. 8–14 The solo violin takes up the ritornello motif α and continues it as if in free improvisation, accompanied only by the basso continuo.

B. 15–18 The three-part tutti takes over the solo part in a new cadential formula and in 16 affirms the home tonality, after which 1 and 2 of the ritornello conclude.

B. 19–31 Solo violin with continuo bass; modulation to relative minor, C♯ minor.

B. 31–45 Three-part tutti, formed from the first bar of the ritornello with its echoed repeat in C♯ minor and 1–4 of the ritornello in the home key, E major. But here the yield of motif α has long expired. This is hardly altered by the fact that the motif is continued by variation.

B. 45–68 Solo violin with basso continuo, modulation to the dominant key.

B. 68–74 Tutti, as in bars 31–45, built on α and its echoed repeat (in B major), bars 1–4 in the home key.

B. 74–87 Solo violin with basso continuo, E major.

B. 87–91 Final ritornello on α and α' and cadential formula from 15 and 16.

The idea of solo concerto form is clearly apparent here; in few works did Vivaldi use the instrumental contrast between solo violin with continuo and tutti so consistently. The solo sections are developed expansively and are copiously inventive, and their relationship to the orchestral sections is such that there are 51 bars of solo against 35 bars of tutti, so that the solo instrument clearly dominates. The ritornello section is less successful; motif α appears in its basic form no less than 16 times, and the nine appearances of the echo effect detract considerably from its effectiveness. The layout of four violins and two violas is in fact not made use of, the tuttis being in three parts, so that a three-part string orchestra with only one violin would have been quite adequate.

It is apparent from these analyses that in Op. III, three very differently laid out types of work are in question: (1) concertos with four violins with short solo sections and groups, having affinities with the Corelli type of concerto grosso, although the ritornello conception is already relatively strongly developed; (2) the double concerto, in clear ritornello form, but with barely developed solo sections, which also have more affinities with Corelli's treatment of the solo group (two violins and continuo) than with the more modern, post-1700, Torelli type of solo and double concerto; (3) the solo concerto with solo sections giving full scope for development and having greater formal weight than the ritornello. The layout of the printed edition is really only suitable for the first type, and it must be doubted whether in fact the adaptation of the solo concertos to an eight-part layout that is essentially alien to their nature was the work of the composer, and also whether these concertos were ever played in such a way. If this should be the case, then Vivaldi must merely have been respecting the tradition of the older practice of antiphonal writing without however basing the structure of the works upon it. From Op. IV on, this arrangement of the parts is no longer to be found, and only occasionally was the composer to write any further concertos 'in due cori'. Thus it can be fairly confidently assumed that the Op. III concertos were composed at a time when Antonio sometimes worked with the San Marco orchestra in place of his father, and that now and again his early compositions were performed there. At this time the great period of music laid out for two or more bodies of performers was already past, but the traditional spatial disposition of the musicians had remained. Vivaldi's Op. III clearly shows this transitional stage in the aftermath of a tradition which, because of different evolutionary aims, had gradually lost its meaning and was later abandoned.

We can get some idea of the enormous effect of the Op. III concertos on Vivaldi's contemporaries by reading in the foreword to the Eulenburg score the fine words spoken by Einstein of that famous passage in the last movement of Op. III, No. 8 where the second violin, playing 'Cantabile solo e forte', makes a contrast to the first violin's semiquaver arpeggios with a melody imbued with passionate rapture: 'It is as if the windows and doors of a stately baroque hall had been opened to welcome in Nature's freedom: a superb pathetic grandeur such as the seventeenth century had not known; a cosmopolitan's cry to the world. It is worth remembering that such must have been known to Bach, and that he, wrapped up in himself, never ventured into this open country.'

JOHANN SEBASTIAN BACH AND VIVALDI

'. . . che ne fu il maggiore estimatore e che seppe (unico probabilmente nel suo tempo) intravedere tutta la grandezza del genio di quel musicista.'*

Alfredo Casella on Bach's relationship to Vivaldi.

In the year 1802 the Bureau de Musique Hoffmeister und Kühnel 'for patriotic admirers of genuine musical art' brought out Johann Nikolaus Forkel's work *Ueber Johann Sebastian Bachs Leben, Kunst und Kunstwerke*. In this, the first biography of Bach, the writer attempted especially to present the development of the master's style, and in several places dealt with the fact that as a composer Bach had no real teacher, but analysed works by older and above all contemporary masters with un-flagging study, and took them as models for his own music. Forkel says: 'Like all first attempts, Joh. Seb. Bach's first attempts at composition were failures. Without any instruction which could have guided him along some path, leading him from one step to the next, he had at first to do as do all those who set foot on such a path without guidance and hope to progress. Keeping both hands as busy as the five fingers will permit, running and jumping up and down the instrument, and keeping this wild state of affairs up until some point of repose is snatched quite by chance; these are the arts that all beginners have in common. In this way they can only become "finger-composers" (or "Hussars of the keyboard", as Bach called them in his later years); in other words, they must first prepare with their fingers what they are to write, instead of dictating to the fingers what they should play. However, Bach did not long remain on this path. He soon began to feel that the eternal running and jumping could never accomplish order, connection and interrelationship in his ideas, and that some sort of guidance was needed if he was to attain such aims. At that time recently published violin concertos by Vivaldi provided

---

* . . . who was his greatest admirer and who perhaps alone in his time could under-stand all the greatness of this musician's genius.

him with just such a lead. He heard them praised as excellent pieces of music so often that he had the happy idea of arranging them all for his keyboard. He studied the treatment of ideas, the relationships of these to each other, the sequences of modulation, and many other things besides. The transformation of ideas and passages intended for the violin and not appropriate to the keyboard also taught him to think musically, so that after his studies he no longer needed to rely on his fingers for his ideas, but could already form them from his own imagination. Thus prepared, it needed only industry and constant practice to progress further, and arrive at the point at which he could not only conceive of an artistic ideal, but could also hope, with time, to achieve it.'

Forkel's contemporaries, who could hardly have known anything of Vivaldi, would not have understood this reference, and indeed it is questionable whether Forkel himself knew all of Bach's arrangements of Vivaldi. However, his information came from the master's sons and from his immediate pupils, and thus must in all probability be based on J. S. Bach's account of his own early development. The fact that Forkel assumes that only after 1720–25 did Bach write any real masterpieces perhaps originates with the same sources of information, and certainly tallies with the master's own stern and self-critical judgment of his early music.

A factually accurate presentation of Bach's evolution as a creative musician and of the influence on him of Italian music was of course impossible in Forkel's lifetime (d. 1818). Certainly, stimulated by his enthusiastic appeal, several publishers—partly independently of each other, partly by unacknowledged reproduction of each other's publications—had begun to publish Bach's works; but their selections, which, moreover, had to be chosen for their potential market in circles of music lovers, had been very dependent on the fortuitous discovery of source material. It was only about the middle of the century that efforts to base a practical and scholarly complete edition on the most thoroughgoing possible investigation of sources were intensified, and in 1850—jubilee year—the Bach Society was founded with this aim in view, the first volume appearing two years later. In the course of the large-scale preparatory work, however, the editions that had been started earlier were continued; thus in 1851, as *Oeuvres complettes Liv. 15*, Peters of Leipzig published in an edition of 100(!) copies this volume: *XVI / Concertos / d'après des Concertos pour le Violon / de / Antonio Vivaldi / arrangés / pour le piano seul / par / Jean Sébastien Bach / publiés pour la première fois / par / S. W. Dehn et F. A. Roitzsch. . . .*

The chief source for this publication was a manuscript 'XII Concerti di Vivaldi, elaborati di J. S. Bach' with the annotation 'J. E. Bach, Lips.

1739'. It had been in the possession of Johann Ernst Bach, a member of a different branch of the master's family who, as an alumnus at St. Thomas's, had also been a pupil of Johann Sebastian. The manuscript then passed to the former Royal Library in Berlin (cat. no. P 280) by way of Georg J. D. Poelchau (d. 1836) who has earned praise as a collector of Bach manuscripts. In the foreword to the first edition, Dehn refers to a further manuscript (P 804), with transcriptions, mainly by Johann Peter Kellner, an ardent admirer of Bach, who copied numerous of the master's works in the years 1725–6. From this source, the concertos Nos. 12–16 were taken for the publication. The 10th concerto of the J. E. Bach manuscript was arranged for organ, and at first Dehn/Roitzsch withheld it from publication; it appeared together with three further organ arrangements (one of them after a concerto by Johann Ernst, Count of Saxe-Weimar, which also exists in a version for harpsichord) that Peters published in 1852 in an edition of 125 copies. Poelchau had collected the manuscripts of these works too, and had acquired from Forkel's estate a copy, in the latter's hand, of a 'Concerto per IV Clavicembali . . . composto da Giov. Seb. Bach', also a reworking of Vivaldi, first published in 1865 by Peters. The works that were accepted as arrangements of Vivaldi in the middle of the nineteenth century, then, comprised seventeen harpsichord concertos, four for organ and one for 4 harpsichords and orchestra, in all, 22 arrangements of 21 works. Besides these, there existed the first movement of an arrangement for organ after Count Johann Ernst in a version for harpsichord.

It was Hilgenfeldt in his book on Bach (1850) who was the first to concern himself with the question of the originals of these arrangements, and he started by identifying the concerto for 4 harpsichords as a Vivaldi composition. (The discoveries of musical scholarship being only very slowly disseminated, the work was still proclaimed to be by Bach on a 1955 gramophone record, Decca AWD 8511!) With this identification, Hilgenfeldt provided the initial stimulus to the Vivaldi researches which now slowly took shape. J. Rühlmann then found sources for other arrangements, and in 1867 he gave a picture of Bach's relationship to Vivaldi which was based on his evidence and whose conclusions certainly differed considerably from those of Forkel. It was quite in keeping with the orchestral conceptions of a time inundated with the spirit of Wagner that Rühlmann should find Vivaldi's orchestral writing poverty-stricken. His second error, resulting from too narrow a source-basis, of finding hardly any thematic work in Vivaldi, has been perpetuated through Schering and W. Fischer to the present time, and has caused Bach to be seen as the herald of classical motivic technique. But Rühlmann's investigations remained an important point of reference for Spitta, Waldersee and Schering, who succeeded in confirming further originals, though these also include works by other contemporaries of Bach.

As a result, the extent of Vivaldi's influence appeared to be more limited but in 1910–11 L. Schitteler and Max Schneider were able to show that a work hitherto taken to be a composition by Wilhelm Friedemann Bach was in fact an arrangement by Johann Sebastian after Vivaldi: this is the Concerto Op. III, No. 11 in D minor by Vivaldi, which Bach reworked in a splendid version in the same key for organ. Wilhelm Friedemann, the gifted but disreputable son, received the score after his father's death as part of his share of the legacy, and noted on the title page 'di W. F. Bach, manu mei Patris descript'. Thus he attributed the work to himself, and made his father merely the copyist! At the end of the nineteenth century the piece was once more arranged, by August Stradal, a pupil of Liszt who died as recently as 1930; his version was published by Breitkopf and Hartel in 1897. This 'arrangement of an arrangement', with a written-out cadenza of seven printed pages, is a very interesting document of the period of Liszt's pianistic heirs, both musically and in its printed layout, as well as conveying to us a listener's impressions (Plate XI). In the foreword, Stradal says: 'The beginning of this organ concerto, with its mighty pedal-point on D and its great crescendo, provided the opportunity to which I was irresistibly drawn of augmenting and slowing down the heaving and rising volumes of sound. The slow swell of this D minor chord also seemed to me like a distant, almost forgotten precursor of the E♭ major at the beginning of R. Wagner's "Rheingold". The large grand pianos of today afford the possibility of increasing the sound from the gentlest ppp to the mightiest fff. With the exception of the introduction, which has been expanded for a few bars from the original [in this case Bach's arrangement!], and the cadenza (which is ad libitum), I have retained the original strictly and exactly, attempting to imitate the power of the organ with broad pianistic writing. . . .' Stradal provided a special foreword for the cadenza: 'I have matched this cadenza to the stormy character of the work. The picture on the title page gives us the basic mood of the concerto, "Storm, dark clouds raging over the firmament, thunder and lightning." On the occasion of one of my concerts in Berlin, the Berlin Nationalzeitung wrote: "The performance of the W. F. Bach Organ Concerto gave us the impression of a great spectacle of nature. We saw mountains totter and trees uprooted by the storm." I believe I may add that I consider this organ concerto by the unhappy and restless W. F. Bach—perhaps a mirror of his disturbed soul—to be the first forerunner of any real artistic account of the magnificent storm-fantasies of Beethoven, Wagner and Liszt.'

Even today, although for over fifty years it has been identified as a reworking of Vivaldi, it is still occasionally performed in public under the name of Wilhelm Friedemann.

Since more recently the eighth concerto of the harpsichord arrangements has been shown by Albert van der Linden to have been a work of Torelli, and the tenth by Jean-Pierre Demoulin as a work of Benedetto Marcello, the present state of researches allows us to divide the originals of Bach's arrangements between six composers; the composers of the models of four of the arrangements have not so far been identified.

Vivaldi	10 concertos
J. E. v. Sachsen-Weimar	4 (one of which appears in two versions)
Alessandro Marcello	1
Benedetto Marcello	1
Telemann	1
Torelli	1
unknown composers	4
	22

The fact that among the composers of the originals are to be found Telemann and a member of the Saxe-Weimar royal family not only enables us to reach an approximate decision about the time and circumstances of Bach's activities as an arranger, but also shows the extent and depth of Italian cultural influence in central Germany. In 1708 Bach had become the court organist at Weimar, the town where his distant relative Johann Gottfried Walther, the composer, and later lexicographer, was also working as an organist. Walther, too, zealously studied works by Italian masters, by Torelli and Albinoni among others, and reworked them in the same way as Bach. No less than thirteen such arrangements by Walther have been preserved. However, in nearby Eisenach the court *Kapellmeister* from 1709–12 was Georg Philipp Telemann, who in an autobiographical sketch has given us a very lively description of this time: 'But all the time, enjoying change, I was also tackling concertos. Here I must confess that they never really come from the heart, though I have already written quite a number of them . . . yet I had to agree with the verdict that in most of the concertos that I came across there was indeed much verbosity and twisting leaps, but little harmony, and even worse melodies, and some of these I disliked because they were uncomfortable for my hand and bow, and because of their lack of the latter characteristics, to which my ear became accustomed through French music; I could not love them, nor was I able to imitate them.'

Here a certain aesthetic opposition between the French and the Italian styles becomes evident, and this was to be played out in all its consequences in subsequent German musical history. Telemann's sparse sympathy towards the latter did not prevent him, however, from writing more than a hundred concertos in the 'italiänischen gusto'!

Count Johann Ernst of Saxe-Weimar was a nephew of the reigning prince. Bach had been temporarily active as a violinist in the father's small court band in Weimar in 1703. The son, a highly gifted musician, was a composition pupil of Walther and a keyboard pupil of Bach, but died when he was only nineteen, in 1715. The only work he left, six concertos in the Italian style, proves him to have been a skilful composer, even though the quality of his music should perhaps be partly attributed to his teacher's 'polishing up'.

We can conclude from Bach's friendly relationships with Walther, Telemann—who was later to be the godfather of Bach's eldest son—and the young count, that their study of Italian music, and above all that of Vivaldi, was the outcome of mutual stimuli. This permits us to place the dates of this preoccupation approximately between the years 1708 and 1717, during which Bach was active in Weimar. It would probably have reached its peak, however, during the years 1709–15.

Many conjectures have been forwarded as to the real reasons for Bach's arrangements. They are keyboard reductions including the solo parts, and in the technical parlance of the time, Bach had 'set down' the original works for keyboard. Obviously their sonorities did not have anything like the scope of the originals, which were certainly played by the court orchestra in the composer's version. Bach must have been aware from the start that the keyboard sonority would be a 'second best', and we can surmise that these keyboard reductions were most likely study versions prepared for himself, for his pupils and perhaps also for other Italian music enthusiasts at the Weimar court. The arrangements for organ probably constitute an exception, for there a source of sonorities that was certainly very different, but still very productive, was available. It had already been the practice in Italy for some decades to play instrumental solos during the elevation of the host in High Mass. The organ works composed 'per l'elevazione' (for the elevation) were replaced by middle movements of violin concertos, when the violin established itself more and more as a solo instrument. This practice seems to have been taken over early in the Protestant North too. A liturgy from the year 1694 says: 'During the Communion, before the German songs begin, a piece of music is played or a motet is sung.' Forkel reports: 'In his time (Bach's) it was usual for a concerto or a solo on some instrument to be played in church during the Communion.' This usage, doubtless also customary in Weimar, must equally have been a stimulus for the arrangements, and Bach himself probably played movements from Vivaldi concertos before or after or in the course of the mass, to the delight of amateurs and connoisseurs attending the court services.

The ten Vivaldi arrangements are based on the following originals:

BWV (Schmieder)	Incipits	Arranged for	Inventaire Thématique Pincherle	First edition	Manuscripts
	RE-WORKING			ORIGINAL	
593	Adagio senza Pedale a due Clav. / Allegro	Organ	2	Op. III/8 in A minor Estienne Roger Amsterdam, ca. 1712 (2 solo violins, strings & continuo)	
594	Recitativo Adagio / Allegro	Organ	151	Op. VII/11 in D major (= Op. VII, Bk. 2, No. 5) Jeanne Roger Amsterdam, ca. 1716/17 (solo violin, strings & continuo)	Turin Giord. V/22 Schwerin No. 3 (5565)
596	Grave	Organ	250	Op. III/11 in D minor Estienne Roger Amsterdam, ca. 1712 (2 solo violins, strings & continuo)	

BWV (Schmieder)	Incipits	Arranged for	Inventaire Thématique Pincherle	First edition	Manuscripts
972	Larghetto / Allegro	Harpsichord	147	Op. III/9 in D major Estienne Roger Amsterdam, ca. 1712 (solo violin, strings & continuo)	Schwerin No. 1
973	Largo / Allegro	Harpsichord	102	Op. VII/8 in G major (= Op. VII, Bk. 2, No. 2) Jeanne Roger Amsterdam, ca. 1716/17 (solo violin, strings & continuo)	Dresden Cx 1024 (= 2389/ 0/56)
975	Largo / Giga Presto	Harpsichord	338	Op. IV/6 in G minor Estienne Roger Amsterdam, ca. 1712/13 (solo violin, strings & continuo)	Landes- bibliothek Darmstadt (destroyed in war)
976	Largo / Allegro	Harpsichord	240	Op. III/12 in E major Estienne Roger Amsterdam, ca. 1712 (solo violin, strings & continuo)	Landes- bibliothek Darmstadt (destroyed in war)
978	Allegro / Largo / Allegro	Harpsichord	96	Op. III/7 in G major Estienne Roger Amsterdam, ca. 1712 (solo violin, strings & continuo)	
980	Largo / Allegro	Harpsichord	327	Op. IV/1 in B♭ major Estienne Roger Amsterdam, ca. 1712/13 (solo violin, strings & continuo)	Uppsala Caps 61: 7

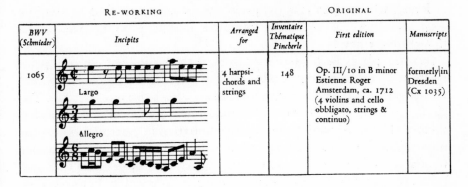

	RE-WORKING				ORIGINAL	
BWV (Schmieder)	Incipits	Arranged for	Inventaire Thématique Pincherle		First edition	Manuscripts
1065	Largo / Allegro	4 harpsichords and strings	148		Op. III/10 in B minor Estienne Roger Amsterdam, ca. 1712 (4 violins and cello obbligato, strings & continuo)	formerly|in Dresden (Cx 1035)

There were also practical reasons for Bach's choice of instruments: for the two concertos for two violins, he needed the organ, for he could only reproduce the free play of the counterpoint if he could give the continuo part to the pedals. In the Concerto for one violin, P. 151, the ritornello has an imitative structure, and here too only the organ is suited to reproducing the three real parts. The other concertos, all for one violin and orchestra, could be arranged for manuals only, and were in the first place thought of as being arranged for harpsichord, though they would also certainly be played by Bach on the organ.

The first concerto (in the Schmieder BWV catalogue No. 593) immediately shows important characteristics of Bach's procedures as an arranger. The model, P. 2, one of Vivaldi's finest works, is formally a double concerto for two violins (see the analysis on pp. 99ff); the designation of Concerto grosso, in general use since Einstein's edition (Eulenburg No. 762), did not come from the composer. Bach retained the same tonality, because the d''' which lies beyond the range of the organ only appears in three places, and is easily avoided by slight alterations. Occasionally typically violinistic figures which were, and still are, difficult to perform in an Allegro tempo on a keyboard, were modified to suit the instrument (Ex. 87). Frequently an octave transposition is used to vary the sonority. Thus, for example, in the middle movement the second solo violin, which enters on the same note as the first, is brought into relief by taking it down an octave, so that the idea of a duet between violin and cello is suggested (Einstein, Foreword to the edition). In general there is with Bach a tendency towards thickening of textures and concentration of motifs. From this there often appear middle parts in close counterpoint, as if for the sheer pleasure of improvisation, which show Bach's mastery (Ex. 88, and also B. 30–33 of the first movement; see also Ex. 92). One is reminded of Reger, who used to take the piano part in sonatas, and, if he was in a good mood, would reputedly improvise middle parts in passages he thought too empty!

In many places Bach's tendency towards thickening-out got to a point where it threatened more fundamental matters. In bars 6–8 of the first movement Bach interchanged motifs at half a bar's distance (Ex. 89). The clearly and rhythmically very accentuated articulation of the original is thereby obliterated, and the semiquaver imitation in particular evokes the impression of 'sewing-machine counterpoint'. It is a widespread mistake to believe that the greatest concentration is achieved by granting a stunted existence to motivic fragments in as many parts as possible. In the contrast between clear articulation and motivic complication that is here so much in evidence, we can also see the contrast between Italian and Netherlands/German musical feeling, and the tensions produced by their confrontation have been an essential factor in the development of European music from the time of Willaert's activity in Venice to that of Verdi and Wagner. Mozart was just as anxious to reconcile them as was Bach, in whose Cöthen instrumental music the seeds of his Weimar studies came to fruition.

If one agrees with Casella that Bach's relationship to Vivaldi was based on the greatest admiration, one must nevertheless admit that Bach was disposed to be extraordinarily critical of his model. He accepted no note as indispensable, without first weighing it in the balance of his artistic intelligence. From this resulted alterations and improvements, particularly in those passages where the model shows tiresome repetitions or sequential treatment of figurations (Ex. 90). The high register of the solo violin here necessitated a transposition from E major to C major! Also excessively underlined symmetrical effects produced by the repetition of bars are avoided by far-reaching alterations (Ex. 91). However, this is nothing more than the sort of diminution that was essential to baroque performing practice, particularly commonly used in sequential passages. Many of Bach's 'interventions' (as they are often called) in Vivaldi's music can be explained by this performance usage. The middle movement of BWV 973 (Ex. 92) is most obvious in this respect.

Far-reaching inferences must be made in those cases where Bach actually does seem to have interfered with the substance of a work, e.g.:

a) in BWV 976 (= P. 240) bar 64 of the model is missing in Bach. He thereby achieves both concentration and a tightening of symmetry;
b) in BWV 594 (= P. 151) virtuoso cadenzas are added to the outer

movements that are not found in the version of Op. VII No. 11
Vivaldi prepared for printing, besides which another middle movement is added;

c) in BWV 980 (= P. 327) the second and third movements do not
conform with Vivaldi's printed work.

These and other departures from the printed editions of the original
works were naturally noticed early on, and have led to very different
opinions. In his analysis of BWV 980, Waldersee holds that one should
be grateful to Bach for having 'thrown this passage overboard', because it
'is one of the most superficial that Vivaldi wrote'. On the other hand,
Schweitzer criticizes Bach sharply: 'Not even the design and the development of the pieces are respected. Sometimes he goes his own way right
after the first bar, then follows the original again for a while, departs from
it anew, comes back to it once more, leaves things out, puts things in, without bothering whether his transcription turns out half as long or twice as
long as the model.' Finally Rinaldi dramatizes his view of the cadenzas
in BWV 594: 'che il Prete rosso avrebbe accettato a denti stretti' (which
the red-haired priest would have accepted with gnashing of teeth).

The situation was clarified by the fact that there were also manuscript
versions of the models of Bach's concerto arrangements, which to a greater
or lesser degree differ from the printed editions. Thus in a Schwerin manuscript the Concerto Op. VII No. 11 contains the cadenza to the first
movement as well as the substituted middle movement, though not the
cadenza to the last movement. In the main Op. IV No. 1 agrees with the
Uppsala manuscript, but Eller has shown by examining details that Bach
could not have known this version either. In comparing printed editions,
manuscripts and arrangements, we may safely draw the following conclusions: in several cases, if not every time, Bach worked from models
which show some marked discrepancies with the printed editions. These
discrepancies therefore might go right back to Vivaldi himself. But that Bach
worked from manuscript models only has one likely explanation, namely
that his work dates from before the appearance of the printed editions.
There are several records of the dissemination of Vivaldi's music in
Germany about 1712, the probable date of the first printed edition of the
composer's concertos. One of the centres of early Vivaldi performances in
Germany was the family of Count Schönborn. Vivaldi works are to be
found at Wiesentheid Castle, in Pommersfelden, the seat of Count Rudolf
Franz Eberwein von Schönborn, whose brother, Johann Philipp Franz,
at that time Provost of Würzburg Cathedral, regularly ordered Italian

music from a Venetian merchant, Ragaznig. In a letter of February 27, 1710, we read: 'to try to get hold of some more rare compositions of Vivaldi and pass them on as soon as possible'. From this we gather that Vivaldi concertos were, already in about 1709–10, known and sought after in circles of German amateurs and connoisseurs, probably including copies of works which were subsequently to appear in print as part of Opp. III, IV and VII. These facts, however, compel us to exercise the greatest caution in any attempt to date Vivaldi's compositions; in general the printed works were hardly likely to have been composed only on the eve of publication. Thus the date of their appearance can only give us the latest possible date of composition, and in no case do we know how long before its publication a work was composed, and indeed even the sequence of opus numbers does not offer a really reliable point of reference. Thus phrases like 'already in Op. III' and 'as late as Op. VI' appearing in literature on Vivaldi, and resultant attempts to trace various developments, should be approached with the greatest caution.

If one examines the profound change which took place in Bach's music from about 1709 on, one is forced to conclude that already in 1802 Forkel had correctly assessed the master's development with regard to the strong influence of Vivaldi. Ex. 93 gives the theme of a canzona from the year 1709. Thirteen years later, in the first part of *Das Wohltemperierte Clavier*, a theme such as Ex. 94 is possible. The canzona theme flows along calmly, and derives from an essentially vocal conception; it has the character of a cantus firmus, and the harmonies—at the service of the polyphonic texture—are of secondary importance. The fugue theme's nature is instrumental and virtuosic, and it is founded on a predetermined harmonic basis; the changes of harmony occur at the strong beats, and give them a special accentuation. The head motif which dominates the whole theme is of Italian provenance, and in fact became a distinctive stylistic trait of Bach's Cöthen period (1717–23); then, 200 years later, it became a favourite figure with composers in the neo-baroque manner. Casella, Pincherle, Engel and others have found thematic reminiscences of Vivaldi in Bach. Many are so striking that a knowledge of the source might be supposed as an absolute certainty (Ex. 95). Others derive rather from a 'germ' structure belonging to the melodic style of about 1700 (Ex. 96). In such cases one can hardly speak of imitation or borrowing. It was much rather the case that Bach and his Weimar friends had taken the works of Torelli, Vivaldi, Albinoni and others so much to heart that they could have quite independent ideas based on the same stylistic foundations. A corresponding example from our own century may help to illustrate this: in his intensive studies of East European folk music, Bartók so assimilated its tonalities, rhythms and melodies that he could no longer say with any certainty of single themes from his *Dance Suite* of 1923 whether they were of folk origin or of his own invention!

But it was more than mere motifs and instrumental figurations that Bach took over from the Italians. In Italian music after about the middle of the seventeenth century, functional tonality had developed more and more, and already in Torelli, though still more in Vivaldi, had led to a clear harmonic ground-plan for large forms. From the concertos, it then infiltrated into all of Bach's music, and in particular, was decisive for the basic structure of the fugue. 'Bach's perfection of the fugue as a form' (W. Fischer) is in the last resort to be considered as a continuation of this phenomenon.

Unlike Schütz, Handel and many others, Bach never had the chance to go to the renowned land of music and learn on the spot about the new style and its concomitant performing practice. But he drank in the spirit of Italian music from the scores of his models in the quiet and privacy of his study. His sincere admiration for them never prevented him from remaining critical; and so in the end he went beyond the Italians in his ceaseless striving for a synthesis between foreign influences and his personal style.

THE VIOLIN CONCERTOS: VIVALDI AS VIOLINIST AND TEACHER

In the second edition of Stevenson's book *Music before the Classic Era*, which appeared as recently as 1962, we read on page 126 the following about Vivaldi's playing of the violin: 'He used what are called the sixth, seventh and eighth positions freely. These positions call for the placing of the fingers much higher up on the finger-board than Corelli ever demanded.' This can be traced to Pincherle, who in his book on Vivaldi reaches the following conclusion about the situation with regard to fingering positions in the first half of the eighteenth century: 'As far as the left hand was concerned, he did not go beyond the 9th position (or the 8th with extension of the 4th finger: Ex., Foà II f.185 final cadenza). Pretty well at the same time, Locatelli risked amazing passages which required the 14th or 15th position, according to the fingering used; at home, in about 1740, the mysterious M. de Tremais did the same.' The decisive work of Locatelli for fingering positions, his Op. III *XII Concerti cioè Violino solo, con XXIV Capricci ad Libitum*, appeared in print in 1733, and in the foreword the composer refers to excellent performances in Venice of these concertos dedicated to 'Girolamo Michiellini, patricio Veneto'. From this Pincherle infers a strong influence of Locatelli on Vivaldi, and even sees in this influence a criterion for a chronological listing: 'If we accept this concerto as dating from our composer's riper years, as is very plausible, we must without doubt recognize here the influence of Locatelli.'

However, there are now two documents which disprove all that and clearly prove Vivaldi's leading role in the development of the violin technique of his time. Herr von Uffenbach, whom we have already quoted several times, recorded in his journal the memory of a visit to the opera at the S. Angelo Theatre on February 4, 1715. There we read: '. . . towards the end Vivaldi played a solo accompaniment admirably, adding at the end a free fantasy, which quite frightened me, for it is scarcely possible that anyone ever played or will play in this way, for he placed his fingers but a hair's breadth from the bridge, so that there was barely room for the bow, doing this on all four strings with imitations and incredible speed . . .' This imaginative description of Vivaldi's violin playing at first seems quite untrustworthy. But Uffenbach was a well-educated amateur, played the lute very well and the violin passably well, and throughout his journal he proves himself to have been a sharply critical observer. Even if Vivaldi certainly did not come within a 'hair's breadth of the bridge', with this expression Uffenbach has still given a true impression of Vivaldi's fingering positions that were so improbable and sensational at the time.

The second document is a Violin Concerto in D major, P. 165, which in the Dresden autograph bears the remark 'Fatto per la Solemnità della S. Lingua di S. Antonio in Padua' (Composed for the Feast of the Holy Tongue of St. Antonio in Padua) and is generally dated as 1712. In the third movement, seven bars before the end, is the direction 'Qui si ferma à piacim:' (Here there is a pause ad libitum), then the cadenza prescribed by it is written out (Plate XII). From the second note of bar 25 on, the composer has inserted a square bracket under the stave which extends as far as the 4th bar before the end. It follows from analogous uses of such brackets and from the two linking passages that this is clearly to be read as an octave transposition upwards. However, this means that as early as 1712, when Locatelli was only seventeen, Vivaldi was using the 12th position. The highest note of this cadenza, the f#'''', however, already lay beyond the fingerboard of the so-called short-necked violins (or rather, violins of the old measure) played in Vivaldi's time. Thus it would seem that Vivaldi had had a longer fingerboard fitted for his own use. If Uffenbach's report is compared with this cadenza, it can even be assumed that at the opera performance in question the Concerto P. 165, with the written-out cadenza, was played: the imitations could refer to the motivic working, and the indication 'on all four strings' perhaps refers to the still relatively rare use of the G string in the double stopping of the tenth bar. But just as astonishing as the technical acumen of this cadenza is its compositional expertise: it begins in 4/4 time, although the third movement is in 3/4 time. The change back to 3/4 comes after 19 bars, but a few bars later, the 4/4 is taken up again and continues to the end of the cadenza. The orchestra's closing ritornello is once more in the time signature of the whole movement, 3/4. This change of beat was necessary because the composer made use of motivic material from the first movement, which is in 4/4 (for the derivation of the single motifs see Kolneder, *Aufführungspraxis*, p. 76). Vivaldi used a similar, though simpler procedure in the Violin Concerto P. 23 (see Kolneder, *Aufführungspraxis*, p. 72). With these, Vivaldi wrote the first so-called 'cyclical' cadenzas, in other words, cadenzas which rework motivic material from all three movements of the cyclic form.

In the cadenza of the Violin Concerto P. 165 two characteristics especially peculiar to Vivaldi are in evidence to a marked degree: the talent for violinistic technique which is conjoined with a highly developed faculty for expanding the possibilities not only of violin but of other instruments as well; and the ability to think creatively with these new possibilities, through which Vivaldi, in his best works, became the stylistic model for a whole era. At first his artistic will manifested itself in violin sonatas, trio sonatas and violin concertos. Whilst after a short time the composition of sonatas was relegated to the background, he remained faithful to the violin concerto throughout his life. We can identify no less than 228 violin concertos from his pen, and 220 of these have been preserved in their entirety. Besides this, several 'Concerti con molti Istrumenti' with a 'Violino principale' are really violin concertos in which only occasionally are the wind instruments used in obbligato fashion, and in the opera sinfonias many of the first movements are laid out like those of violin concertos. Altogether there are about 260 concertos with one solo violin, not including the so-called chamber concertos. In 36 other works the violin is used as a solo instrument in different instrumental combinations, 25 of these being double concertos for two violins, one a concerto for three violins and in five works four violins are used (including four concertos in Op. III). This constitutes the largest contribution any composer has ever made to the violin repertoire. It is clear that in such an incredibly large number of works of a single kind every one cannot be first-rate; and violin concertos, in particular, were written by the master as a matter of routine under the pressures of his creative commitments.

It was precisely in the violin concerto that a certain danger lurked for the composer in this respect. In the years of Vivaldi's creative activities the technical possibilities of playing were expanded in an unprecedented way by imaginative violinists; a comparison between the works of Vivaldi, Fr. M. Veracini, Geminiani, Locatelli and others, and those of Torelli, and Corelli clearly shows the stages of development from one generation to the next. In particular, the playing of chords, with a good number of varied ways of arpeggiating, playing in extended positions, effects of bowing

technique, such as staccato, detached bowings and bariolage

had occupied the inventive spirit of numerous violinist-composers. Sometimes there was too great a temptation to give precedence to these violinistic possibilities over compositional substance, and in many works whole solo sections consist of broken chords without any sort of motivic eventfulness. Only a composer with as strong an urge towards motivic structuring as Bach invariably avoided this danger in his violin works. But critics of Vivaldi have alighted on just these somewhat insubstantial works of the master, and in the literature since Waldersee—generally copied from him—one constantly meets with assertions such as that formulated by Wilhelm Fischer in Adler's *Handbuch der Musikgeschichte*: 'The melodic style of the soli, where they were not developed from the tutti sections, was of a purely figurative character (scale passages, broken chords, arpeggios, double stopping, open-string effects).—As a rule, the writing in Vivaldi's Allegro form is homophonic . . .' In the interests of a 'black-and-white' contrast, passages of extremely differing construction from Vivaldi and Bach are juxtaposed as examples. This view is only acceptable with severe reservations, since it is founded on an acquaintance with only a small part of Vivaldi's output, but it does give an indication of the dangers which, in his weaker works, Vivaldi did not always avoid.

In order to provide the solo section with a wealth of motivic material, there was firstly the possibility of taking over the head motif from the ritornello, or some other ritornello motif, into the solo and of working it in a quasi-improvisatory development. This is none too frequent in the solo violin concertos, but can nonetheless be found in a whole series of works. Ex. 97 shows it in a very interesting form. If solo sections were developed in chordal figurations, there was the possibility of compensating

Sonetto Dimostrativo
Sopra il Concerto Intitolato
L'ESTATE

DEL SIG.re D. ANTONIO VIVALDI

A   Sotto dura Staggion dal Sole accesa
    Langue l'huom, langue 'l gregge, ed arde il Pino;
B   Scioglie il Cucco la Voce, e tosto intesa
C   Canta la Tortorella e 'l gardelino.

D   Zeffiro dolce Spira, ma contesa
    Muove Borea improviso al Suo vicino;
E   E piange il Pastorel, perche sospesa
    Teme fiera borasca, e 'l Suo destino;

F   Toglie alle membra lasse il Suo riposo
    Il timore de' Lampi, e tuoni fieri
    E de mosche, e mossoni il Stuol furioso!

G   Ah che pur troppo i Suoi timor Son veri
    Tuona e fulmina il Ciel e grandinoso
    Tronca il capo alle Spiche e a'grani alteri.

X. Facsimile of the *Sonetto Dimostrativo* for the *Summer* Concerto, Op. VIII, No. 4, P. 336.

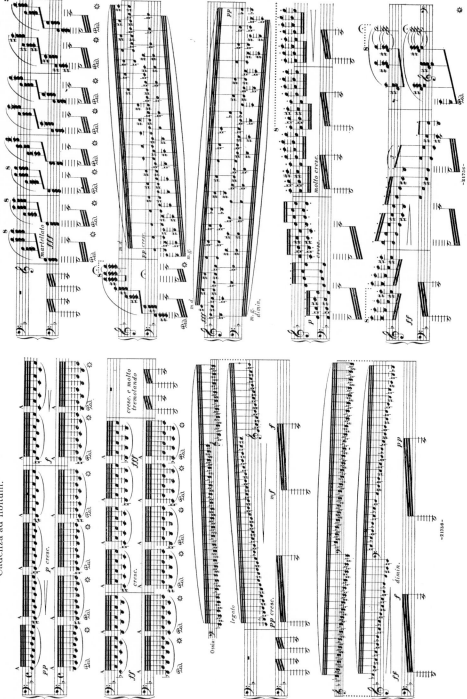

Cadenza ad libitum.

for this by having a copiously motivic orchestral accompaniment, and thus by shifting the weight of the musical argument to a certain extent to the orchestra. This happens in an ideal way in the D minor Violin Concerto P. 272: a syncopated motif from the ritornello is taken over in the solo sections I and II. In the solo III, the soloist takes up a motif from the second ritornello group note for note, and continues it in an arpeggio figuration, accompanied by a motif in complementary rhythm in the first violin, motivic syncopated sequences in the viola and a bass composed with rhythmical concision (Ex. 98). It is regrettable that Vivaldi's critics did not include such works in their analyses. The work in question, P. 272, is one which forms part of the old Dresden collection, and thus has been accessible all the time.

The composer's imaginativeness in developing new possibilities of playing arpeggios seems to have been inexhaustible. Often he simply wrote out the chords and left it to the performer to deduce the arpeggio. But in many passages the first bar is written out, and the composer has thus given a model for unmarked passages. In Kolneder, *Aufführungspraxis*, pp. 79–82, fourteen possibilities are shown, taken from Vivaldi's works; such a number shows how unsystematically Vivaldi approached this question. The 21-bar Larghetto that is inserted between the second and third movements of the Concerto for four violins Op. III, No. 10 in B minor, P. 148 (Ex. 99), shows how interested Vivaldi was in possibilities of contrasting simultaneous sonorities when playing arpeggios. In his arrangement (BWV 1065) Bach has changed the typically violinistic arpeggios of the first solo violin (transposed to A minor) into pianistic ones (Ex. 100). If the key permitted open strings to be included in the arpeggio, particularly interesting variants could arise, as in the first movement of a Violin Concerto in D major, P. 200: a pedal-point in cellos and basses, three-part quaver chords in the violins and violas, and on top, a descending broken chord in the solo violin, in which the open strings are precisely indicated with the note-tails pointing upwards (Ex. 101). In such passages the E string is often specified with the direction 'Sopra il Cantin' or 'Sopra il Canto'. The other strings are designated as if vocal parts; a passage in the third movement of the *Summer* Concerto (Op. VIII, No. 2 = P. 336), where arpeggios are to be played on the two lower strings, bears the remark 'Sopra il Tenore e Basso'. Vivaldi often used the G string as a pedal-point in chordal figuration. This was still relatively rare at the time, apparently because the technical demands of manufacturing well-sounding silver strings were only gradually being met. In the Violin Concerto P. 14 there is a passage which is to be played throughout in the arpeggio figures given for the first two demisemiquaver groups (Ex. 102).

In order to recruit open strings for playing arpeggios in 'awkward' keys, so-called *scordatura* was practised, literally 'putting out of tune', in other words, changing the tuning of single strings to suit the key. Vivaldi prescribes this in four violin concertos: P. 154 (Op. IX, No. 12) B minor ; P. 215 (Op. IX, No. 6) A major ; P. 229 A major (d°); P. 368 B♭ major .

It is strange that with such a liking for chordal writing, double stopping in the sense of uniting two approximately equal melodic lines is to be found relatively seldom. In the Violin Concerto P. 171, already used as our Ex. 50, the second solo section is developed in two parts (Ex. 103).

Ex. 102, taken from the Concerto P. 14, is provided with written-out fingerings. The necessity of occasionally giving such aids for his pupils offers us insights into the master's way of playing, because it is true that a composing virtuoso always subconsciously bases his invention on his own manner of playing. Accordingly we must imagine that, at least during the years in which playing the violin had not yet been pushed into the background by his activity as a composer, Vivaldi was a violinist with a highly developed bow technique which found expression not only in *jeté* bowing, staccatos and flying staccatos, but also in a very refined manner of playing arpeggios with unusual bowing techniques. His essential strength, however, probably lay in a very agile left hand, which mastered the entire fingerboard with complete sovereignty and accomplished particularly wide stretches without difficulty. To judge by his fingerings, Vivaldi must already have been a fairly secure adept of a technique which is constantly spoken of as a modern refinement, that of changing to a higher position by moving the lower fingers up (with a closing movement of the hand and a subsequent transition to the normal position) and by stretching out the upper fingers and then drawing up the hand without going through the motions of a real change of position. (In changing to a lower position the corresponding movements are reversed.) With this in mind, the fingering in P. 403 should be examined closely (Ex. 134). The Violin Concerto in E major, Op. IX, No. 4, P. 242, shows large stretches over the fixed supporting finger (Ex. 104).

A low-lying stretch of an eleventh that at first sight appears almost unplayable is composed precisely according to the possibilities of the violin (Ex. 105). In fact, stretches of this sort are not possible for a normal hand if one first places the first finger and then tries to stretch the fourth finger upwards. However, if one first places the fourth finger and reaches down with the first, amazing stretches are possible. A work that is very interesting from the violinistic point of view is the Violin Concerto in B♭ major, P. 396. In the first solo of the first movement the solo violin enters with a major tenth in the first position. The notation indicates clearly that the soloist does not join in the ritornello, but instead is left free to prepare the difficult finger position. The orchestra and solo parts are notated on one stave (Ex. 106). Then the left hand stretches further in tenths until in bar 17 the sixth position is reached. This must be retained in bars 18 and 19, so that the first finger is prepared for supporting the arpeggios from bar 20 on. A similar passage, but with an eleventh, occurs in the second solo of this movement. Here too the preparation of the fourth finger is allowed for in the composition; the hand travels higher in a harmonic sequence, and the stretch for the eleventh then becomes easier (Ex. 107). Even today many violinists would say with Uffenbach of such passages that they 'quite frighten' them.

An essential formal element of the violin concertos which is only to be found in embryo in the concertos for other instruments is the solo cadenza. It stands at the end of the last solo section, and is an extension of the harmonic cadence with which in fact every solo section finishes. Because of the special position of the entry of the final ritornello in the tonic key, the solo cadenza has a double function, namely that of harmonic preparation (generally with a pedal-point on the dominant) and that of the virtuoso improvisatory and developmental working of the movement's motifs. Quantz says of its historical development (XVth Chapter, §2) that it came into use 'several years before the end of the previous century'; 'between 1710 and 1716, or thereabouts, the cadenzas customary at present, in which the bass must pause, became the mode'. The so-called 'perfidies', probably for the most part improvised insertions in instrumental works that are preserved in some copies written out by Torelli, represent an early form of them. Vivaldi played an essential part in the further development of the solo cadenza, which is closely related to the evolution of solo concerto form. It is particularly fortunate that as a teacher he was occasionally compelled to write out such a cadenza. The ability to improvise them was in fact not so widespread even in the baroque period as is generally believed, and Benedetto Marcello joked about the sort of *maestro de' concerti* who played a gigantic cadenza 'quale porterà seco già preparata' (which he brought with him ready prepared).

In Vivaldi there are several possible ways of giving structure to the cadenza, whose great formal importance is in preparing the entry of the final ritornello:

1) The cadenza is conceived as an organic part of the movement. An excellent example is the first movement of the D minor Violin Concerto P. 293. A 31-bar ritornello developed from a rhythmically concise motif opens the movement. After the first solo in F major (relative major), it is curtailed to ten bars, and enters after the second solo in the relative major of the subdominant (B♭ major), further abbreviated to eight bars. The third solo leads directly to a 27-bar arpeggio passage in the solo violin, under which, however, ritornello I appears, shortened only by the final phrase and played p. This episode ends on a fermata in the dominant and leads to a further solo section of 14 bars. Here the written-out cadenza is enclosed by two solo sections which are in the same key and form a certain unity with it. A new 4-bar final phrase closes the movement. Here Vivaldi anticipated the modern attempt to incorporate the solo cadenza into the composition of a movement, and produced a masterly solution (Ex. 108). In a similar way, the cadenza-like development in the Violin Concerto in C major, P. 14, is built into the course of the movement (see Ex. 102). At the end, the tempo generally broadens, and the readoption of the main tempo for the closing ritornello was so natural that it was only seldom indicated.

2) The normal case was the freely improvised cadenza. In the score the orchestra has the following direction: 'Qui se ferma à piacimento' (Here there is a pause ad libitum), and occasionally before the final tutti is the remark 'poi segue' (then follows). A cadenza such as this is once even required in a middle movement. In the 'Con^to con 2 violini obligati' in C minor, P. 436, both the soloists join with the continuo bass in a trio in the middle movement. On the crotchet before the final chord a fermata is marked in all parts, and also a trill in the two violins, with the indication 'a piacimento'.

3) Probably for the use of pupils, perhaps also occasionally to fix such a cadenza definitely, Vivaldi sometimes wrote them out. In all we have nine longish cadenzas by Vivaldi:

P. 14	Dresden 0/59	Turin
P. 23	Dresden 0/98	Turin
P. 165	Dresden 0/74	Turin
P. 167	Dresden 0/85	—
P. 169	Dresden 0/94	—
P. 228	Dresden 0/43	—

P. 244	—	Turin/Paris
P. 271	Dresden 0/79	Vienna
P. 368	—	Turin

The fact that seven of them have been preserved in Dresden also suggests that it was a question of study material for Pisendel, or at least that he was particularly interested in these written-out cadenzas and wished to possess them. Of these nine cadenzas, P. 165 has already been given (Plate XII), two others (P. 14 and 23) are printed in Kolneder, *Aufführungspraxis*, pp. 70 ff., and that from P. 228 has been published by Landshoff in Peters Edition (No. 4206). In the simplest type, as for instance in P. 23, the cadenza combines a longish succession of chords arpeggiated over a dominant pedal-point, played in strict tempo, with a shorter section generally headed Adagio or Andante, which as a rule is built up of very interesting harmonies and concentrated modulatory sequences, and leads to the final trill. But we have already seen that Vivaldi also wrote 'cyclical' cadenzas (p. 117).

Vivaldi's special significance as a composer lies in his output of concertos, of which rather more than half are violin concertos. In these, basing himself on Torelli, he not only gave his contemporaries important models in formal structure, but also decisively advanced violin technique. Up till about his 35th–40th year he had been one of the best violinists of his time, but thereafter probably abandoned playing to a certain extent because of his activities as an operatic *maestro*. His regular activity as a violin teacher at the Ospedale continued till about the same time, and as a result of it his orchestra of girls soon occupied a leading position in Venice. On August 29, 1739, Charles de Brosses reported: 'Of the four ospedali, the one which I most often and with greatest pleasure frequent is the Pietà; it is also the best in the perfection of its orchestral playing. What precision of performance! Only here does one hear that unique bow stroke which is so unwarrantably celebrated at the Paris Opéra. La Chiaretta must surely be Italy's finest violinist . . .'

The fact that we scarcely know the names of any famous pupils is first and foremost related to the fact that women at that time did not stand much chance as instrumentalists and the violin-playing girls of the Pietà generally left the institution to get married. But violinists like Pisendel came to Vivaldi when they were already fully-fledged virtuosos, and in these cases the teacher–pupil relationship was probably confined to suggestions which would concern truly violinistic questions much less than those of interpretation and the processes of composition.

THE WORK

THE CELLO CONCERTOS

At the time when Vivaldi began to write concertos, the cello was valued as a powerful and, compared with the double bass, a clearer-sounding orchestral bass, and also as a continuo instrument, but was still only used to a very small extent as a solo instrument. The most important place where the instrument flourished was Bologna, where in the second half of the seventeenth century Petronio Franceschini (d. 1680) and his pupil Domenico Gabrielli (d. 1690) were active as cellists in the S. Petronio orchestra as well as being composers of local importance. The fact that the latter was dubbed 'Minghino dal Violoncello' shows how unusual it was for a musician of rank to play the cello. Both these masters of their instrument were active in Venice from time to time, so that in this town too we may assume that cello playing had attained a relatively high standard already in the seventeenth century. The rise of the cello as a concertante instrument in Northern Italy is closely connected with the work of the cleric Giuseppe Maria Jacchini (d. c.1727), a pupil of Gabrielli, who belonged to the same orchestra as his teacher. He is said to have excelled especially in the art of diminution and Herr von Uffenbach was deeply impressed by his playing. Under 21 Martii 1715 Uffenbach remarks in his journal, in Bologna: 'After this concert a virtuoso played on his own with a simple bass, or violon cello, by name Jacquini . . . he is in fact the first to have progressed so far on this instrument, and therefore is famous in all Italy.' From the report it is clear how unusual it still must have been in 1715 to hear a soloist on the cello. It is a pity that Uffenbach does not tell us which of his works Jacchini played. His 'Concerti per camera à 3 e 4 strumenti con Violoncello obligato' Op. IV, Bologna 1701, are generally recognized to have been the first cello concertos, but with regard to technical demands as well as to their inventiveness and conception they are relatively underdeveloped pieces of little value.

In view of the close musical relations between the Northern Italian towns it is very probable that Jacchini's Op. IV had very soon after its appearance stimulated Vivaldi to transfer the style and form of the already existing first violin concertos to works for the cello. As is shown by the master's abundant production for this instrument, it attracted Vivaldi's particular interest. It may be assumed that he was well acquainted with cello technique from his own experience, and had perhaps even given instruction on the instrument at the Ospedale della Pietà, for right up to the time of Verdi it was usual in Italy (and elsewhere) for all stringed instruments, woodwind and brass to be taught by one master for each group.

THE WORK

In all Vivaldi composed 36 concertos with a solo cello, namely:

27 for cello solo
  1 for 2 cellos
  3 for violin and cello
  2 for 2 violins and cello
  1 for 1 violin and 2 cellos
  2 for 2 violins and 2 cellos

In a further series of works the instrument is required as an obbligato within a larger ensemble, but used more according to the concerto grosso practice as a support for a concertino group.

There are a few—even if relatively uncertain—points of reference for dating Vivaldi's cello concertos. This is important because the same two decades that separate Jacchini's Op. IV from Bach's solo suites (c. 1721) brought an increased interest in cello playing as well as in composition for the instrument, in which Vivaldi certainly played his part. For various reasons, the master's first cello concerto is held to be a Concerto in C minor, P. 434, and indeed it may have been one of his first solo concertos. Its layout, notation and style are peculiar and seemingly archaic. The first violins are notated in the soprano clef, the second play in unison with the violas, and the orchestral texture is in three parts throughout. None of this is found again in Vivaldi's music. The soprano clef is enigmatic, and it could be supposed that the work was conceived for high violas or viole da gamba and the designation of instruments on the score was only added later. The orchestral prelude barely shows any characteristics of Vivaldi's typical ritornello material, and is laid out rather in the style of an older trio sonata, with the technique of suspension underlining the old-fashioned impression. The solo sections are almost without exception accompanied by continuo bass, and only in one solo does a brief two-part episode between violas and solo cello develop. The principal motif is strongly reminiscent of the old Venetian canzona style, appearing also occasionally outside the ritornello as a supporting bass for the solo section; in its frequent recurrence, its effect is weakened somewhat by note repetitions, and in any case it shows very little of the rhythmic élan of the Op. III concertos. A fugato-like layout of the ritornello is also prominent in the third movement, and equally points back in its general style and material to the older model of the trio sonata. Contrary to Vivaldi's practice of abandoning the fugato at the return of such ritornellos for reasons of tension, it is retained in two further ritornellos—a factor that brings to the movement a certain corpulence. From a formal point of view, the middle movement, built in ritornello form, is of interest:

Ritornello I	Orchestra	5 bars	C minor
Solo I	Cello, cont.	3½ bars	C minor → G minor
Ritornello II	Orchestra	2 bars	G minor
Solo II	Cello, cont.	4 bars	G minor → E♭ major
Ritornello III	Orchestra	2 bars	E♭ major
Solo III	Cello, cont.	4 bars	E♭ major → C minor
Ritornello IV	Orchestra	3½ bars	C minor

With such a formal layout only short-breathed development is possible in the Adagio tempo, and this is particularly noticeable in the solo sections. Elsewhere Vivaldi did not use the ritornello form in such a pronounced way for slow middle movements, so that this movement has a markedly experimental character.

But with all these reservations, this work already far surpasses Jacchini's Op. IV in the quality of its ideas and of its formal structure, though it is especially in his demands on playing technique that Vivaldi goes far beyond anything the Bologna master required of the cellist. With great mobility of the left hand, already shown by the predominance of semi-quaver triplets and demisemiquavers, the solo part is taken up to c'', whereas Jacchini at most ventured into the region of the fourth position. An acoustical property that the cello shares with the bassoon is the penetrating power of its low notes, whose exploitation has led to a kind of writing which outlines melodic lines in a sort of simulated two-part style. This demands of the player not only a well-developed technique of detached bowing, but also a thoroughgoing familiarity with the various positions on all four strings.

Another cello concerto of Vivaldi can perhaps be given an early dating by reason of its formally experimental nature: this is the Concerto in E minor, P. 119. The first movement begins with an 11-bar Adagio with solo cello and solo bassoon, which is followed by 13-bar orchestral section in continuous quavers and motivically unified (see Kolneder, *Solokonzert-form*, pp. 74 f.). The same sequence appears six times altogether, the formal sections later being curtailed; solo concerto form is recognizable in the layout of modulations. In the second movement the process is reversed, the solo cello beginning in Allegro tempo in the manner of a toccata in continuous semiquavers; the course of the movement is interrupted by short chordal Adagio insertions from the orchestra. With their contrast of tempo these insertions are reminiscent of the older canzona structure to an even greater degree than the formal sections of the first movement. In their regular succession of relatively short-limbed episodes the effect of both movements quickly becomes wearisome; elsewhere Vivaldi did not use a formal layout of this sort. It is probably not too far off the mark to suppose that these were cases of unsatisfactory formal experiments.

The seven cello concertos that are a unique constituent of a large music library of the aristocratic Schönborn family at Schloss Wiesentheid, Pommersfelden, form a group that is fairly unified stylistically and approximately datable. It is to Fritz Zobeley that credit is due for first having pointed to these. We owe the preservation of the manuscripts and possibly even the existence of the concertos in the first place to the musical enthusiasm of Count Rudolf Franz Eberwein von Schönborn, one of the typical cultivated music-lovers of his time. Apparently born in Mainz in 1677, he and his six brothers received an excellent education in which music had a precisely allotted share. '. . . after eating he may amuse himself with the lute or the guitar until his teacher of French language arrives' we read in the schedule the father worked out for one of his sons. At the age of eighteen Rudolf Franz Eberwein went to Rome for three years to study, and there got to know Corelli and Pasquini, taking instruction on the violin. On the way home he spent some time in a number of towns, having instruction in elementary musical theory, in flute-playing, and also on other musical instruments; he retained a servant in Florence to carry a violoncello, and heard eight opera performances in Venice in February 1696. Perhaps he there met Vivaldi, who was eighteen at the time. After periods of study in Leyden, Paris and Vienna, everywhere making the acquaintance of musicians and buying music, he returned to Wiesentheid in 1701 to manage his estates. He himself took part in the 'house music' as a passionate and able cellist, had his strings sent from Rome and in the course of time acquired about a hundred cello concertos for his own use. His brother, who in 1710 had already ordered Vivaldi's work for him in Venice, again on June 15, 1712, placed an order for 'a dozen of the latest concertos by Vivaldi, Lotti and Pollaroli'. Thus it can be assumed that the Vivaldi cello concertos in the Wiesentheid Library were acquired at about this time, and perhaps Vivaldi composed some of them 'expresse'—as he himself once said—for the Count.

In the layout of the Schönborn concertos the ritornello and the solo section are clearly distinguishable from each other almost throughout, and in general the solo cello is accompanied only by the continuo bass, the orchestra participating but seldom in the accompaniment of the solo. Such a procedure was probably the result of aural experience of string ensembles, where the participation of violins and violas in the accompaniment of a solo all too easily masks the sound of a low-lying string soloist. A further peculiarity of these concertos is the very dense working of excellent ritornellos where the second violin is given a highly involved part (Ex. 109). With regard to playing technique, the Schönborn concertos are confined to the limits of what was still accessible to an accomplished amateur of the instrument. In the C minor Concerto the solo instrument is taken up to a♭′, in the D minor, B♭ major and G minor concertos b♭′ is often touched on, but c″ is only required in two places. Thus the works were to be played throughout in the normal fingering positions with some stretches. Since double stopping appears only in one movement, and there for only a few bars, and bowing techniques such as staccato and bariolage (cf. p. 118) are not exploited, the repertoire of musical figuration remains fairly limited. Vivaldi uses the instrument in cantileno style in the tenor register, or in toccata-like passages of figuration, but demands great skill in broken chords; and in playing of arpeggios he makes relatively extensive demands on bowing technique (Ex. 110).

Later developments, as far as can be judged from a doubtful chronology, appear to have been such that Vivaldi, perhaps stimulated by players with special tonal qualities or even instruments having particularly strong sonority, gradually started to use the orchestra more and more in solo sections, that he also transferred to the cello technical details familiar to him from the violin, and finally that he also significantly extended the previous capabilities of the instrument with regard to fingering positions. Such tendencies can be clearly seen in several cello concertos in the Turin collection. In this group of works what is striking is the frequent use of staccato over short groups of notes and also over groups of up to eleven notes, the detached bowing specifically indicated by wedge-heads, as well as the use of non-adjacent strings in semiquaver movement, which presupposes a particularly flexible handling of the bow (Ex. 111). There are amazing examples of the extension of fingering positions, and in the Concerto P. 180 even f♯″ is reached. In many respects one of Vivaldi's maturest works is the A minor Concerto, P. 35. In the last movement, over a pedal a, an ascending line is taken up to e″, and joined to this is a descending sequence which can only be performed cleanly and musically by means of a thumb attachment (Ex. 112). This way of playing is said to have been introduced by the Italian cellist Francischello, whom Geminiani heard in Rome in 1713, and who lived in Naples after 1725 and in Vienna after 1730. Quantz heard him in Naples in 1725 and was very impressed by his playing, but does not give us any particulars about his technique.

It is quite conceivable that Vivaldi got to know this master of the instrument during his opera season in Rome (1723–4) or even in Naples, and was persuaded by him to write cello concertos with extremely virtuosic playing technique. This would mean that Vivaldi was the first to exploit the thumb attachment in works of significance. Moreover this way of playing is said to have been taken to France by a cellist who had been born in Florence of German parents, J. Baptiste Stück, who then called himself Batistin; there, it was described for the first time by Michel Corette in his *Theoretical and practical method for learning perfect playing of the cello in a short time*, printed in 1741, the year Vivaldi died.

Vivaldi's cello concertos, apart from a few weaker pieces, are compositions of great musical worth. Even though their dating is not thoroughly certain, they may fairly definitely be ascribed to those two decades which were so essential to the rise of the cello as a solo instrument, and in their standards of playing technique they reflect the most important stage in the history of cello playing.

THE CONCERTOS FOR VIOLA D'AMORE

Vivaldi wrote no original concerto for the viola, and did not even use the instrument in a solo group. On the other hand he seems to have been particularly partial to the silvery tone of the viola d'amore, a sonority produced by the sympathetic strings that pass under the bridge, tuned in exactly the same way as the playing strings, vibrating together with them. In all, we have six solo concertos for the instrument, a concerto for viola d'amore and lute, and the viola d'amore is used once in a concerto 'con molti Istrumenti'. Furthermore, it is included several times as an obbligato solo instrument in vocal works. The concertos mentioned are the following:

P.	Title	Key	Tuning
37	'Con^to con Viola d'Amor'	A minor	*[musical notation]*
166	'p. viola d'amour à 5'	D major	*[musical notation]*
233	'concerto P. Viola d'amore'	A major	—
287	'Con^to con Viola d'amore'	D minor	*[musical notation]*
288	'Con^to con Viola d'Amor'	D minor	—
289	'Con^to p. viola d'amore'	D minor	*[musical notation]*
266	'Con^to con viola d'amor, e leuto e con tutti gl'istromenti sordini'	D minor	—
286	'Con^to con Viola d'Amor 2 Corni dà caccia, e 2 haubois tutti sordini e fagotto'	F major	*[musical notation]*

The composer uses a six-stringed instrument, and generally indicates the tuning required. He is particularly exact about the Concerto P. 289, prescribing 'Accordatura senza Scordatura'. From this it follows that for Vivaldi D minor was the normal tuning. With one exception the instrument is always notated in the treble clef, and the real pitch of the melodies is between about a'' and d'''. One concerto (P. 233) is notated in the alto clef, but it is clear from the whole layout that it should be read an octave higher. In the middle movement of the Concerto P. 287, written for viola d'amore and bass, Vivaldi began to write the upper part too in the bass clef, but turning the page reverted again to the treble clef. Moreover the movement is crossed out and replaced by another which is added after the last movement. The first solo from P. 289 is typical of Vivaldi's way of writing for the instrument. The bass is given to the violins, and the keyboard instrument has a rest here. This happens especially often in the viola d'amore concertos, and recommended itself not only for reasons of sonority, but also because full chords would have been superfluous in view of the writing for the solo instrument, which is often in two parts (Ex. 113).

So that the viola player should not entirely go wanting, the composer himself allowed for a performance on that instrument of the concerto we have just been considering. On the left hand side of the title we read 'Viola' and in the course of the first solo, the copyist's direction 'Qui in vece di scrivere à 2 Corde scrivete solamente le note di sopra' (Instead of writing in two parts here, write only the upper notes). Several times similar remarks are to be found in the course of the work. Vivaldi frequently provided for such 'ad libitum' performances on a solo instrument, but in doing so generally made more alterations than here.

THE CONCERTOS FOR RECORDER AND FLUTE

When in 1718 Johann Joachim Quantz became an oboist and violinist in the so-called Polnische Kapelle of the Saxon Elector August II, whose duties extended to Dresden and Warsaw, he soon recognized that he had no particular prospects on these instruments, changed over to the flute, and in 1719–20 took instruction from Pierre Gabriel Buffardin, the first flute of the Dresden Royal Band. In his book *The Present State of Music in Germany*, Burney says of this time: 'The scarcity of pieces, composed expressly for the German flute, was such, at this period, that the performers upon that instrument were obliged to adopt those of the hautbois or violin, and by altering or transposing, accommodate them to their purpose, as well as they could.' From the standpoint of the year 1772, when Burney undertook his journey to Germany, the 'flute' naturally meant the transverse flute.

Vivaldi's output for this instrument goes back to a time when, after acoustical improvements to which above all the French Hotteterre family of woodwind players and instrument makers had contributed, it was only just gradually becoming a court instrument. Above all, in decent chamber music the recorder, with its character more attuned to the lower-keyed 'concert pitch' of the time, was regarded as the more pleasant instrument because it was less obtrusive. If the transverse flute gradually ousted its quieter rival this was not because it corresponded better to the technical demands of the new concertante style; in this respect the instrument, which still had hardly any keys, was in no way better equipped than the recorder. It was much rather the more penetrating and (with regard to its dynamic range) more versatile tone of the transverse flute which soon made the less agile expressiveness of the recorder seem old-fashioned. Already in 1722, when the Bishop of Würzburg, Johann Philipp Franz von Schönborn, was given a recommendation for a musician 'who made an especial profession of the bassoon and the recorder', he answered that he was 'only interested in him if he was a good player of the German flute—for the other is of little consequence'. At about this time the transverse flute had finally established itself.

Vivaldi wrote works for both instruments, and like Bach and other contemporaries distinguished between them by using the terms 'flauto' (= recorder) and 'flauto traverso' (occasionally also 'Flauto Traversier' or 'Flaute travers'). A work of particular interest with regard to the composer's attitude to the instrument is his Op. X, *VI Concerti / a Flauto Traverso / Violino Primo e Secondo Alto Viola / Organ e Violoncello / Di / D. Antonio Vivaldi / Musico di Violino, Maestro del Pio Ospitale / della Citta di Venetia e Maestro di Capella / di Camera di S.A.S. Il Sigʳ Principe / Filippo Langravio d'Hassia Darmistabt*. The work appeared in print in 1729–30 and comprises the following concertos:

	Title	Turin Manuscript
No. 1, P. 261	La Tempesta di Mare	Giordano VIII/p. 353
No. 2, P. 342	La Notte	,, VIII/p. 343
No. 3, P. 155	Il Gardellino	,, VIII/p. 332
No. 4, P. 104		— —
No. 5, P. 262		Giordano VIII/p. 347
No. 6, P. 105		,, VIII/p. 308

The fact that Op. X contains three concertos with programmatic titles has already been dealt with in connection with the master's programme music. The Turin manuscripts of five works from Op. X are particularly valuable for the history of the flute, since in their instrumentation they show considerable departures from the printed versions:

P. 261 Flauto Traversier, Haubois, Violino, Fagotto, Basso
P. 342 Flauto Traversier, 2 Violini, Fagotto, Basso
P. 155 Flauto Traversier, Aubois, Violino, Fagotto, Basso
P. 262 'à Flauto Solo' (with 2 violins, violas, basses)
P. 105 Flauto, Aubois, Violino, Fagotto, Basso.

Thus four of these works were originally chamber concertos, three of them with transverse flute and one with recorder, and a further one was a solo concerto for recorder. There is no doubt that the Turin manuscripts represent older versions; from this, we may deduce the historical facts about Vivaldi's Op. X with a good deal of certainty. It is not yet known who wrote the first solo concerto for the transverse flute; perhaps it was Quantz himself. Whether it was he who stimulated Vivaldi to compose concertos for the transverse flute—they met in Venice in 1726—is doubtful. It was probably rather the Amsterdam publisher, observing the growing popularity of the transverse flute as a solo instrument, who had the obvious idea of ordering flute concertos from Vivaldi. The master had probably not yet written any original concertos for the flute, otherwise it would have been easy for him to delve into his music cupboard and satisfy the publisher's wish. But just then he did not have time to write any. Thus it is easy to see why only one concerto, P. 104, is a genuine flute concerto. For the rest, he relied on adaptations. With P. 262 this was no problem, but it was not quite so easy with the four chamber concertos: here the oboe had to be replaced by a violin, a viola had to be added and the bassoon eliminated. Besides this change of instrumentation there were also structural problems, which would lead to poor acoustical effects. Namely, in the chamber concerto the violin part is taken by only one player; the composer can readily use it on equal terms with the flute in chains of thirds or dialogue passages. But in orchestral performance the violin, in such cases, would have a greater weight of sound in relation to the woodwind instrument which, without any structural change in the composition, has now become a soloist. A close comparison of the two versions shows that in many passages the printed edition is inferior to the first version, and it is possible that Vivaldi did not himself prepare the arrangement for printing but simply gave a pupil general instructions for doing this. A real adaptation would probably have required extensive alterations for which the composer did not have time. In the D major

Concerto P. 155, *Il Gardellino*, the intensive participation of the strings in the solo accompaniments can be explained by the original version, which used quite a different ensemble. Thus in performances from the printed edition there is a constant danger that the strings will swamp the solo instrument. Hence in passages such as that after bar 69 of the first movement it is advisable to perform the violin part by one violin alone as in the first version. Also in the first movement's opening ritornello, the flute in the Turin version plays an octave higher with the oboe (violin), and the flute figure was added later. The peculiar key relationships in the Concerto P. 262, too (1st movement F major, 2nd movement G minor, 3rd movement F major), do not occur in the first version, where the middle movement is in F minor. The more detailed evidence about Vivaldi's Op. X perhaps allows us to date his flute compositions with greater certainty. It seems that before 1729–30 the composer had written solo Concertos only for the recorder and had used the transverse flute only in chamber concertos. In that case the solo concertos for transverse flute came after that date, when recorder concertos would probably have been less expedient.

Besides the Op. X, there are the following flute concertos by Vivaldi:

3 solo concertos for flautino (P. 78, 79, 83)
2 solo concertos for recorder (P. 77, 440)
4 solo concertos for transverse flute (P. 80, 140, 203, 205)
6 chamber concertos with recorder (P. 81, 198, 204, 207, 402, 403)
6 chamber concertos with transverse flute (P. 82, 206, 322, 360, 404)
1 concerto for 2 transverse flutes (P. 76)
3 incomplete concertos for transverse flute (P. 139, 141, 142)

Besides these, the Cello Concerto P. 118 also exists in a second version for transverse flute; furthermore, 'flauti' are used in several 'Concerti con molti Istromenti', and in a 'Salve Regina' recorders and transverse flutes are even used alongside each other. Finally Vivaldi especially included the recorder in bucolic scenes in his operas, often even as 'flauti in scena', thus on stage. In *Tito Manlio* and in *La Verità in Cimento* 'flauti grossi' also appear.

With regard to their use, the recorder and the flute were kept somewhat distinct from each other, the former being frequently taken up to f''', and even occasionally to f♯''', whilst e''' is the upper limit for the flute. At the other extremity, the recorder's low f' is retained as a rule in the flute concertos as well, so that most of the flute concertos can also be played on the recorder. Occasionally technical simplifications are indicated, but these were probably always intended for the player, and do not permit any sort of inference about the instrument. In certain works Vivaldi demands of the recorder player a really virtuoso technique in arpeggio figures which are clearly derived from stringed instruments (Ex. 114).

It is still not entirely clear which instrument was meant by 'flautino'. Two of these concertos are notated from f' to f''', and the third from e' to f'''. They are apparently written for a recorder whose range is an octave higher than the alto flute, thus for that instrument which Praetorius called a 'Gar Klein Exilent', and whose actual sounds go up to f''''. The flauto piccolo (= flageolet) which appears in two cantatas of Bach had the range g'' to a''''. Vivaldi also used the flautino in operas, for example in *La Verità in Cimento* in an aria with flautino obbligato. The flauto grosso was certainly a tenor recorder. In an aria from *Tito Manlio* with '2 Flauti grossi', the instrument is notated in the treble clef and only used between e'' and c'''.

As a small notational peculiarity one might mention a stroked grace note which actually appears over the note. Perhaps it is meant to be cut particularly short (Ex. 115).

The Concertos for Oboe, Clarinet and Bassoon

In his *Geschichte des Instrumentalkonzerts* (1905), Arnold Schering wrote in the chapter 'The earlier solo concerto': 'After the first stage of simple superficial imitation of the Italians had been overcome, national characteristics began to become noticeable in the German concerto. Whereas Italy had from the start preferred the string (violin) concerto, it was now purely wind, or wind and string concertos that held sway in Germany. There, wind instruments had of old been the recipients of a special sympathy. Open-air ceremonies, serenades, 'table music' and the sounding of signals depended on the constant training of good wind players, and since the town wind bands which nurtured young talents paid particular attention to this, the development of string playing lagged behind somewhat.' Here he has described the circumstances which explain the predominance of the violin in Italy and that of wind instruments in Germany. In more general terms, such as have been reproduced by later writers, the Italians were soon seen as the nation of string-players, and the Germans as wind-players, and this point of view has cropped up again and again to the most recent times. How false it is is shown not only by the abundant use of the trumpet in Bologna, for instance, and especially by Torelli, but above all by the wide scope of Vivaldi's output of concertos

XII. Cadenza from Violin concerto in D major, P. 165, 3rd movement.

I L
T E A T R O
ALLA MODA

O   S I A

METODO ficuro, e facile per ben comporre, ed efequire l'OPERE Italiane in Mufica all'ufo moderno.

Nel quale

Si danno Avvertimenti utili, e neceffarja Poeti, Compofitori di Mufica, Mufici dell'uno, e dell'altro feffo, Impreffarj, Suonatori, Ingegneri, e Pittori di Scene, Parti buffe, Sarti, Paggi, Comparfe, Suggeritori, Copifti, Protettori, e Madri di Virtuofe, ed altre Perfone appartenenti al Teatro.

D E D I C A T O

D A L L' A U T O R E D E L L I B R O

AL COMPOSITORE DI ESSO.

Stampato ne' BORGHI di BELISANIA per ALDIVI.
VA LICANTE; all'infegna dell'Orfo in PEATA.
Si vende nella STRADA del CORALLO alla
PORTA del Palazzo d ORLANDO.

E fi riftamperà ogn'anno con nuova aggiunta.

XIII. Title page: *Il Teatro alla Moda.*

for wind instruments. He not only supplied the recorder and the transverse flute with concertos, but also the oboe, the bassoon—to an amazing extent—and even the newly developing clarinet (Johann Christoph Denner, *c.* 1700), which was known to him at least from 1716. It may be doubted whether the idea of writing them came from Vivaldi's orchestra of girls, although de Brosses tells us of the girls in the Ospedali: 'Moreover they sing like angels, play the violin, the flute, the organ, the oboe, the violoncello, the bassoon; in short, there is no instrument so large that it could frighten them.' Apparently there were in the orchestras of the Count of Hessen-Darmstadt, the Duke of Lothringen and Count Morzin particularly good wind players whom Vivaldi had to provide with virtuoso show-pieces.

It is evident that the oboe played a large part in his music. In about 1700 the instrument already had a long evolution behind it, and was one of the basic members of the seventeenth-century orchestra. On account of its penetrating tone it recommended itself especially for open-air music. Vivaldi uses different designations for the instrument: Hautbois, Hautboy, Houbois, Aubois, Oboè. One could clearly suppose that these terms represent a series of developments, which might provide points of reference for a chronological listing of the works. With a composer who had travelled so far and from time to time had also worked with the orchestras of foreign princes, the choice of term may also have been a concession to the particular usage at any given occasion. We know of Vivaldi:

10 concertos for oboe (P. 41,* 42, 43,* 44, 91, 187, 264, 306, 331, 334)
3 concertos for 2 oboes (P. 53, 85, 302)
1 concerto for oboe and bassoon (P. 129)
1 concerto for oboe and violin (P. 406)
2 concertos for violin and 2 oboes (P. 165, 210)
1 concerto for violin, organ and oboe (P. 36)
1 incomplete concerto for oboe (Wiesentheid)
3 bassoon concertos arranged for oboe (P. 50, 89, 318)

Of the concertos for solo oboe, several appeared in print in the composer's lifetime: P. 264 in a collection *Harmonia Mundi* with Walsh and Hare, London; P. 331 and 334 as the first and seventh concertos in Op. VII—in other words, as the first work in each half. Each time the

---

* In the first and second movements of these concertos, the ritornello sections are the same, the solo sections differ. Their final movements are completely different.

title reads 'Uno è con Oboe'. Three further violin concertos which appeared in print are designated by the appropriate note as oboe concertos ad libitum; these are Op. VIII, No. 9 = P. 259, Op. VIII, No. 12 = P. 8 and Op. XI, No. 6 = P. 339. Furthermore there are seven chamber concertos with oboe, and in the concertos 'con molti Istromenti' the oboe appears eight times in a smaller concertino group and nine times in a larger.

The Concerto P. 54 is indicative of the practice of the time: it is written for three violins, two oboes, viola, bassoon and basses, the bassoon being treated in the outer movements as a non-obbligato instrument. However, the Largo is laid out in three parts for two recorders and bassoon; in other words the oboists changed instruments and played the middle movement on recorders.

Whereas the ad libitum concertos show very little exploitation of the properties of the violin, and were thus also possible on the oboe, Vivaldi shows in the arrangement of bassoon concertos for the oboe that he was very familiar with the nature of the two instruments and their effective potentialities in the style of the time. That of the Bassoon Concerto P. 318 was undertaken with great care, and occasionally even the whole orchestral score is rewritten. Having a somewhat smaller range, the strength of the oboe lies in its expressive solo register, whilst for the bassoon it is above all the low register and its characteristic staccato that are exploited (Ex. 116).

In the ripieno concertos, the oboe is occasionally also used to reinforce the violins (P. 301). Rudolf Eller has given a precise description of another case in his edition of the Dresden Violin Concerto in G minor, P. 351 (Breitkopf and Härtel, PB 3593): the score has no oboes, but in the orchestral material oboe parts are found; they were apparently added later and only occasionally are treated in obbligato fashion.

Vivaldi also used clarinets in three concertos. Their exact titles are:

P. 73 'Con^{to} con 2 Hautbois 2 Clarinet, e Istrom^{ti}'
P. 74 'Con^{to} con due Clarinet 2 Hautbois e Istrom^{ti}'
P. 84 'Con^{to} P la Solennità di S. Lor^{zo}'

In the score of the third concerto the following instruments are specified: two Hautbois, two Claren, two Flauti, two Viol^{ni} di Con^{to}, two di Ripieno, Viola, Basso e Fagotto. It is clear from the work's middle movement that Claren meant clarinets, because there a 'Clarinet' is called upon to perform in the basso continuo.

The use of the instrument in three concertos as well as in the oratorio *Juditha* (1716), thus at a time when the clarinet was believed to have still only been in the experimental stage of its development, seemed to be very improbable, and it has constantly been maintained that these must have been Clarini, in other words high trumpets. As recently as 1959 Norbert Loeser wrote: 'The clarinet did not yet exist in Vivaldi's time, therefore it was to the flute, oboe and bassoon . . . that he referred.' Right away the first solo passage of the Concerto P. 74, however, leaves no doubt that the trumpet here is quite out of the question (Ex. 117). The instruments used were in C, and the key of all three concertos is C major; the '2 Claren' of the oratorio were in B♭, and the aria concerned is in B♭ major. The range covered extends up to c''' and b♭'', and its extent downwards cannot be definitely decided. As was practically every other instrument, the clarinets too were sometimes used for the so-called 'Bassetchen' (see p. 77) which was notated in the bass clef without regard to the instrument's range.

Vivaldi seems to have had a particular liking for the bassoon. His series of compositions for the instrument comprises:

36 solo concertos (P. 45, 46, 47, 48, 49, 50, 51, 52, 55, 56, 57, 69, 70,
71, 72, 89, 90, 128, 130, 131, 137, 298, 299, 300, 304, 305, 307,
318, 381, 382, 384, 386, 387, 401, 432, 433)
1 concerto for oboe and bassoon (P. 129)
1 concerto movement for bassoon (P. 303)
1 concerto for oboe, arranged for bassoon (P. 41/43)

Besides these, the insttument is used in nearly all the chamber concertos and in all the 'Concerti con molti Istromenti'.

In the chamber concertos, the bassoon is principally used in conjunction with the cello (or bass), but as a rule in such a way that it has its own passages over the basic notes (Ex. 38). In this way Vivaldi remained true to the practice of gifted bassoonists for whom the basic outline simply formed a foundation for improvisation. In the concertos for larger ensembles the instrument often combines with two higher wind instruments to form a three-part group that is used in alternation with other groups.

In Vivaldi's time the bassoon had only two keys for the notes which lay too far out of the player's reach. This makes the technical demands in the composer's concertos even more amazing; they are still technically challenging works today, and in the fast movements require above all a highly developed staccato. Writing for cello, the composer was already familiar with the exploitation of deep notes in melodic outlines. A passage from the Concerto P. 318 (also arranged for oboe) shows this

THE WORK

characteristic (Ex. 118). At that time C was the instrument's lowest note, and Vivaldi generally extended it upwards as far as g'', and in many concertos to a''.

Occasionally in the bassoon concertos there are the rudiments of solo cadenzas. For these, the old singers' rule that the cadenza should not exceed the length of one breath held good in the early eighteenth century. In the wind concertos Vivaldi frequently built up through-composed cadenza-like developments over the dominant pedal-point as a preparation for the final ritornello, but he also often indicated the possibility of a short improvised cadenza by fermatas (Ex. 119).

In dealing with solo concerto form we have already pointed to one characteristic of the wind concertos coming from the contrast between wind sound and string sound: since the danger of masking the sound of a wind soloist with the tutti strings was relatively small, the motivic interest in the solo accompaniment is generally greater in wind concertos than in string concertos. The examples given in Kolneder, *Solokonzertform*, pp. 64–49, are a very early anticipation of the classical era in their layout, both in dialogue passages and in their manner of development.

THE CONCERTOS FOR BRASS INSTRUMENTS

When in about 1700 or shortly afterwards Vivaldi began to write solo concertos, there was already in Italy a flourishing tradition of using brass instruments. In church music, opera and courtly musical performances, the trumpet was a symbolic instrument 'ad maiorem dei gloriam', as well as to that of secular princes; in opera, the horn was an indispensable prop for depicting hunting life, and the trombone could embellish scenes of the underworld in a colourful way, as well as serving to express the dignity of priests. The adoption of trumpets and horns in solo concert works was nonetheless subject to limits resulting from the restricted number of notes that a 'natural' instrument could yield. Even before 1700 composers had already confronted this problem, and one can study their different solutions in the genre of the trumpet sinfonia, to which much thought had been given; these solutions generally include that of not venturing too far from the main key of D major or C major, and giving the necessary tonally contrasting sections to the strings. The formal design of the solo concerto, with modulating solo sections and the return of the ritornello on different degrees of the scale, increased this problem vastly and seemed to make the use of solo brass players impossible.

In the light of this, Vivaldi's single trumpet concerto, the Concerto for two trumpets in C major, P. 75, is one of the most interesting works for the study of his treatment of form and his ability to overcome the difficulties of his material. In this three-movement work, the middle movement is confined to a six-bar string transitional passage, for obvious reasons. With regard to the notes used, it is striking that the third and fourth overtones (g, c′) do not appear, and the fifth (e′) only appears once. This confirms Mahillon's view that the clarino players used particularly flat and narrow-bored mouthpieces, which facilitated the production of the high notes, but made the low notes unusable. Vivaldi uses only the following eleven notes: e′, g′, c″, d″, e″, f″, f♯″, g″, a″, b″, and c‴. With such a small supply of notes it proved expedient to reduce the scope of the solo sections compared with the ritornellos, and in the first movement the proportion is $27\frac{1}{2}$ to 54, in the third movement 61 to 74. However, this was only possible if the ritornellos were especially copiously endowed from the motivic point of view. In that of the first movement, the trumpets are also included right from the start, so as to give the work a festive splendour in the first bars. In the first solo, Vivaldi uses all the tricks of his trade to conceal the deficiency of notes at his disposal: imitation, staccato thirds in semiquavers, interplay of dynamic contrasts, note repetition (Ex. 120). With a tutti interjection, still in the tonic, he gives the soloists a breathing space—this is the last ritornello group—, and the modulatory F♯ has already entered in the bass two bars before the first trumpet uses it for a cadence. Compared with the beginning, ritornello II is not shortened, but it soon modulates from the dominant G major to the relative minor of the dominant, E minor. Two of the contrasting tonalities that are necessary in solo concerto form are thus combined in one ritornello. In this way the tonic acquires sufficient value again to be used uninterruptedly from bar 55 to the end. In the last movement the procedure is similar, except that in ritornello II the relative minor of the tonic instead of that of the dominant is modulated to, and from bar 81 on, the trumpets hint at A minor for a few bars, before completing the modulation back to the tonic (Ex. 121).

Vivaldi always used the horn in pairs, both in two double concertos (P. 320 and 321) and in the following concertos for larger ensembles:

P. 265	2 horns, 2 oboes, 2 bassoons (all concertos with strings)
P. 267	2 horns, 2 oboes, bassoon; violin and cello obbligato
P. 268	solo violin, 2 oboes, 2 horns, bassoon
P. 273	solo violin, 2 horns, 2 oboes, bassoon
P. 286	viola d'amore, 2 horns, 2 oboes, bassoon
P. 444	Concerto grosso à 10 (with 2 horns in D)

The horn also appears in two sinfonias, frequently in operas and in two cantatas, including one 'in Lode si S.A.S. Pr. F. d'Armstatt'.

P. 320, in F major, is written for horn in 'high F', in other words having the fundamental F. The instrument is used from its 3rd to its 13th partial (without the 7th), so that there were only ten notes at his disposal: c', f', a', c'', f'', g'', a'' bb'', c''', d''' (notated in C). In keeping with this small number of notes, the composer remained in the home key even more than in the trumpet concerto, the dominant being touched on only for a very short time. The compositional means used in finding material for the two horns are much the same as in the trumpet concerto (Ex. 122). The composer has solved the problem of the middle movement with a Largo for solo cello and continuo bass.

In the Concerto P. 321 there is a notable instance of his use of the horn. Here Vivaldi had horns in 'low F' (today's normal tuning) at his disposal—in other words with the fundamental F'. Using the notes c', e', f', g', a', bb', c'', d'', e'', f'', g'', a'', bb'', c''', he has gone completely outside the normal range, f' already being the eighth partial (the e' appears only at one point as a minim, and could be taken as a stopped eb', the seventh overtone). But this means that Vivaldi demanded of his player a range extending to the 24th partial. At no time was this technically possible, so that the composer must have allowed the possibility of ad libitum playing throughout almost all the work: or rather, that of recomposing the part for the horn's actual range. A few bars from the first solo of the first movement will serve as an example (Ex. 123). The two horns also play in the middle movement, a Larghetto in 12/8 time.

In works like P. 268 and P. 273, which are really violin concertos, and in P. 286, a viola d'amore concerto, the horns are used as soloists relatively sparsely, but their diatonic, fanfare-like melodies have a very enlivening effect by way of contrast. Often they make up a trio with the bassoon, and are juxtaposed with other trio groups in dialogue. In many passages with long-held notes in the horns it is possible to recognize a tendency which led to a new function for the horn in classical and romantic instrumentation. P. 265, the only copy of which was brought to light in the Hessische Landesbibliothek in Darmstadt, was unfortunately destroyed in the war together with copies of eight other Vivaldi works.

Vivaldi used two trombones in a concerto only once, if the 'Trombon dà Caccia' of P. 319 really were trombones. In its structure, the work is a violin concerto with two oboes, bassoon and these dubious hunting trombones, which in any case are given relatively little work to do and are used in the manner of horns. The work has a peculiar title, 'Con^{to}

THE WORK

P.S.A.S.I.S.P.G.M.D.G.I.M.B.,' which Pincherle supposes to be a jesting dedication to Pisendel (Per Sua Altezza Serenissima il Signor Pisendel Giorgio . . .)

THE CONCERTOS FOR PLUCKED STRINGS

On December 26, 1736, Vivaldi wrote to his protector, the Marchese Guido Bentivoglio d'Aragona in Ferrara: 'Non posso esprimere l'ardente desiderio che nutro di venire a Ferrara solo per ossequiare V.E. Supplico V.E. aver la Bontà di farmi avvisato se più si diletta di mandolino' (I cannot express my ardent desire to come to Ferrara simply and solely to pay my respects to Your Excellency. May Your Excellency let me know if He is still pleased with the mandoline). If the Marchese answered in the affirmative, then it is quite probable that on the eve of a large operatic undertaking, for which he needed his patron's assistance, Vivaldi wrote for him the two mandoline concertos, P. 134 for one mandoline and strings and P. 133 for two mandolines and strings. The composer was already well acquainted with the instrument from the time of his oratorio *Juditha*, where it is included as an obbligato solo instrument in an aria. In the eighteenth century it was not played with the modern tremolo, but with single strokes; Vivaldi however, often used the note repetition characteristic of the mandoline.

In the Concerto P. 134, the conception of the string ritornello is already mandoline-like (Ex. 124), and the composer states in the subtitle 'Si puo anco fare con tutti i violini pizzicati' (It may also be played with all the strings pizzicato). In both concertos, the bass is often given to the violins and violas, and in the solo concerto, the direction 'Vio^{lo} Solo' (= cello solo) is to be found several times, whereas in the double concerto the organ is specified as a continuo instrument. Occasionally, in passages where there are leaps over several strings which are impossible to perform beyond a certain tempo, simplifications are given. The first solo of P. 133 (Ex. 125) is typical of Vivaldi's way of writing for the instrument. By reading the score, one can barely imagine how these few notes will sound, but the actual sonority is so bewitching by its very spareness that one has to admire the master for having taken all this into consideration. Moreover, the work gains a great deal if the two soloists are placed at some distance from each other.

A further work of Vivaldi's with two mandolines is the first of the four concertos which were performed before the Elector of Saxony, Friedrich Christian at the Ospedale della Pietà in 1740. It bears the title 'Concerto con Due Flauti, Due Teorbi, Due Mandolini, Due Salmò, Due Violini in Tromba marina et un Violoncello'. Here again we find the theorbo that Vivaldi had already used in *Juditha* and which was to be retained as a continuo bass instrument till the turn of the century on account of the particular charm of its sonority.

Besides this deep lute, Vivaldi also used the lute in its normal tuning, namely in two concertos and two trio sonatas. The 'Con^to con 2 violini, leuto e basso' in D major, P. 209, was perhaps conceived for a chamber ensemble; the lute is the solo instrument, and the violins have a pronounced ripieno function. The other concerto, P. 266, was also played before the Elector of Saxony in 1740 and in the memorial volume preserved in Dresden bears the title 'Con^to con viola d'amor, e leuto, e con tutti gl'istromenti sordini'. Perhaps the Elector had brought with his entourage the famous lute virtuoso Sylvius Weiss? In Vivaldi's works one looks in vain for really characteristic lute writing, or polyphonic writing suited to the instrument. In the Concerto P. 209 the lute is kept in a relatively high register and written for mostly in one part, three-part chords from which arpeggios are to be derived being notated in the way familiar to the composer from the violin. Today, Vivaldi's lute works are mostly played on the modern guitar, and sound very well on this instrument. One should not object to such a transfer, for the master himself gave plenty of suggestions for such ad libitum versions.

THE CONCERTOS WITH SOLO KEYBOARD INSTRUMENTS

In general Vivaldi meted out fairly shabby treatment to the keyboard instruments. Only recently has Gian Francesco Malipiero discovered the only harpsichord piece Vivaldi is at present known to have written. It seems that neither the rigid sound of the harpsichord nor that of the organ meant very much to the composer, whose ideas and shapes were governed primarily by the expressive tone of the violin. Certainly both instruments were for him indispensable aids to the execution of the continuo bass; but even there he often enough excluded the harpsichord with a specific indication as having too intrusive a sound. But what interested him about both instruments was their charming sonorities in the upper registers, particularly in fast movement or in playful broken chords.

The only work with a concertante harpsichord is a 'Con^to Con molti Istrom^tt' in C major, P. 87, to which little attention has so far been paid. In the first catalogue of his works, Rudge gives as the ensemble 'str'; Rinaldi, who apparently only worked from Rudge in his catalogue, read the 's' for a '5' and made the work a 'Concerto per cinque trombe'

Op. 53, No. 3. Finally, in his *Inventaire thématique*, Pincherle gives the instrumentation as 'Quatuor et bois' (Four-part strings and woodwind). The autograph score specifies the following instruments: three violins (i.e. sometimes also three solo violins), 1 system in the alto clef (= viola), Hautbois, two Viole Inglesi, Salmoe, two Flauti, two Cembali, Violoncelli et altri Bassi (thus, double basses and bassoons) and in the final movement also two Trombe. For this enormous ensemble the master only had ten-stave paper at his disposal, on which he tried somehow to accommodate exactly what he wanted done.

At the beginning the two harpsichords play in unison with the basses, and only in bar 25 do they emerge as soloists; from there on they continually join in with smaller or larger episodes in the interplay of alternating instrumental groups. The first solo insertion is itself characteristic of Vivaldi's conception of sound (Ex. 126), and the aurally very charming way in which the master handles the two harpsichords in the middle movement has been described on p. 76. Here it should be mentioned that in modern Italian writings in particular, the continuo bass harpsichord is often mentioned in a work's title in such a way that one might suppose it to be used as a solo instrument. Thus Rinaldi (p. 229) speaks of a 'Concerto in si minore per cembalo, violino solo e archi', where the proper title should be, as in the Ricordi catalogue, 'violino solo, archi e cembalo'.

Of the five concertos with solo organ, P. 274 is also not clear in its specifications. Pincherle writes in the *Inventaire thématique* 'Concerto con organo, à 4', and on p. 104 of his book he calls it 'Concerto con organo', and a few lines later in fact gives it correctly as 'violin solo, quatuor à cordes et orgues', though he puts the organ last as though it had a continuo bass function. The instrumentation of the other four concertos is:

P. 36   'Con^{to} p. Viol^o Organo et Hautbois ò pure 2 Violini et Hautbois' (or also 2 violins and oboe)

P. 226   'Concerto in due cori con flauti obligati' (with concertante organ in the second orchestra)

P. 309   'Con^{to} con 2 Violini et 2 Organi obligati' (only one movement)

P. 311   'Con^{to} à Viol^o et Org^o'

In all these compositions the organ is treated as a basso continuo *and* a concertante instrument. Since in solo passages, apart from a few broken chords, the instrument is written for in the upper stave in only one part, this part—as is indicated in the subtitle of P. 36—can be taken over by a violin without further ado. In a spare stave of page 1 under the score itself the following remark appears: 'Questo basso volendo cambiare l'oboe in violoncello' (This bass will alter the oboe part to a cello part), so that altogether four different groups of soloists are possible. Two passages from the first movement show typical treatment of the organ (Ex. 127), which is taken up to c'''. The sonorities of the work are full of charm, the three solo instruments alternating for the most part in small groups, and often being used in the same register so that only their timbre differentiates them. The middle movement, where the orchestra is silent and the basso continuo is given to the lower stave of the organ whilst the upper stave forms part of a three-part texture, is especially attractive. In every instance Vivaldi will probably have always used a very bright organ registration.

Pincherle has given two examples from the Concerto P. 274 (pp. 104 f.) which show essentially the same procedure. In P. 311, a genuine double concerto, the two soloists play together in long solo episodes and frequently exchange parts in the same register. Three bars before the end of the third movement appears the direction: 'Qui si ferma à piacimento del Viol° et Org° poi segue.' The master crossed this out, perhaps after a performance in which the double improvisation did not entirely correspond with his wishes.

It is regrettable that of P. 309 only the first movement exists, because in its layout and exploitation of possibilities this is a masterpiece. It is written 'in due cori' in such a way that two string orchestras, each having a solo violin and an organ, form two completely self-contained ensembles. We may clearly suppose that the movement was intended for St. Mark's. The suggestion of utilizing spatial relationships in such a compositional structure was already inherent in the existence of the two separate organs. Vivaldi has the two organs playing by turns, as well as the two violins; but he also combines violin and organ in different groupings. The finest sound effects arise when all four solo instruments alternate with each other in short motivic figurations in a high register.

THE CONCERTOS FOR SEVERAL INSTRUMENTS

Analysis of Op. III, Vivaldi's first printed concertos, has shown that some of these works were closely related to the older Corelli-type concerto grosso, for which the modern term group concertos has been coined. A characteristic of this genre is a concertino group—frequently consisting of three instruments (two violins and continuo bass)—which is contrasted with the orchestra in short alternations. In the formal respect, it was modelled on the older church sonata and suite, often freely intermixed. But in Op. III there are also very clearly defined solo concertos. Since from Op. IV on the concerto grosso type disappeared completely from his printed works, it can be assumed—although the dates of the single concertos of Op. III are not known—that the instrumentational and formal traits belonging to the concerto grosso appear only at the beginning of Vivaldi's output of concertos.

However, there are a greater number of concertos by the composer in which two or more soloists are involved, though these concertos may be fundamentally different in form from the old concerto grosso. As did Torelli in his Op. VIII, Vivaldi took over the new genre of the solo concerto form for works with two or more soloists. In order to distinguish between these two types, it is necessary to discard the term 'group concerto', which refers only to the ensemble, and use instead the term 'Concerto grosso' for the older type and a phrase such as 'Concerto per due oboi' for the new type, since these terms can also relate to the form of the works. In such circumstances we can see again and again that the old masters, alleged to be so obscure in their terminology, really knew exactly what they were doing when they gave their works titles. The term 'Concerto doppio' (double concerto) that was occasionally used by Vivaldi's contemporaries but never by himself, also corresponds exactly to the case in hand insofar as it is a question of two instruments. If the concertino group was constituted of more than three or four instruments, Vivaldi would generally call such works 'Concerto con molti Istromenti', and occasionally something like 'Concerto a 10 obligati' (P. 359). The latter concerto is interesting for the number of instruments given: solo violin, solo oboe, 2 recorders, 2 oboes and four-part strings, with all the bass instruments—that is, cello, double bass, bassoon and harpsichord—counted as one instrument! Thus the indication 'obligato' does not always necessarily refer to a solo instrument.

If we include the concertos from Op. III, but not the chamber concertos and those 'in due cori', there are altogether 76 concertos by Vivaldi for two or more solo instruments. Of these 76 concertos, 25 only are for two violins, being generally designated by Vivaldi as 'Concerto con due violini obligati', and also occasionally as 'Concerto con due Violini concertati'. Sixteen further works are double concertos for different instrumental groups:

P. 238, 308, 388 for violin and cello (all concertos with strings)
P. 311   violin and organ
P. 406   oboe and violin

P. 266	viola d'amore and lute
P. 411	two cellos
P. 133	two mandolines
P. 76	two transverse flutes
P. 53, 85, 302	two oboes
P. 129	oboe and bassoon
P. 320, 321	two horns
P. 75	two trumpets

Of the works with three and more soloists, P. 73 and P. 74 (two oboes and two clarinets), P. 135 and P. 188 (two violins and two cellos), P. 278 (three violins), P. 367 (four violins) and finally 17 works 'con molti Istromenti' are of particular interest. Almost all these compositions have in common the use of ritornello form for the outer movements. For the solo sections, they make use of very different possibilities: a) group solos; b) predominance of single instruments in single solo sections; and c) dialogue treatment. A typical example of the latter type is the Concerto for two mandolines, P. 133 (Ex. 125).

The way in which Vivaldi experimented with the form is shown in another double concerto, the 'Conto con due Aubois' in A minor, P. 53. Here the ritornello is in six parts, the solo oboes are used in it as obbligato instruments, and the texture is clearly divided into three groups (Ex. 128). After 13 bars, passagework in semiquavers begins, being played by the two oboes and the violins in unison. This formal section modulates to the relative major, C major, whereupon in bar 23 ritornello II, having the same structure as ritornello I, enters. The whole movement is laid out in this sequence, solo sections and ritornellos alternating in this manner.

The way the composer introduces three soloists first one after the other and then combines them in a unified sonority can be studied in a 'Concerto con 3 violini di concerto' in F major, P. 278 (Ex. 129). The work is one of Vivaldi's strongest inspirations, and in the middle movement he has given us a masterpiece of magical violin sonorities (see Kolneder, *Aufführungspraxis*, p. 117).

The greater the number of soloists, the greater is the number of combinatory possibilities. In a 'Conto con due Clarinet 2 Hautbois e Istromtt', P. 74, in the first solo section of the last movement, at first the two clarinets and the two oboes alternate with each other, then there is a dialogue between the first clarinet and the first oboe, then follow two-bar groups of oboe and clarinet, and finally the first oboe plays a ten-bar solo

THE WORK

passage (Ex. 130). A ten-part Concerto P. 385, whose original title was *Con^(to) Funebre / Con Hautbois sordini e Salmoe / e Viole all'Inglese / Tutti li Violini e Violette Sordini / Non però il Viol° Principale* (all the violins and violas muted, though not the solo violin), is particularly rich in contrasting timbres. Solo sections on the violin interchange with those in which different combinations alternate with each other in brief interjections. To correspond with the peculiarity of these upper-part groups' sonorities, the bass is for the most part split up among different instruments.

THE CONCERTOS 'IN DUE CORI'

St. Mark's Cathedral in Venice, with its two facing choirs, each of them furnished with an organ, stimulated composers from the time of Adrian Willaert on to adopt the technique of so-called 'chori spezzati' (divided choirs). The unusual typographical layout of Roger's Amsterdam edition of Op. III shows that in his youth Vivaldi probably felt close affinities with this antiphonal way of writing, but that he had scarcely derived any structural consequences from it, apparently because his development tended more towards solo concerto form and antiphonal writing did not really interest him at that time. However, a number of reports of official ceremonial concerts with Vivaldi's works allow us to conclude that as a recognized master he constantly received commissions for such occasions, which would naturally be held in the official church, the Cathedral of St. Mark's. As a thoughtful and effective builder of forms, and above all as a master of sound effects, Vivaldi again took up the antiphonal style connected with the place at a later stage in his development, though now he recognized and exploited the compositional possibilities it afforded.

Altogether we have eight vocal works by Vivaldi which are already in their titles described by the composer as being laid out 'in due cori', and one of them is the *Dixit Dominus* which will be discussed in the chapter on the sacred music. Besides these there are four instrumental concertos using antiphonal technique, and these are:

P. 14 in C major. 'Printed at the expense of Gerhard Frederik Witvogel, organist at the new Lutheran Church in Amsterdam' during the composer's lifetime, in a collection of music by different composers. Also preserved in manuscript in Dresden and Turin. The Turin manuscript bears the title 'Con^(to) in due cori Per la S. S^(ma) Assontione di M.V.' (Concerto with two orchestras for the Assumption of the B.V.M).

P. 164 in D major. In manuscript at Dresden and Turin with different middle movements, the Turin score having the title 'Con^{to} In due cori Per la S. S^{ma} Assontione di M.V.'.

P. 226 in G minor. In manuscript in Dresden with the title 'Concerto in due cori con flauti obligati' (with concertante organ in second orchestra).

P. 368 in B♭ major. In manuscript at Turin with the title 'Concerto in due Cori con Viol^o scordato Del Vivaldi'.

In addition there is a single movement, P. 309, laid out in two choruses.

The fact that three of the four concertos are preserved in Dresden gives rise to the supposition that the Dresden court supplied the commissions and the large Dresden orchestra provided the stimulus, indeed the Violin Concerto P. 383 (with two recorders, two oboes and bassoon added to the strings) bears the title 'Con^{to} del Vivaldi p. l'orchestra di Dresda'.

In the antiphonal vocal works the orchestra too is generally handled antiphonally, as for instance in a 'Domine in due Cori à 8 Con Istrom^{ti} Del Vivaldi'. The form of the work is in three parts, the two outer movements, whose antiphonal conception is most effective, being contrasted with a central soprano solo of intimate sonorities, in which two three-part string orchestras first alternate with each other in 'spezzati' fashion, and then are combined in a unified body of sound (Ex. 131).

Seen from the standpoint of antiphonal construction, a concerto such as P. 164 represents a relatively early stage of development. It is a violin concerto with two four-part string orchestras; in the spatial arrangement the soloist was presumably placed close by the first orchestra, which is also treated as the principal orchestra and undertakes the accompaniment of the solo. Only in the ritornellos is the second orchestra written for independently, and alternates with the first orchestra in short exchanges. The violinistically very interesting Violin Concerto P. 368 is conceived in the same way. In its concentration of structure and exploitation of the solo instrument's virtuoso possibilities with a written-out cadenza, the work is one of the master's best violin concertos, though in its antiphonal technique it barely surpasses P. 164.

A work that is laid out in a genuinely antiphonal way is the Violin Concerto in C major, P. 14. It is already evident in the imitatively developed ritornello of the last movement that Vivaldi here has set about making compositional use of the possibilities inherent in the use of two orchestras (Ex. 132). But even in the solo accompaniment, the second orchestra is treated throughout as the equal of the first.

THE WORK

THE ORCHESTRAL CONCERTOS AND SINFONIAS

Vivaldi wrote a fair number of generally three-movement works for strings, only occasionally augmented by auxiliary wind instruments; in these either no solo instruments predominate, or only episodically do single instruments emerge from the tutti as soloists. For this type of work, which seems to cover his entire creative career, he himself did not use a common terminology. Following the older usage he called it a 'Sinfonia', but often simply 'Concerto', or even 'Concerto a quattro', or again 'Concerto ripieno'. Yet with these different names no subtle difference of genre was being defined. Several of these works have been preserved in two copies and are referred to in one as a sinfonia, in the other as a 'Concerto' or 'Concerto à quattro'. Besides, the title 'Concerto à quattro' simply means a 'Concerto without soloists', and yet Vivaldi generally headed his violin concertos 'Concerto à cinque': in other words, a work for solo violin and four-part strings. Charles de Brosses discerned the type exactly when he heard such works, which were new to him, in Venice. On August 29, 1739 he wrote to his friend M. de Blancey: 'Here there is a kind of music which is not known in France and which seems to me better suited than any other to Bourbonne's garden. They are large concertos in which there is no solo violin. Quintin can ask Bourbonne whether he would like me to bring him a supply.'

The term 'sinfonia' points to a work being used in the theatre; in fact operatic practice in the later seventeenth and early eighteenth centuries made abundant use of sinfonias. One would be given as 'Sinfonia à prencipio' (= overture) at the beginning, others were used as entr'acte music, and single movements were required perhaps as music for storm scenes or to accompany lyrical scenes, but often merely to fill out the pauses needed for scene changes. When around 1700 the solo and concertante elements obtruded more and more into the operatic sinfonias, the solo concerto gradually supplanted the sinfonia in the theatre as being by far the more interesting genre for the listener. Thus we know from Uffenbach's journal that in performances of his operas Vivaldi played violin concertos as insertions, and his pupil Pisendel played one of his teacher's concertos (P. 268) as interlude music during his stay in Venice. Moreover, this custom died hard, and Mozart's violin concertos were still 'inserted' into Salzburg theatrical performances.

With regard to form Vivaldi also based his concertos without soloists on the design to which he kept in the solo concertos. In this way the traditional title 'sinfonia' began to have little meaning, and Vivaldi found a name for his orchestral concertos in the term 'Concerto ripieno', though it appears only in his own music. Ripieno is the Italian word for full, stuffing, and 'il ripieno' can also mean 'the stopgap'. In Quantz, Ripienist is simply the term for an orchestral musician, and 'Of the Ripieno Violinists in Particular' is Quantz's title for that chapter which deals with the tasks of the accompanying violinist.

With the description 'Concerto ripieno' Vivaldi had already provided an excellent solution 250 years ago to a terminological problem that has constantly been tackled up to the most recent times. In his *Geschichte des Instrumentalkonzerts* Schering coined the modern term 'concerto-symphony', which unfortunately combines two concepts which were subject to drastic changes and have acquired a completely new meaning, above all since classical times. He says of this nomenclature: 'The name "concerto-symphony" has been introduced for this instrumental genre, here treated in its own right for the first time, for it indicates at the same time the newly appearing characteristics of the concerto as well as the difference from the older polyphonic "sonata" and emphasizes its links with the church.' Boyden proposed 'concerto-sonata', but Giazotto had anticipated him in his book on Albinoni with the description 'sonata-concerto'. Boyden then suggested the worthwhile possibility 'ensemble-concerto', and Bukofzer's expression 'orchestral concerto' is perhaps even better, having been given such a distinct imprint in our century by an important work of Bartók's.

Altogether Vivaldi left 47 such works, of which 28 are preserved only in Turin, and two only in the library of the Paris Conservatoire; ten further works exist in the two libraries, the rest being in Rostock, Uppsala and Vienna. The fact that the library of the Paris Conservatoire possesses twelve of these concertos is perhaps attributable to the fact that de Brosses obtained the relevant commission from his friend.

In all these works the lack of a soloist and thus of solo sections threw up special problems for the composer. For these, Vivaldi found three solutions:

1) The self-contained orchestral ritornello is taken, according to the usual design, through the tonalities I–V–VI–I: in other words, only the orchestral framework of the solo concerto is given. This was perhaps the least interesting solution, and was possible only if the ritornello was in itself constructed with abundant motivic material and could appear as if new at every entry by means of considerable variation.

2) Between the ritornellos, interludes with new motivic material or with a further developmental treatment of the ritornello motifs are inserted.

3) These interludes are of such great scope that the ritornello itself loses some of its formal importance and more or less merely constitutes the frame for a free, concertante style of orchestral writing.

All these types of concerto ripieno movement are copiously exemplified in Vivaldi. One of the most interesting examples is the first movement of P. 60 in A minor, which Vivaldi specifically described as 'Concerto ripieno'. The 13-bar ritornello is clearly divided into three motivic groups. As ritornello II it is curtailed to the first group; as ritornello III it is even further reduced; and as the closing ritornello IV it is expanded once more in the home key. The interludes are developed from ritornello motifs, but these are so freely evolved that in their content they do not anticipate the return of the ritornello and thereby detract from its effect.

It seems that Vivaldi occasionally attempted to compensate for the lack of possibilities of motivic contrast by a particularly rich harmonic layout. The first movement of a Concerto ripieno P. 400 is designed according to the following harmonic plan: B♭ major—D minor—G minor—C minor —E♭ major—B♭ major; however, despite the rich variety in the modulations, the effect of the six appearances of the ritornello, in the absence of real development in the interludes, quickly becomes tiring.

In single movements we can find a formal method in which the ritornello design is only apparent as a kind of background, but which, in its motivic contrasts and strong reprise effect seems like an anticipation of the structural principles of the classical composers. In the 'Concerto à quattro' in A major, P. 235, the brio of the string writing is so reminiscent of Mozart's early symphonic style that one might readily suppose the work to be typical of Vivaldi's late style, and equally readily think it probable that Vivaldi had a direct influence on Mozart. Yet there is no evidence for either supposition.

Vivaldi's concerti ripieni are as a rule in three movements, and a relatively unimportant middle movement in ternary Lied form or in a plain chordal form is often followed by a dance movement or a dance-like movement laid out in two repeated sections, occasionally even by a fugue. These fugues are always excellently worked pieces and show Vivaldi's basic schooling in the traditional craft of composition. Often a fugue appears already as an introductory movement (P. 127) and perhaps in so doing underlines the liturgical use for which such a work was designed, as an instrumental introduction to a solemn mass. A 'Concerto à quattro' of the Vienna Estensisch Collection (P. 145) bears the heading 'Intro-dutione', which suggests its use as an overture in the theatre or as an opening voluntary in church. A feature of P. 127 is that its title 'Concerto' was later replaced by the word sinfonia. The same unstable terminology is shown by a Dresden sinfonia (Pincherle No. 4) for two oboes, two horns, bassoon and strings which can be found in Turin in a four-part string version, whose formal structure would identify it as a concerto ripieno, and which bears the title 'Concerto'.

In the form as a whole, pairs of movements are often linked together. Thus, for instance, P. 86 (Concerto madrigalesco) is in four movements, but the first and third, of respectively twelve and eleven bars, both designated as Adagio, end with half-closes and have the function of slow introductions to the following movements, which are fugues. The second movement of this work, a double fugue opening in two parts, shows the strength of Vivaldi's thematic writing in fugue (Ex. 133).

If a solo instrument emerges from the tutti, either episodically or at regular intervals, the result is a hybrid form based on the concerto ripieno and the solo concerto. Thus in the first place, with its Adagio and Allegro fugue, P. 407 is a genuine concerto ripieno. As its third movement there is a Largo for solo violin and continuo bass such as often appears in the violin concertos, and the final movement is a real solo concerto movement for violin and orchestra. In a three-movement Concerto P. 301 (with oboes) even the first movement is a solo concerto movement. The work certainly bears the title 'Concerto ripieno', but its three movements are those of a solo concerto. Where in a real concerto ripieno the formal sections between the ritornellos were more thoroughly developed, a solo group could be included ad hoc to perform these sections. In the Concerto ripieno in D major, P. 197, suchlike solos and tuttis were marked, though they were then crossed out again. This was none other than the 'chorweise umbwecheln' (antiphonal exchanges), a way of performing so charmingly described by Praetorius.

A whole series of these works is striking for being written in a small number of parts: often the viola is missing, and often first and second violins play for long stretches in unison; single movements are even in only two parts whilst the violas play in octaves with the cellos and basses. The frequent regular semiquaver movement in the upper parts with typically violinistic figurations would suggest that many of these works were conceived by Vivaldi as orchestral studies also, and were used as such. Certainly his pupils hardly had the opportunity to practise undisturbed on their own; from the reports of contemporaries we know that for instance in the so-called conservatoire of Naples dozens of string and wind players would practise away together. In such circumstances, orchestral works written as studies were a good way of increasing the technical abilities of individuals whilst working in a group.

Vivaldi's formal methods in the concerti ripieni were also singled out by other composers of his time. Thus the penultimate movement of Handel's Concerto grosso Op. VI, No. 5 is constructed in a way strikingly analogous to some movements by Vivaldi. We do not know to what extent Handel was familiar with Vivaldi's music, but it is very probable that the two masters met personally during the years 1708-9, when Handel was staying in Venice.

The large number of concerti ripieni included in Vivaldi's total output shows that this genre was of particular interest to him, probably in the first place because he needed such works for the upbringing of his orchestra, and perhaps also because he did not always have a good soloist at his disposal. Almost throughout, these works are very carefully composed, and the autographs show numerous corrections, undertaken partly during work itself, and probably partly only after its completion. Works that are particularly affected by such rewriting are P. 175, 191, 230, 280, 313 and 361; it is particularly directed to shortening—the composer was evidently quite conscious of the danger of losing tension through the absence of a soloist.

THE CHAMBER CONCERTOS

When Vivaldi had taken over the Torelli type of solo concerto movement and defined it more sharply in numerous works, this form had become so central to his concerns that, though it had originally arisen from the opposition between a soloist and the orchestra, he adapted it for other types of ensemble. This gave rise to many problems, and in solving them the composer constantly gave proof of his sense of formal construction. It was relatively simple and straightforward to take over the new formal scheme for works in which two or more soloists were set against the orchestra, for the wealth of experience from the concerto grosso practice was already there to be drawn on. The problem in the concerto ripieno was, so to speak, the reduction of the solo group to nil, because then an essential element of solo concerto form, the contrast of ensembles, disappeared. However, Vivaldi undertook yet another experiment with the form, namely that of writing concertos for soloists without orchestra. There are some 15 works by him written for this type of ensemble, and also four flute concertos from Op. X in an earlier chamber version. In these he generally used two or three instruments in the soprano range, adding to them a continuous bass which, however, was sometimes shared by two instruments, for example 'fagotto' and 'basso', whereby the former would fill out the simple bass line according to the practice of diminution. The construction was designed as in ritornello form, generally in such a way that the ritornello was performed by all the instruments, whilst individual instruments alternated in the solo sections. In this way the ritornellos often had a trio-sonata-like structure, and this group of works occupies a unique position between chamber music and orchestral music, though Vivaldi generally used the title 'Concerto' for them. Three of these works, to be found in the Saxon Library, Dresden, are in fact entitled 'Sonata'. One of them (Q/9) is particularly interesting, being also preserved in Turin, but there headed 'Concerto' (P. 360).

Pincherle concerned himself on several occasions with this position between two genres and with the obscure terminology. In connection with his discussion of the sonatas he writes: 'To these one might add 9 other manuscript compositions for 3, 4 and 5 instruments with the title concerto, which are more precisely hybrids between the concerto and the sonata. The ensemble corresponds to a chamber music group: 3, 4 or 5 soloistic performers; but the form is that of the concerto (allegro–adagio–allegro), as is the thematic style, and generally a privileged instrument is in the foreground', and in the thematic catalogue he says of a work such as P. 198 'à 3, flauto, violino, fagotto e violoncello (rather, trio sonata, despite the title Concerto)'. However, Vivaldi's title is legitimate, because formally the outer movements are solo concerto movements. The problem can be solved quite simply by deciding to use the term 'chamber concerto' for this group of works, since this implies both Vivaldi's description of the form and also the chamber music ensemble.

According to the title, P. 198 is written for recorder, violin and bassoon or cello ad libitum. The eleven-bar ritornello begins in the manner of a trio sonata and then continues with the usual sequence of motivic groups. In the first solo section the two upper instruments alternate in short interjections. In ritornello II, which is abbreviated to six bars, all three instruments combine again. The next formal section is a solo episode of 16 bars for the recorder, accompanied by only the bass. After the return of the ritornello (III), again played by all the instruments and curtailed to six bars, there follows a solo episode for the violin, which by virtue of its length (21 bars) and its technical demands—using arpeggio playing in the seventh position—might take its place in any violin concerto. To this is joined a transitional passage of five and a half bars, whose importance is above all modulatory. After a ritornello IV reduced to three bars, there is a further solo section for the recorder, and the opening ritornello is repeated to end with by means of a D.C. (da capo). The bass which continues through the entire movement is not figured at all, but with regard to the solo sections it is self-evident that it must be performed by a melody instrument and a harmony instrument. (Unfortunately this necessity is not always acknowledged in modern editorial practice!) The work is a genuine chamber concerto for recorder, violin and continuo, both instruments being treated as soloists, and the three together representing the orchestral tutti in the ritornello.

The first movement of P. 402, which Vivaldi headed 'Con^{to}' and wrote in three parts for Flauto, Hobois and Fagotto, shows in its construction a departure from this pattern. Here the recorder is treated as a concertante instrument throughout, the oboe is only used in the ritornellos, and the bassoon plays the continuo bass throughout, the use of a harpsichord being taken for granted.

Yet another type is exemplified by a 'Concerto' P. 403 for Flauto, Aubois, Violino, Fagotto and Bass (= continuo). The role of the ritornello is fulfilled by a formal section which, although by bar 23 it has modulated to the relative minor, extends as far as bar 31 and is developed according to the principle of motivic juxtaposition. These motivic groups, however, are already given to different solo instruments or different groups, thereby largely eliminating the contrast with the subsequent real solo sections (Ex. 134). Here the concertante element has infiltrated into the ritornello, and by virtue of its characteristic sound has imparted to it a strong luminosity, though also breaking it up extensively. In the short phrases of the alternating solo groups, the work has acquired a distinct concerto grosso character.

These three types, which differ so much among themselves, show how thoroughly Vivaldi confronted the formal problems and structural possibilities of a concerto for soloists without orchestra. Moreover, this conception occupied many composers in the eighteenth century. In a concerto for four unaccompanied violins Telemann has given us another attempt to solve it, and J. S. Bach, probably stimulated by his Vivaldi arrangements for keyboard instruments, in his *Italian Concerto* represented the tutti–solo contrast on the harpsichord; also, Matteo Zocarini did the same for cello and continuo (harpsichord) in his Concertini. It can only be guessed whether all of them were working directly under the influence of the Vivaldi chamber concerto model. The fact that such works, although never printed in the composer's lifetime, travelled to Dresden and Paris, makes it look as if this type of work was nonetheless well known.

An unusually laid-out work, the 'Con^to' P. 199, probably does not belong in the chamber concerto category. In the outer movements it is written in three parts for violin, viola and continuo, and formally clearly divided into ritornellos and solo sections. In the violin part, the ritornellos are marked 'Tutti', and the solo sections 'Solo', the viola being silent in all the solo sections. These instructions clearly designate a concerto for violin and three-part string orchestra. All the same, the work can also be performed by a solo trio ensemble (bass on cello and harpsichord), the violin's solo sections being sufficiently differentiated in instrumentation by the absence of the viola.

The middle movements of these chamber concertos are generally kept very short, and as a rule are written for one solo instrument and figured bass. In P. 403, the solo instrument is the recorder, and the bass is not specified, though the writing suggests the bassoon rather than the cello. Occasionally the master's intimate medium inspired him to a particularly thorough formal conception of the middle movement; that of P. 402 might find a place in any trio sonata. In such compositions Vivaldi seems to have enjoyed recalling the sonata output of his youth (Ex. 135).

THE OPERAS

Vivaldi as an Operatic Composer and his Background

In about 1600, as a result of the efforts of circles of aristocratic amateurs, opera was born in Florence, and for decades it remained a much-admired but exclusively princely spectacle. Republican Venice seems at first to have taken up a stance which tended to reject this new art form. When the first great creative genius of the opera, Claudio Monteverdi, became the *maestro di cappella* of St. Mark's in 1612, he had for many years no opportunity of publicly performing his musico-dramatic works in the city where he practised his profession. If he wrote further works despite this, they were composed exclusively as commissions from Northern Italian courts.

But when Venice got to know the marvel of the 'dramma per musica' at first hand, the popular spirit of the city, enjoying magnificent pageantry, plays, masquerades and intrigues, took hold of the new possibilities of operatic presentation so enthusiastically that Venice soon became the leading operatic city in all Italy. In 1637 something happened there that would scarcely have been possible anywhere else: in the part of the city near the S. Cassiano church the aristocratic Tron family opened an opera

house in its palace, which was accessible to the entire populace on payment of an entrance fee. The rush of all sorts of people who until then
could only have heard with amazement about opera performances must
have been enormous; for a few decades later there were already seven such
theatres. A new profession began to flourish, that of the impresario:
business-like, cunning to the point of unscrupulousness, but also constantly on the look-out for new works with drawing power in order to
survive in the face of rival enterprises. Since in those days an operatic
work, once it had been laid aside after a few performances, could hardly
be played again on the same stage, or at least not without fundamental
revisions, there was a huge demand for skilled librettists, and for composers who could turn their hand over rapidly. If a work fell through at
its première—and this happened often, despite the gondoliers who were
given free passes as claqueurs—a substitute had to be scrambled together
in a few days, for singers, dancers, orchestral musicians and machine
operators were hired under contract and would demand to be paid. It so
happened that occasionally three composers would be simultaneously writing one work, each doing one act, and that composers borrowed from
older works, and would even assemble a concoction from foreign works.
Today the figures of operatic productions on record seem almost un-
believable, and can only be understood by acquaintance with the special
circumstances: between 1680 and 1700, 150 operas were performed in
Venice—that is, seven or eight works a year. From 1700 to 1743, thus
roughly during the time of Vivaldi's creative activity, 432 operas were
performed, in other words about ten a year. (By comparison, the modern
operatic repertoire comprises about 60 works!) In this way, skilful composers could always find work, and vied with each other in record-
breaking efforts. Thus Carlo Francesco Pollaroli wrote no less than 70
operas between 1685 and 1722, an average of two every year, and this
was in addition to his activities as an organist, second *maestro di cappella*
at St. Mark's and teacher at the Ospedale degli Incurabili! Such a bulk
of production by librettists and composers was only possible, however,
because they had gradually worked out rigid rules for their craft, which
permitted them to produce operas to measure, more or less off the
conveyor belt. Indeed, these rules gradually acquired so much of the
status of laws that to break them already jeopardized the reception of a
work, and in any case invited the antagonism of the singers and led to
severe tensions with the ensemble; for after all they were hardly calculated
to diminish envy and ambition among the 'stars' in the slightest. To us,
who in operatic questions are strongly inculcated with the romantic

creative concepts of Wagnerian times, according to which every work derives its laws from the particular nature of the material it brings into play, some of these 'rules of the craft' seem very strange: in every work six or seven scene changes had to occur; three principal roles were obligatory, and each of them had to have five arias—a pathetic aria, a bravura aria, an 'aria parlante', one of moderate character, and one brilliant; singers of second-rank roles were given only three arias, and those of smaller roles only two, and prima donnas were zealously watchful lest some small role might have a bravura aria; arias of the same character in close succession had to be avoided, and two pathetic arias together were strictly forbidden. But this was less for artistic reasons than to avoid giving rise to increased rivalry among the singers. The arias were linked by long recitatives, whose dramatic purpose we find hard to understand today because we know that as a rule they were not listened to at all. In Italy—and not only there—one went to the theatre in order to meet people, one conversed aloud, ate and drank in the boxes, and played board- and card-games. This social intercourse was only interrupted when a star began an aria. In the midst of the applause, previous occupations were once more reverted to. Obviously the recitatives had the purpose of resting the singers and of spreading out the raisins well in the cake, so as not to glut the public and overtax it with too much attentiveness.

It is clear that in such circumstances, in which the composer, as the obedient servant of singers and public, was to some extent forced into the new role of the purveyor of the now indispensable music, it was hardly possible for musico-dramatic masterpieces to be produced. But for all that, the average quality was amazingly high, and one has the impression that for all their preoccupation with fulfilling their obligations on the production line the composers often enough spared a thought for the almost imaginary connoisseur who yet might occasionally find himself actually in the theatre. The time at which Vivaldi gradually grew up into Venetian operatic life and then became a busy *maestro* and even impresario, was favourable—owing to the state of the market—towards the routine production of operas which might satisfy the immediate needs of the public, but not towards the creation of works which could claim validity for all eternity.

When his dramatic first-born was put on stage, Vivaldi was already thirty-five, an instrumental composer of European celebrity and a much esteemed virtuoso, teacher and *maestro di cappella*. It would be thoroughly mistaken to suppose that at the time he had barely come into contact with the theatre, and hence had no operatic experience, as a consequence of his clerical standing and of his activities at the Ospedale della Pietà. In the seventeenth and eighteenth centuries it was nothing extraordinary for priests to work in opera orchestras, and in Venice a close relationship between church music and operatic life had already resulted from the fact that the choruses for opera performances, and some of the soloists too, were largely enlisted from the St. Mark's Cathedral choir. Vivaldi will probably have already worked in the orchestra at an early age, in musical performances at different Venetian theatres, particularly when it was not a case of firmly contracted groups of players but of orchestras which may have been brought together for one or other of the three seasons—that is, the carnival or Winter season, from December 26 to March 30, the Ascension or Spring season, from Whit-Monday to June 31, and the Autumn season, from September 1 to November 30. And yet it seems that at first no one in Venice had very much confidence in Vivaldi's abilities as a dramatic composer, for his first commission came from Vicenza. The opera *Ottone in Villa*, performed there for the first time in 1713, must however have been a great success; we know of several revivals. Above all, the composer had now become worthy of Venetian commissions. Already in the following year the S. Angelo theatre in Venice was putting on Vivaldi's *Orlando finto pazzo*. Subsequently this theatre regularly kept the composer busy. Vivaldi seems to have quickly found his feet in the operatic field, for as early as 1715 Uffenbach described him as an 'entrepreneur' (contractor). Apparently he had hired the theatre for the first performance of the opera *Nerone fatto Cesare* and had engaged a company to perform it there. The work is in fact a pastiche, assembled from works of several composers, and Vivaldi contributed twelve arias to it. In the year 1715 the composer also drew up a dedication for the libretto of the opera *Luca Papirio* by Predieri, generally only the concern of the theatrical contractor.

His rapid transformation into an impresario can be explained by the contemporary situation. In total contrast to today's ideas, the composer was by no means the most important person in an operatic work and its performance, and he was not always even mentioned by name; in any case he ranked far behind the singers, the dancers and even the *ingegnere di scena*, the *ingegnere di decorazioni* and the *capo d'illuminazione* (stage designer, chief scene painter and lighting director). The fact that at the Hamburg opera in 1725 a composer received 50 florins for his score, whilst 100 florins was provided for procuring the principal actor's helmet, may have been a particularly blatant exception, but it does give some idea of how the producer of the music was valued. As a rule the composer stipulated in his contract that he should be given the direction from the harpsichord of a certain number of performances, for only his fee as *maestro di cappella* could compensate him to a certain extent for his work as a composer. If a composer wished to benefit from his works, it was virtually essential to take the same steps as did Handel, namely to gather the management into one's own hands. Vivaldi seems to have possessed a high degree of the necessary organizational skill and the indispensable business ability to do this. It is not known to what extent he was regularly active as an impresario; but, outside Venice, he seems to have usually brought out his works in his own productions—as we know from the Ferrara affair of 1737. The few preserved letters, all from the years 1736–37, give an insight into the operatic life of the time. They are addressed to the Marchese Guido Bentivoglio d'Aragona, who lived in Ferrara and was an active friend and patron of the arts. This man sent his impresario 'sig. ab. Bollani' (thus a man in holy orders) to Venice in order to get together an especially good opera company with Vivaldi. The master himself could not go to Ferrara because he was tied by a contract to the S. Cassiano theatre, which had tried in vain to reduce his usual fee of 100 sequins to 90. He promised to arrange two older operas for performance in Ferrara, in fact to do this in his own hand (tutte adatte e compite dalla mia penna), whereas otherwise such matters were as a rule left to someone else. It is evident from the composer's performances that every composition was reworked for each new production, because the scores had been so tailor-made for the singers of the first performance that the performers of a new version were quite justified in wanting an adaptation. Vivaldi complained of impresarios who had little experience (di poco prattica), and soon began to have difficulties with the abbot Bollani. The latter, when one opera had been completely prepared, constantly wanted to have another, and only paid a part of the fee, although Vivaldi, out of regard for his patron, had been content to accept only the expenses of a copyist, and he remained impassive to warning letters. Finally Vivaldi unleashed his tongue on Bollani: this man did not understand the business of the operatic impresario, and did not know where to spend or where to save. And he reproached him with engaging singers according to their contacts and not for their quality. In a letter from Verona, the composer tells of the success of his opera *Catone in Utica*. Only six performances had taken place, but the attendances had been so good that the costs had already been covered. If the work continued to run successfully, no small profit could be counted on. He advised that the work should not be given in the next Ferrara carnival, for at that time the ballet alone would cost 700 louis, whilst in the Summer, that is, the close season, it could be had at any price he cared to name. For the opera performances of 1737 in Ferrara, which, as we already know, did not take place, Vivaldi had engaged the dancer Coluzzi; but she had run away from her parents and married the dancer Pompeati, a wretched fellow in every respect. This had thrown all the plans into confusion. We learn on this occasion that in order to compose a ballet—following the directions of the choreographer and the dancers!—and to rehearse it, at least 16 to 18 days were necessary.

Vivaldi's operatic output has been the object of very different evaluations, and negative or strongly restrictive remarks are strikingly abundant in the reports of contemporaries. This is strange, for if perhaps his operas do not rank in quality with the best works of, say, Handel or Alessandro Scarlatti, they still maintained the average level usual at the time and must have been successful enough for coolly calculating impresarios to engage the composer again and again, and for himself to be able to venture into performing them at his own financial risk. In order to understand this extremely critical attitude towards Vivaldi as an operatic composer, we must bear in mind that after about 1710 he had become known throughout all Europe through the really revolutionary nature of his concertos, and soon afterwards had created a sensation with the style of his Venetian performances. It was natural for people to expect something extraordinary from his operas too, and to be disappointed if these high hopes were not fulfilled. In many of these judgments can be detected the cliché that has always been so detrimental to the evaluation of creative personalities: namely that Vivaldi, considered firstly as an instrumental composer, could not possibly have been capable of writing vocal works. It is typical that arguments of this kind, which depend on the proviso that composers are pigeon-holed into strictly isolated categories, have come from two well-known composers of instrumental music who themselves wrote no works for the stage. The following dubious thinking is from Quantz: 'But finally, as a result of excessive daily composing, and especially after he had begun to write theatrical vocal pieces, he sunk into frivolity and eccentricity both in composition and performance . . .'; and Tartini made the following pronouncement on the relationship between instrumental and vocal music: 'These two types differ from each other in such a way that what is right for the one cannot be so for the other. Everyone must limit himself to his talent. I have been asked to compose for the Venetian theatres, but have never wanted to do so, because I know that a throat is no fingerboard. Vivaldi, who wanted to work in both spheres, was always hissed in the one, and achieved very great success in the other.' But if the public hissed an opera in those days, it was apparently condemning rather the bad singing than the actual composition. Tartini's one-sided view of the purely instrumental composer thus scarcely echoed the real public esteem for a composer of operas who had been successful for 26 years; on March 23, 1727, Abbé Conti wrote to Madame de Caylus from Venice: 'Vivaldi has brought out three operas in less than three months, two for Venice and the third for Florence; the latter has re-established the theatre of that city and has brought in a lot of money.'

The most interesting source for a critical presentation of the situation of the opera in Venice, and Vivaldi's position in the theatrical life of his native city, is the satire *Il Teatro alla Moda*. The ample title (Plate XIII) reads: 'The theatre as is fashionable today, or a sure and easy method for composing Italian operas well, and for performing them in the modern manner. Containing useful and necessary directions for poets, composers, singers of both sexes, impresarios, buffa parts, tailors, pages, supers, prompters, copyists, patrons and mothers of female singers and other persons belonging to the theatre. Dedicated by the author of the book to its composer. Printed by Aldiviva Licanto in the Borghi di Belisania at the sign of the Bear in the Barque. Obtainable in the Strada del Corallo at the gate of the Palazzo d'Orlando. The book will be reprinted each year with supplements.' The headpiece shows a small boat propelled by an oarsman, the rudder of which is steered by the feet of an angel playing a violin. In the front of the boat, on a supply of provisions—a cask of wine can be seen among other things—stands a bear, wearing a coat and waving a flag. Contemporaries who kept in touch with Venetian affairs soon knew that the author of the wittily written little book was none other than Benedetto Marcello. Six years younger than Vivaldi, this composer, who was of aristocratic birth and liked to call himself a 'nobile dilettante', was indeed always playing a lively part in Venetian musical life, though he never practised music as a profession, spending his life in the civil service, both at home and elsewhere. It was precisely this independent position outside the professori (professional musicians) that enabled him to take a critical interest in operatic life and to censure its weaknesses with harsh scorn.

It had long been suspected that the enigmatic names on the title page were word-plays on personalities of the Venetian scene, but at last G. F. Malipiero succeeded in identifying them when by chance he came upon a copy of the booklet in which the early owner had added the key figures, who were well known to him. The author had at the same time hidden and revealed the targets of his satire with the anagrammatic deformations typical of written pamphlets of this kind: Aldiviva = A. Vivaldi; Licante = Canteli, a female singer at the S. Moise theatre; Borghi di Belisania—Borghi and Belisani, two male singers of the S. Angelo theatre; the bear (Orso) represented the impresario Orsatto of the S. Moise theatre; the pun 'in Peata' is aimed at Modotto, the impresario of the S. Angelo theatre. The violin-playing priest/angel is of course Vivaldi, steering the S. Angelo (the angel's wings) theatre to success. Moreover, a note in Malipiero's copy tells us that the booklet appeared in December, 1720.

The fact that Vivaldi, who up till that time had written thirteen operas in eight years, could be such a prominent figure in a satire on opera, goes to show his leading position in Venetian theatrical life, for an outsider would scarcely have been chosen as its butt. But it would be quite wrong to associate everything the writer says about composers directly with Vivaldi. Marcello's scorn is rather maintained at such a general level that his satire goes beyond the time and place of its immediate targets to concern itself with operatic life in general and all modernistic and snobbish artistic tendencies. The librettist, Marcello says, should be as little burdened as possible with a knowledge of ancient poets, but should expatiate at length about aesthetic problems in his foreword, calling to witness Sophocles, Euripides, Aristotle and Horace. He should choose as dedicatee a person rich rather than cultured, and should share the cash reward for his dedication with the intermediary. In the Epistola dedicatoria expressions such as libertà, animo generoso (freedom, magnanimity) must appear, and it must close with the author kissing the fleabites on the legs of His Excellency's dog as an act of deepest respect. (This was probably a very evident joke at the expense of Vivaldi's dedicatory style; in the foreword to Op. II, we read: 'You have descended from your throne, and this condescension has permitted Your Highness to console him who, deeply obeisant, confesses himself unworthy to kiss even the lowest step of your throne.') The composer should ask the impresario how many scene-changes he wants, and he must pad out each preceding scene with dialogues, recitatives, and ariettas, so as to prepare for the extensive scene transformations. The recitatives need not necessarily have any inner relationship to the arias and the arias should be long enough for their opening to have been forgotten in the middle. In order to make sure of the performance, many visits are advisable, and one should not forget to include those to the prima donna's mother and to her 'Protettore'.

A great deal of technical ability is only cumbersome to the composer, and he should not dwell on working out choruses and duets, but should write everything as much as possible in unison, or at the octave, and over pedal-points; above all he should use effects like pizzicato, con sordino etc, and not write over-learned overtures with fugues and real themes, but should compose the first movement in the French manner and the last as a minuet, a gavotte or a gigue. However, if the impresario is not happy with the music, the composer should tell him that the score contains a third as many notes more than usual and took the composer almost fifty hours to compose. The composer is recommended above all to be on good terms with the entire cast, right down to the last super, and when dealing with, say, a castrato, always to proceed with his hat in his hand one pace to the rear, and constantly to bear in mind that even the least of them might in the opera portray no less a personage than a general or a captain of the royal bodyguard.

The most detailed chapter in Marcello's lampoon is naturally that on the singers, but he does not spare the musicians, who, regardless of each other and of the solo voices, contribute their embellishments, the dancers, the supers, the prompters—in fact none of the vast personnel of an opera. Some instructions for the impresario are of particular interest. The modern operatic contractor should have technical knowledge of none of the spheres of theatrical life. But in the production of the libretto he should take care that every tragic event should get its happy end, and if two prima donnas appear in the piece, he should persuade the librettist to provide two roles which not only have the same number of recitatives but also have an identical number of syllables. If the work is to open on stage on the twelfth of a month, it is sufficient to commission the composer on the fourth. The latter should only work in haste, and should not bother himself about parallel fifths and octaves or other errors of composition.

It is precisely clues like these which show that the real target of the lampoon was hardly Vivaldi himself, but much rather his less important colleagues. Yet in spite of its exaggerations it is typical of the Venetian operatic situation in the first decades of the eighteenth century, and paints in vivid colours the circumstances in which Vivaldi had to work as a composer of operas.

SURVEY OF VIVALDI'S OPERATIC OUTPUT

Altogether we know of 48 operas by Vivaldi, distributed over the years 1713–39, so that the composer wrote on average almost two operas a

Title	First Performed	Libret-tist	Copies in	Remarks
1. *Ottone in Villa*	1713 Vicenza	Lalli	Turin	
2. *Orlando finto pazzo*	1714 Venice S. Angelo	Braccioli	Turin	
3. *Nerone fatto Cesare*	1715 Venice S. Angelo	Noris		by several composers, 12 arias by Vivaldi
4. *La Costanza trionfante degli Amori e degli Odi*	1716 Venice S. Angelo	Marchi		
5. *Arsilda Regina di Ponto*	1716 Venice S. Angelo	Lalli	Turin	
6. *L'Incoronazione di Dario*	1716 Venice S. Angelo	Morselli	Turin	
7. *Tieteberga*	1717 Venice S. Moisè	Lucchini		
8. *Il Vinto trionfante del Vincitore*	1717 Venice S. Angelo	Marchi		only in part by Vivaldi
9. *Artabana Rè de' Parti*	1718 Venice S. Moisè	Marchi		revised version of No. 4
10. *Scanderbegh*	1718 Florence Teatro della Pergola	Salvi		
11. *Armida al Campo d'Egitto*	1718 Venice S. Moisè	Palazzi	Turin Acts 1 & 3	2 arias in Act 1 by Leo
12. *La Candace o siano Li Veri Amici*	1720 Mantua Teatro Arciducale	Silvani/Lalli		
13. *La Verità in Cimento*	1720 Venice S. Angelo	Palazzi/Lalli	Turin	
14. *Gli Inganni per Vendetta*	1720 Vicenza Teatro delle Grazie	Lalli		
15. *Filippo, Rè di Macedonia*	1721 Venice S. Angelo	Lalli		only Act 3 by Vivaldi
16. *Silvia (Pastorale)*	1721 Milan Nuovo Teatro Ducale			
17. *Ercole sul Termodonte*	1723 Rome Teatro Capranica	Bussani	Paris Cons. 7 arias	
18. *Il Giustino*	1724 Rome Teatro Capranica	Beregani	Turin	
19. *La Virtù trionfante dell'Amore e dell'Odio ovvero Tigrane*	1724 Rome Teatro Capranica	Silvani	Turin Act 2	only Act 2 by Vivaldi
20. *L'Inganno trionfante in Amore*	1725 Venice S. Angelo	Noris/Ruggieri		

Title	First Performed	Librettist	Copies in	Remarks
21. *Cunegonda*	1726 Venice S. Angelo	Piovene		
22. *La Fede tradita e vendicata*	1726 Venice S. Angelo	Silvani		
23. *Farnace*	1726 Venice S. Angelo	Lucchini	Turin Acts 1 & 2 in 2 versions	
24. *Dorilla in Tempe* (*melodramma eroico-pastorale*)	1726 Venice S. Angelo	Lucchini	Turin	
25. *Ipermestra*	1727 Florence Teatro della Pergola	Salvi		
26. *Siroe, Rè di Persia*	1727 Reggio	Metastasio		
27. *Orlando furioso*	1727 Venice S. Angelo	Braccioli	Turin	
28. *Rosilena ed Oronta*	1728 Venice S. Angelo	Palazzi		
29. *Ateneide*	1729 Florence Teatro della Pergola	Zeno	Turin	
30. *L'Odio vinto della Costanza*	1731 Venice S. Angelo	Vitturi		rearrangement of Nos. 4 and 9
31. *Semiramide*	1731 Verona			
32. *La Fida Ninfa*	1732 Verona Teatro Filarmonico	Maffei	Turin	
33. *Montezuma*	1733 Venice S. Angelo	Giusti		
34. *Sarce*	1733 Ancona			
35. *L'Olimpiade*	1734 Venice S. Angelo	Metastasio	Turin	some numbers from other works with text altered
36. *Griselda*	1735 Venice S. Samuele	Zeno/ Goldoni	Turin	
37. *Tamerlano*	1735 Verona	Piovene	Turin (as *Bajazet*)	only in part by Vivaldi
38. *Adelaide*	1735 Verona Teatro Filarmonico			doubtful title, possibly identical with No. 29
39. *Aristide*	1735 Venice S. Samuele	Goldoni		
40. *Ginevra, principessa di Scozia*	1736 Florence	Salvi		
41. *Catone in Utica*	1737 Verona	Metastasio	Turin (no Act 1)	

Title	First Performed	Librettist	Copies in	Remarks
42. *Rosmira*	1738 Venice S. Angelo	Stampaglia	Turin (as *Rosmira fedele*)	compiled by Vivaldi after various composers; arias by 5 composers in Act 1, including Handel
43. *L'Oracolo di Messenia*	1738 Venice S. Angelo	Zeno		
44. *Feraspe*	1739 Venice S. Angelo	Silvani		

Works whose dates of performance are not known:

45. *Il Teuzzone*		Zeno	Turin	one aria from
46. *Tito Manlio*		Noris	Turin (2 copies)	No. 18
47. *Demetrio*				
48. *Alessandro nell'Indie*				

year over 27 years. The sources for our knowledge about these works and their performances are the 19 preserved scores, the librettos which in those days the librettist would as a rule have printed and dedicate to a patron, and in some cases reports of performances of works of which neither the score nor the libretto has been preserved. As with the concertos, the numbers sometimes given for the operas differ slightly. Vivaldi often reworked an older work under a new title, often took over bits from older works by himself or by others, and often only collaborated on one act, so that opinions as to whether the work concerned was really original or not can also differ. Many authors also include with the stage works a five-part cantata *Il Mopso*, which was perhaps performed on the stage as well.

VIVALDI'S FIRST OPERA, *OTTONE IN VILLA*

The work was composed in 1713, probably on commission from a Venetian impresario for a performance in Vicenza. As librettist a certain Sebastiano Biancardi had been engaged, a former bank employee from Naples, who had fled his home town on account of embezzlements, and had taken the plunge in Venice; thus his nom de plume, Domenico Lalli, was probably not chosen for entirely poetic reasons. Lalli was a much-occupied librettist and Vivaldi collaborated with him several times.

THE WORK

From its libretto, one can see in *Ottone in Villa* the stamp of mass-produced goods, such as were so prodigiously consumed in the Italian theatre at that time. Ottone is a fictitious Roman Emperor, staying at his country seat. Cleonilla, whom he loves, certainly takes full advantage of her position, but in turn seeks the favours of Ostilio after she has dismissed her old admirer Caio. However, Caio was formerly the lover of Tullia, who in fact still loves him and appears disguised as Ostilio. The intrigue, in which a real and a faked love letter play a part, is vigorously drawn out by the artful Cleonilla, and the trusted Decio tries in vain to warn the Emperor of her and of imminent political danger, which, however, is only hinted at incidentally. After the usual developments, everything works out for the best. The piece is a neat little comedy of situation, which, skilfully composed, would have provided material for a tightly organized little comic opera or operetta. But to meet his commission, Lalli padded out this meagre dramatic substance into a three-act opera, and the work's weaknesses, arising from the discrepancy between substance and proportion, were already present before the composer had even started his work.

The choice of clefs in the score is interesting: the part of Ottone is notated in the alto clef, and was apparently intended for an alto castrato; those of Caio and Ostilio/Tullia are notated in the soprano clef, and were probably soprano castrato parts. In all, five characters appear:

Ottone (Roman Emperor)	Alto
Cleonilla (loved by him)	Soprano
Ostilio/Tullia	Soprano
Caio (loved by Tullia, but loves Cleonilla)	Soprano
Decio (confidant of the Emperor)	Tenor

The work has no chorus, the heading Coro for the closing number referring to the ensemble of five soloists, all of whom are deployed in the dramatic dénouement in the last scene. In the whole piece, no change of scene is necessary, and the indication 'scena' in the score simply means an entrance.

The first act is made up of eleven scenes, each consisting of a recitative and aria. All the arias are solo arias, and they are well apportioned among the characters, in accordance with the dramatic conventions: Cleonilla and Tullia have three each to sing, Ottone and Caio two each, and the subsidiary role of Decio is given only one. In the first scene Cleonilla brings us in on her well ramified love life, and her aria speaks of her hopes of love in the Spring. The second scene brings together Cleonilla and Caio, and she tells him that she now prefers Ostilio. In a passionate aria, Caio nonetheless professes inalienable love for Cleonilla. They are both joined by Ottone (third scene), who would like to forget the heavy burdens of government by going away to the country with Cleonilla. But she pretends to be disconsolate and reproaches him for having neglected her for his political affairs, telling him in her aria that only in his constancy can her soul find repose. Ottone, who does not suspect Caio's love for Cleonilla, is alone with him in the fourth scene, and asks him to appease his beloved. In an aria he expresses his regret about the troubled soul of his supposed *cara fida*, for which he blames himself. Scene five: Caio meets Tullia, who is dressed as Ostilio. Ostilio, allegedly a friend of Tullia, reminds Caio of her true love for him, and Caio explains 'solo Cleonilla è l'Idolo mio' (Cleonilla alone is my idol). In the sixth scene Tullia is alone; she swears vengeance on Caio and gives free vent to her feelings of jealousy in an aria. In the seventh scene, Cleonilla is together with Ottone and Decio, who brings the Emperor news of unrest in Rome; but the latter wants to remain with Cleonilla. In the eighth scene (Decio, Cleonilla and Ostilio/Tullia), Cleonilla wants to know what is being said in Rome about the Emperor's love for her. Decio can tell her nothing good. 'L'alto splendore del puro onore non si raquista se t'ama un Rè' (She who is loved by a King will not win the high splendour of true honour) she sings in her aria. Cleonilla is then alone with Ostilio/Tullia (ninth scene) and confesses her love. Tullia sees in this new development a chance for her revenge on Caio, and proceeds to engage in the appearance of protestations of love, with all necessary reticence, but also makes mention of Caio. Then Cleonilla says candidly that she disdains Caio. There follow pledges of love, and a passionate aria 'nel cor sempre constante amante' (lover always constant of heart). Caio has overheard all this, and Ostilio/Tullia gloats over his grief (scene ten). In the final scene Caio is alone, now aware that Ostilio is his rival and despairing over Cleonilla's betrayal. With this the first act, in which practically nothing has happened, comes to an end. In a loose sequence of scenes, only emotional states have been discussed and sung of in arias. There has been no duet, no ensemble, no finale effect, and the act might just as well have ended a scene earlier. The characters come and go, generally without the slightest semblance of dramatic necessity, such as might have come from an inner connection in the treatment of the scenes. The only point at which the narration of the proceedings is complemented by a visual situation is that in which Caio overhears the conversation between Cleonilla and Ostilio/Tullia.

The second act brings a scene that was a favourite in Baroque operas:

Ostilio/Tullia, hidden behind a knoll, answers Caio as a voice of the spirits. The latter has written an ardent love letter to Cleonilla. In reading it, she is surprised by the Emperor. He reads the letter, believes her unfaithful, as Decio has already in vain tried to persuade him, but she protests that it is only a letter for Tullia that she was entrusted with, and offers to write a reply to it. In this reply she tells Caio he is out of luck because Tullia loves him no more. The Emperor shows the perplexed Caio his letter to Cleonilla, and then her reply. Whilst the Emperor is once more convinced of Cleonilla's fidelity, Caio considers the letter a trick and still entertains hopes of her.

In the third act, the action at first stands still for a long time. In a love scene Cleonilla approaches Ostilio/Tullia, Caio surprises them; the cunning Cleonilla cries for help, and Ottone and Decio rush to the scene. Cleonilla simulates anger, but Caio reports to the Emperor the scene he has just witnessed. The latter answers 'Immobil sono' (I am transfixed). Now Ostilio/Tullia, the Emperor's supposed rival for the attentions of Cleonilla, announces her wish to speak, and explains that the latter is innocent, the traitor being Caio. As she is not believed, and is threatened with the Emperor's vengeance, she finally admits that she is not Ostilio but Tullia. Now Cleonilla's innocence is finally established, the Emperor asks her forgiveness and joins Caio and Tullia in marriage. Caio has no choice but to lead the ensemble in the final scene with the words 'Grande è il concento' (Great is the contentment).

The whole sequence from Caio's appearance at the love scene to the happy ending is a gigantic recitative of 121 bars; here Lalli missed the opportunity of building up a grandiose finale of entanglement and extrication. But such a task would either have been beyond his abilities or impossible to work out in the time at his disposal. For the first performance Vivaldi followed the textual model word for word without correcting the libretto's undramatic and musically relatively unsuitable passages by making alterations in its layout. As is known from the report of Goldoni, as an experienced operatic maestro he later no longer accepted a libretto's weaknesses without further ado, but himself had a say in its dramatic development. When *Ottone* was revived in 1715 and 1729, Vivaldi was well aware of the deficiencies of the text, and tried at least to tighten it up with deletions. In the score, there are constantly indications for the conductor and for the copyist, such as 'Questo non si dice', 'qui non si scrive' and 'non si suona' (This is not said; this is not written; is not played), and the recitatives above all are markedly abbreviated. In this version, Ottone's part is also, for instance, transposed in part by the

indication 'un tuono più alto' (a tone higher). In fact, for the third performance many of the gaps were filled again, and against crossed-out arias
the note 'qui si scrive' (this is written) may be found.

Whereas in the recitatives Vivaldi did not surpass the average level usual
at the time, the arias, apart from some weaker numbers, are throughout
distinguished, abundantly inspired music. In form almost all of them are
built as da capo arias in ternary form, A–B–A, a type which already
recommended itself strongly because the indication D.C. saved the
maestro a lot of working time (and copyists' fees!). But often this type
of aria is transformed in a way that is characteristic of the stage Vivaldi
had then reached as a composer. In the first aria of the work, 'Quanto
m'alletta la fresca erbetta' in G minor (Cleonilla), the 13-bar opening
ritornello of the orchestra is composed entirely in the style of a concerto.
Between the five entries of the solo voice are more or less long orchestral
sections, which are all developed from the ritornello. Occasionally motivic
material from the ritornello is taken over in the accompaniment to the
solo. Thereby the middle section, which in D.C. form has a function of
contrast, is absorbed into the composition, and the soprano aria becomes
a solo concerto movement in miniature for soprano and orchestra. Thus
the new formal type, the solo concerto movement, also permeates the
operatic aria. Schering, who at the time of preparing his *History of the Solo
Concerto* (first edition 1905!) can only have known isolated arias from
Vivaldi's operas, recognized the stylistic position of the master with
admirable accuracy. He wrote: 'from 1713 on we find him as an opera
composer. A comparison of his operatic output with his instrumental
works would yield extremely valuable results, but unfortunately all of
Vivaldi's operatic scores seem to have been lost. Several preserved arias
give us an idea of his dramatic style. Even if all previous conclusions were
to prove fallacious, a glance at these would prove the common basis on
which aria and concerto took shape at this time. The exposition of a
mood by the orchestra, its continuation by the soloist, orchestral interjections, renewed outbreak by the individual, and after a more discreet
intermediate mood a return to the opening ideas: this was how the aria
was identified at the beginning of this chapter. Vivaldi combines it with
the instrumental concerto, though reciprocally he does not omit either to
mix in those instrumental elements, e.g. (Ex. 136), which appear in such
great number that the whole piece might cheerfully be given to a violinist
and called "Violin Concerto". Vivaldi's unprecedented fertility in both
spheres explains this handling of the two types, which often proceeds
towards mutual identity. . . .'

Vivaldi's vocal style, which Schering demonstrated with an extreme example, is, however, not to be explained simply on the basis of a transference of instrumental figurations. Much rather it is the structural factors which to a large extent also govern the programmatic works that are operative here. In the first place, the texts used are kept very brief throughout. The text of the first aria of *Ottone in Villa* reads:

Quanto m'alletta	L'un con l'odore	(How much the fresh grass
la fresca erbetta	m'inspira amore	gladdens me, what joy the
quanto à me piace	l'altra col verde	lovely flower holds for me.
il vago fior.	ampie di sperme	The one with its scent exhorts
	l'amante cor.	me to love, the other with
		its greenness fills the loving
		heart with hope.)

If with its 19 syllables the first stanza has to provide the weightier main section of the aria, recourse must be had either to the technique of textual repetitions or to the 'stretching' of the singer's part in the aria by spacious melodic developments on single syllables. Of course, Vivaldi was familiar with both techniques, but in the case in question he lengthened the text by an unusual procedure which might in fact be termed permutational transposition, not only of the single phrases, but even of single words:

(first solo entry, 8 bars) Quanto m'alletta la fresca erbetta la fresca erbetta quanto à me piace quel vago fior quant à me piace quanto mi piace quanto m'alletta la fresca erbetta il vago fior.
(second solo entry, 8 bars) Quanto mi piace quanto m'alletta la fresca erbetta fresca erbetta vago fior quanto mi piace il vago fior.
(third solo entry, 7½ bars) Quanto m'alletta quanto mi piace la fresca erbetta il vago fior la vaga erbetta il vago fior.
(fourth and fifth solo entries, 5 and 9½ bars, developed from the second stanza).

In Vivaldi, as in other operatic masters of the time, certain padding words were used, which also added to the dramatic accentuation. If for instance the text read 'non posso amarti' (I cannot love you), this would be varied textually to give a heightened effect: 'no, no, non posso amarti'.

In the development of the vocal line one often finds a type of motif which at first one might consider in Schering's sense instrumental. Thus, for instance, in an aria of Ottone, the first aria of the second act (Ex. 137) (As the wave, with deep and fearful gorge, aroused by winds and storms, raging and roaring, surges there in the lap of the sea, so sighs the heart, assailed by haughty fear, perplexed, excited, astray, and can rest no more for jealousy). The starting-point for the construction of this aria is the portrayal of a storm in the manner of the master's *Tempesta* concertos, but the turmoil of nature is an image of the soul agitated in grief. The musical invention serves the portrayal of this state of mind down to the last note. All these excited semiquaver and demisemiquaver figures are naturally played by instruments, but they are not primarily instrumental figurations, but rather aural symbols for states of mind. If at first they appear in the orchestral introduction, which in this aria too has the character of a ritornello in the sense of a solo concerto movement, and then are taken up by the solo voice, it is fundamentally wrong to speak of instrumental figurations having been transferred to the vocal line. Vivaldi's instrumental and vocal styles have, rather, a common root, namely the composer's heightened emotional tensions, which led to strongly rhythmed motivic language, for which his first and most obvious means of expression was the stringed instrument. In the present aria the violin figures in bars 1 – 10 are no 'broken triads' but symbols in sound of natural turmoil and, equally, of spiritual agitation (bars 42 ff., 46, 59, 68, 77, 88). The motivic groups at bars 11–17 (and again at bars 27, 71, 94), which have a similar expressive function, are frequently to be found in the composer's concertos, appearing, for instance, in the *Winter* concerto from *The Seasons* at the textual line 'Al Severo Spirar d'orrido vento' (At the severe uproar of the frightful wind) and were to become an important figure in the Bach concertos showing Italian influence, as for instance in the first movement of the Fourth Brandenburg Concerto. The run at bar 18, imitated in the bass, symbolizes in the traditional manner both lightning and the agitation it arouses in man, and from bar 72 on, at the word 'agitata', it is spotlighted and developed. The tremolo-like figure, played by all the strings in unison from bar 51 on, characterizes the words 'tremendo' and 'stringendo' in the text. But even such an apparently superficial imitative device as the low C at 'profundo' (bar 27) is an immediately effective aural symbol; and anyone feeling that the quaver rest (French: soupir = crotchet rest, demi-soupir = quaver rest) at the word 'sospiro' (bar 116) is a mere play on graphic symbols should remember that in such cases it was always the resemblance that was present in the first place, the term being coined later.

The orchestral apparatus in *Ottone* is expectedly simple, entirely in keeping with the sort of impresario's opera which strove to require the least possible necessities of a performance, so as not to jeopardize the real objective—a clear profit for the 'entrepreneur'. In the overture already two oboes are added to the normal layout of the string orchestra, though they are used only in few places in the work, so that the whole opera could by and large be played by the string orchestra. In one number this is complemented by two flauti (thus, recorders). Since at this point the oboes are silent, it may be supposed that, as was common practice at the time, the oboists also played the recorders and would change instruments for this scene.

In accordance with the Italian custom, the sinfonia is in three movements. The first movement, for which the score specifies two oboes, solo violin and string orchestra, is laid out as a somewhat freely constructed solo concerto movement. However, in the very first solo section, as in the further solo episodes, two solo violins are used; thus it is in fact a double concerto movement; the two oboes are for the most part treated in unison with the orchestral violins, and emerge only occasionally from the tutti with small two-part interjections. The second movement, Larghetto, in the minor key, is developed in Lied-fashion in two repeated sections $\|: \frac{A}{8} :\|: \frac{B}{4} :\|$ plus $\frac{A}{8} :\|$, but the repeats are rescored: in each first time the two 'Oboè soli' play, supported in the bass by the violins: 'Viol^{ni} suon^{no} il Basso senza bassi' (the violins play the bass without the bass instruments), and the repeat is played tutti. The unspecified last movement, probably to be played Allegro, is built formally in the same way as the middle movement, the two A sections being melodically identical, so that the last movement is a variation of the Larghetto in the major key.

In the arias, the texture is generally thin as in chamber music, and the violas are brought into play only in a few numbers. Of the two violins, one is as a rule following the vocal part—this perhaps proved advisable for supporting the more uncertain singers—so that the texture even in the orchestrally accompanied parts of the arias scarcely exceeds three-part writing. Arias such as Ex. 137 would already strike the listener as an expressive high-point simply by the wealth of their sonorous resources. The bass is worked out carefully throughout and frequently has a motivic connection with the upper part, or participates in representing the subject by means of symbolic motifs (Ex. 137, bars 19, 21–23, 27–32, 41, 50–56, 64 f.). The following aria of Cleonilla from the first act of the opera seems in its pervading two-part canonic layout like a movement from a chamber sonata, and its bass line is reduced by the indications 'non si suona' (is not played) and 'si suona' (is played), which appear several times (Ex. 138).

It is the third scene of the second act that is the most sumptuously provided with specific aural allurements: this is the scene of Caio and Tullia, who is hidden behind a knoll and answers him as a voice of the spirits. Caio feels himself abandoned: 'L'ombre, l'aure e ancora il Rio, Eco fanno al dolor mio sé questi solo, ò Dio, qui son presenti' (The shadows, the wind and the stream too echo my grief, they alone, O Lord, are present). Corresponding to the spatially separated characters, a small group from the orchestra is occupied as a stage band and has the task of depicting the whispering air and the murmuring brook ('Flauti in Scena, 2 Viol^{ni} in Scena'). But two solo violins are also prominent in the orchestra itself. The dramatic situation with the expressive contrast between Caio and Tullia gave the composer the idea of a very free formal structure with a juxtaposition of small formal components in strongly contrasting tempi. The aria, or rather the musical scena, is built up as follows:

3/4Ad^o	And^{te}	Ad^o	All^o	Ad^o	All^o	And^{te}
1 bar	5 bars	1 b.	3 b.	2 b.	3 b.	7 b.

Ad^o	All^o	unspecified, probably		4/4	3/4All^o	Largo
7 b.	17 b.	Largo —5 b.		1 b.	6 b.	9 b.

To sum up, we can say of Vivaldi's first opera that the composer squandered a profusion of excellent music on a libretto which surpasses the day-to-day standards of the time neither in its general layout nor in its details. The lack of dramatic development, of ensemble work and of finale technique offered the composer no opportunity of providing anything more than an oratorio-like succession of recitatives and arias. The chances for a revival on stage of this music are correspondingly very small. On the other hand, a recording for the gramophone, in which moreover all visual distractions are excluded, and where the recitatives could be drastically curtailed, could rescue this valuable music for the listener of our time. The credible vocal presentation of the role of Ostilio/Tullia would still remain a problem.

OPERATIC MAESTRO IN VENICE: FIRST SUCCESSES ABROAD

The performance in Vicenza had brought a new sphere of Vivaldi's activities to the notice of Venice. It was to be expected that one of the Venetian impresarios would quickly try to acquire for his theatre this creative force which promised so much success. The most interesting offer came from Modotto, the operatic contractor of the S. Angelo theatre, who was to appear a few years later as the oarsman on the title page of Marcello's lampoon. Vivaldi wrote his next opera for his house, and remained faithful to it, with some interruptions, right up to his last datable stage work, *Feraspe* (1739).

With the first *scrittura* (operatic commission) for Venice, the opera *Orlando finto pazzo*, Vivaldi knew what was at stake for his continued operatic career. In many respects, the work represents a mighty step forward from *Ottone*. The librettist, Dottor Grazio Braccioli, was a skilled man of the theatre with a certain knack for giving the stage action increased dramatic tension and effectiveness. The multiple amorous intrigues between the seven characters, some of them appearing in disguise, take place in a *Magic Flute*-like ambience in the domain of the Fairy Queen Ersilia; choruses of priestesses, temple servants, nymphs and fauns broaden the sphere of action and provide opportunities for impressive visual and aural effects. In the recitatives, the attempt to give individual characterizations, not only by means of the accompaniment but also by the melodic line of the singing voice and by the harmonies, is constantly striking. An accompagnato of Ersilia from the first act shows this tendency clearly. In a scene of magical incantations, romantic sound-colours are given out, while a recitative is accompanied in the bass register (Ex. 139). (Strange signs and a magic circle I write here on the ground. On these I turn three times towards dawn, three times when the menacing night draws near, and with my foot I stamp three times on the ground. By this magic herb that I scatter . . .)

Throughout, the orchestra is more copiously laid out than in *Ottone*, and it is also treated with greater variation of its colouristic resources. A whole aria is accompanied by pizzicato strings (bass: solo cello in the tenor register and 'senza Cembalo'); in a choral scene a string orchestra is placed on stage, besides which a small distant orchestra is used in the manner of an echo.

The libretto of this work is an attractive document of the time; it was printed shortly before the performance and dedicated by the author to the General of the Imperial Infantry Karl, Margrave of Baden—with many misprints in its title. The title page reads:

'Orlando / Finto pazzo / Dramma per musica da rappresentarsi in / S. Angelo / l'Autunno 1714 / del Dottor / Grazio Braccioli / Dedicato / a S.S.S. il Sig. Prencipe / Carlo Margraf / de Baden / Hocberg, Co. de Spovheim, / e l'bersdein; Sig. de Rotelvi Baden Weiler / Lahr, e Mahlberg. Gen. / dell'Arme, e Collonello / d'Infanteria di S.M. dell' / Imperatore . . .'

THE WORK

The dedicatory preface is dated November 10, 1714, and the 'Umilissimo Devotissimo Servitore' (most humble and devoted servant) Grazio Braccioli apologizes for his 'povera Musa' (poor Muse), trembles in 'confuso rispetto' (embarrassed respect), but in view of 'la generosa magnanimità' (generous magnanimity) ventures nonetheless 'di consacrare a Vostra Altezza Serenissima questo drammatico componimento' (to dedicate to Your Serene Highness this dramatic work). After the dedication, the librettist continues 'Al Lettore' (to the reader) and gives a small introduction to the action and the text. Then the characters are introduced:

Orlando   il Sig. Anton Francesco Carli, Virtuoso della Serenissima gran Principessa Violante di Toscana;

Ersilia   Regina Maga, che dal Boiardo è detta Falerina innamorata di Brandimarte, e di Origille creduta Ordauro. La Sig. Margherita Gualandi detta la Campioli;

Tigrinda   innamorata di Argillano. La Sig. Elisabetta Denzio;

Origille   innamorata di Grifone, che si finge uomo sotto nome di Ordauro. La Sig. Anna Maria Fabbri;

Argillano   Campione eletto da Ersilia, ed innamorato della stessa. Il Sig. Andrea Pacini;

Grifone   innamorato di Tigrinda, che si finge donna col nome di Leodilla. Il Sig. Francesco Natali;

Brandimarte   amico di Orlando, amato da Ersilia, che si fa credere Orlando. Il Sig. Andrea Guerri.

Coro di Sacerdotesse di Ecate, e di Ministri del Tempio di Pluto.
Coro di Ninfe e Fauni.

(Orlando—Mr. A.F.C., singer at the court of Her Serene Highness the Grand Duchess Violante of Tuscany—; Ersilia—Fairy Queen, called Falerina by the Boyards, loves Brandimarte and Origille, thought to be Ordauro. Miss M.G., called C.—; Tigrinda—loves Argillano. Miss E.D. —; Origille—loves Grifone, pretends to be a man named Ordauro. Miss A.M.F.—; Argillano—chosen warrior of Ersilia and in love with her. Mr. A.P.—; Grifone—loves Tigrinda, pretends to be a woman named Leodilla. Mr. F.N.—; Brandimarte—friend of Orlando, loved by Ersilia, gives out to be Orlando. Mr. A.G.—; Chorus of priestesses of Hecate and priests of the temple of Pluto. Chorus of nymphs and fauns.)

Such a commentary on the action in the list of characters itself was necessary in the case of such complicated goings-on on stage, with many erotic cross-currents among the characters, three of whom also give themselves out to be different people. This was all the more so when the audience barely listened to the recitatives in which the actions were presented. In this work as much as in *Ottone* it is interesting to find a preference for roles in which a man is dressed as a woman and vice versa. They were dependent on castrato voices in which there was, in fact, a great deal of virile resonance, and which often were given masculine roles to sing. Here, librettists made skilful use of the castrato voice to produce complications and interesting situations with faint sexual undertones.

The next opera performed under the name of Vivaldi, *Nerone fatto Cesare* (1715), is a compilation of music by several composers, Vivaldi contributing twelve arias, and thus producing the main portion. The rest had already been composed to the same libretto of Matteo Noris twenty-two years previously. This librettist too, who wrote more than 50 opera texts, was more than once a collaborator of Vivaldi's. When Herr von Uffenbach asserted in his journal under February 19, 1719, that he had heard the opera *Agrippina* by Vivaldi, he doubtless meant *Nerone* and had remembered the work by the name of another of its main characters.

The opera *L'Incoronazione di Dario*, to a much-revised text by the author Adriano Morselli, poses a chronological problem which, though small, is important for Vivaldi's time. Its performance is generally given as having been in 1716. In the libretto there is the remark 'Dramma per musica da rappresentarsi al Teatro di Sant'Angelo per terza opera del carnevale dell'anno 1716' (opera for the S. Angelo theatre, to be the third work of the carnival season of the year 1716), but the printer has given on the title page 'In Venezia MDCCXVII'. This is not necessarily an error, for the carnival season began on December 26, and Vivaldi's opera was played as the third in the season. The printer's declaration even says that it was first performed in the month of March. In fact, the Venetians still reckoned by the old calendar in Vivaldi's time, and according to this the year began with March 1. Thus the performance must have taken place in the year 1717, 'more veneto' (Venetian style), that is, after March 1, but before March 31, the closing date of the carnival season. Differing dates that have been given regarding Vivaldi are often caused by ignorance of these peculiarities of the calendar.

The unknown reviser of the libretto—he doubtless worked according to Vivaldi's directions—believed, moreover, that he should justify the alterations. In the foreword he says 'Eccoti l'Incoronazione di Dario, opera del Sig. Adriano Morselli già da molti anni defonto. Se la ritrovi in qualche parte mutata, e per le arie, e per gli caratteri de rappresentanti, non si è fatto ad altro fine, che per accomodarla all'uso moderno del Teatro, e alla compagnia che deve rappresentarla; vivi felice' (This is the opera *The Coronation of Darius* by Mr. Adriano Morselli, who has now been dead for many years. If you find it changed, in the arias and in the character of the dramatis personae, this has been done only with the purpose of making it more suitable to the modern theatre and to the cast which plays it. Fare thee well!). Its subject is interesting, providing in its fusion of political with private life many possibilities for dramatic development. After the death of the Persian King, Cyrus, there are three pretenders to the throne: Darius, supported by the satraps, Oronte, the people's favourite, and the captain Arpago, the army's candidate. Darius wishes to make his way to the throne by marrying Statira, Cyrus's elder daughter, and in doing this he seeks the help of Argene, the younger daughter. The latter, however, is herself in love with Darius, and wants to acquire a husband and kingdom for herself. After many entanglements Darius is crowned at the side of Statira.

The work begins with a recitative accompanied in the low regions of the strings, in which the ghost of Cyrus speaks to his daughters (Plate XIV—on the left at the top is the seal-like sign of the composer, made up of the letters A Vivaldi).

As a special instrumental attraction, a small cantata is added, having as accompaniment a viola d'amore, given in the score as a Viola all'Inglese ('Qui Segue Cantata in Scena con Viola all'Inglese'—Here follows a cantata on stage with Viola all'Inglese). This probably referred to an English Violet, a somewhat larger variant of the viola d'amore, which had double courses of sympathetic strings. The instrument was chosen to portray the tender world of feeling of dawning love. The recitative ('Il cor mio celar non posso, e palesar non oso'—I cannot conceal my heart and dare not make it known) is followed by an aria, in which the solo instrument is treated in virtuoso style, and at the end of which appears the direction: 'Segue Cadenza con Viola all'Inglese' (There follows a cadenza with the English violet).

The opening of the second act is typical of a concern for profounder expressiveness; the conversation between Dario and Argene is introduced by an Arioso of Dario (Ex. 140) (Tyrant Love, leave off from tormenting me; you have already roughly and cruelly laid this faithful heart in chains). One has the impression of being confronted with a page from a Bach cantata, so closely do the two masters approach each other here, not only in the conception of bass lines of this kind, but also in the technique of interrelating the parts.

179

With the opera *La Costanza trionfante degli Amori e degli Odi*, Vivaldi conquered another Venetian theatre, the S. Moisè, which kept him busy more than once in subsequent years. The piece was reworked two years later, given at the same theatre under a new title and in 1731 underwent a further revival at the S. Angelo theatre after similar alterations. We know of a performance in Mantua in 1720. It is regrettable that this music is lost in all its versions; for to all appearances the composer thought a great deal of it.

The master's growing reputation as an opera composer could now be seen from allusions in the librettos, and authors did not neglect to use the personage of the composer to make propaganda for the performance. Thus we read in the libretto of the opera *Arsilda regina di Ponte* (1716): 'La musica è del celebro virtuoso di violino il signor D. Antonio Vivaldi' (The music is by the famous violin virtuoso . . .), in that of *Tieteberga* (1717): 'La musica è del sempre celebre sig. D. Antonio Vivaldi' (The music is by the far-famed signor . . .), and in the 'Avvertimento al lettore' (Notice to the reader) for *Artabano rè de' Parti* (1718), the author of the libretto, Antonio Marchi, goes still further: 'La virtù musicale del signor Don Antonio Vivaldi che esige allora tutta l'ammirazione, può maggiormente ora impregnare la tua attenzione per applaudirlo avendolo di nuove adornato' (The creative force of . . . which has already commanded all admiration, can now lay claim to your attention to an even greater extent, that you may accord him applause for having enriched the work with new ideas). The dedicatees of the texts are also of interest, for alongside the Italian nobility we find amongst them 'S.E. il signor Baron Federici Girolamo di Witzendorff signore di Zeger e Seedorff' (*L'Armida*) and the *consigliere aulico* (Privy Councillor) to His Majesty the Czar 'S.E. il conte Sava Wladislavich' (*La Verità in Cimento*).

Vivaldi's reputation as an operatic maestro, which established itself more and more in Venice in the five years after 1713, naturally soon reached the leading operatic centres in Italy, and even abroad. In 1718 came a commission for the Teatro della Pergola in Florence. The opera *Scanderbegh* is the first work in which he collaborated with the poet Antonio Salvi, one of the most prolific librettists of his time, who also wrote the texts of two further operas Vivaldi composed for that city. Now his activities outside Venice began to increase: in 1718 *La Costanza trionfante* was given—perhaps in the presence of the composer—in Munich; 1720, with the performance of *La Candace o siano Li Veri Amici*, probably saw the start of several years of activity in Mantua; in the same year followed *Gli Inganni per Vendetta* in Vicenza, in the following year there was the pastoral *Silvia* in Milan, for a celebration of the birthday of the Empress Christine, and in the years 1723–4 Vivaldi was active for three seasons in Rome, and reaped triumphant successes. In between there were constantly performances in Venice. In all, during these extremely active years 1718–24, eleven operas came into being. It seems that these works were also thoroughly good business successes; for Vivaldi's impresarios could afford to engage the best singers in Italy, who at that time were mostly in the service of highly placed members of the occupation forces. In the libretto to *Fillippo rè di Macedonia* (Venice 1721) the following singers are named:

> La Sig. Ant. Margherita di Merighi virtuosa della Sereniss. Gran Principessa vedova di Toscana, Governatrice di Siena; La Sig. Chiara Orlandi, virtuosa di S.A.S. il Sig. Duca di Massa Carrara; La Sig. Anna M. Strada virtuosa di Camera di S.E. il Sig. Conte Colloredo, Governatore di Milano; Il Sig. Girolamo Albertini virtuoso di S.A.S. il sig. Principe Carlo Langravio d'Assel Cassel; La Sig. Antonia Laurenti, detta Coralli virtuosa di Camera di S. Maestà il Re di Polonia; & Il Sig. Antonio Barbieri, virtuoso di S.A.S. il Sig. Principe Filippo Langravio d'Hassia Darmestat.

From this middle creative period, which also includes some works written for Venice in the years 1725–6 (four operas in 1726 alone!), relatively little has come down to us. The Turin scores and some arias in the Paris Conservatoire show an inconsistent level of composition. In his haste to fulfil a commission, sometimes—if singers came in late—at the last minute before the performance, Vivaldi wrote music rapidly in a routine way, and this music met only the demands of the moment. On other occasions he worked very carefully. Gentili has shown that a Quartet, which closes the first act of the opera *La Verità in Cimento* can be found in two different versions in a Turin volume of cantatas in the Foà collection. The strongly concertante part played by the orchestra is constantly striking. Thus for instance in *Ercole sul Termondonte* (Rome 1723) there is an aria 'Ama la tortorella' (The love of the turtle-dove) with a solo violin on stage and another in the orchestra. A piece of great violinistic interest is a 'Salterio' in the opera *Il Giustino* with solo violin.

The libretto for *Ercole* is in fact by Don Giacomo Francesco Bussani, 'canonico regolare alla Carità di Venezia', and that of the opera *La Virtù trionfante del Vincitore* (Rome 1724), to which Vivaldi contributed only one act, is by Abate Francesco Silvani—a proof of considerable participation by the clergy in Roman operatic life too. A peculiarity of the performances of Vivaldi in Rome was the fact that all the roles were performed by men. In the Papal city, women were not allowed to appear on stage and had to be replaced by castrati.

In the choice of subject matter there was in Venice itself, with its wealth of connections with the Orient, a certain preference for the affairs of Eastern potentates—whether historical fact or fiction—as well as for the Egyptian scene. In connection with the Turkish siege of Vienna (1683) and the heavy fighting of the Venetians with the Turks which lasted until the Treaty of Passarowitz (1718), Turkish subject matter was more and more topical in the Italian theatre. In *La Verità in Cimento* the Grand Sultan Mamud has to choose between two women, *Il Giustino* is about a siege of Constantinople, and finally *Cunegonda* takes place at the time of the Crusades with the Sultan of Egypt as antagonist. Once, as the action took place in Norway (*La Fede tradita e vendicata*—1726), the names, which the Italian singers must have found unpronounceable and which could therefore scarcely be used in vocal music, were romanized. The libretto comments '. . . il dramma presente, in cui si mutano per comodo della musica in nomi di Umle in quello di Grimoaldo, in quello di Ricimero quello di Ataulfo, e quello di Scandone in quello di Rodoaldo' (. . . the present drama, in which for the sake of the music's ease of singing the names Umlo, Ataulfo and Scandone are changed to Grimoaldo, Ricimero and Rodoaldo).

In *Farnace* (1726) Anna Girò, as she is called in the libretto, appeared for the first time in Venice in an opera by Vivaldi. This singer, so talented particularly as an actress, had already made her Venetian début two years previously. With the 1726 performance began her close artistic collaboration with the composer, which included performances not only in Venice but also in the other operatic centres of Italy. In the score of *Farnace* is that aria 'Nell'intimo del petto il dolce e caro affetto' (the sweet and dear emotion in the breast) which is so typical of Vivaldi's aural imagination and spirit of inventiveness; here he anticipated the development of orchestral technique by a century and a half. The composer used in addition to the strings a Corno di Caccia (hunting horn), which had hitherto been almost exclusively a symbolic instrument for hunting scenes; here it is already used in the same way—with a pedal effect—as in the classical and romantic orchestra. Beginning with bar 32, a note has to be held as long as thirteen bars. In order to make possible this expressive effect demanded by the text, Vivaldi at the beginning of the aria (Plate XV) gives the indication 'Questo pedale del Corno non deve mai mancare; per tanto devono suonare due Corni . . . sempre Piano affino uno lascia

XIV. First page from the score of the opera *Incoronazione di Dario.*

XV and XVI. From *Farnace*.

prendere fiato all'altro' (This pedal point in the horn should never be missing; therefore two horns must play, always piano, so that one can give the other an opportunity to take his breath). Suchlike practices were forgotten or remained unheeded, and were rediscovered anew towards the end of the nineteenth century to be used in modern orchestral writing.

At the beginning of the ninth scene of the first act the transition from a harpsichord-accompanied recitative into an accompagnato is typical of a recitative technique which by now had become very refined. After a halting recitative permeated with rests in the vocal part as well as in the harpsichord, the direction appears in the score 'Qui bisogna fermarsi un poco senza Suonare, poi Segue Subito' (Here one must pause a little without playing, then follow on immediately) (Plate XVI).

THE CULMINATION OF THE OPERATIC OUTPUT

The last decade of Vivaldi's activities as an opera composer, which was overshadowed by the shattering personal events of 1737, brought a constant succession of one or two operas a year; and for the single year 1735, four performances of works to which Vivaldi at least contributed. The dates of performances in cities like Verona (five times), Florence (twice), Ancona (once), as well as eight performances in Venice and also several revivals of older works do not show in the slightest the decline in public esteem which has constantly been asserted, and which might be attributed to a decrease in his creative powers or to merely routine composition. If in attempts to revive Vivaldi's operas in our time it is precisely works from this creative period that are chosen, this speaks for a special quality in his late works. Thus Alfredo Casella, at that time artistic adviser to the 'Settimane senese', chose for the first modern performance of a Vivaldi opera, on September 19, 1939, L'Olimpiade, first performed in 1734 at the S. Angelo theatre; and La Fida Ninfa of the year 1732 was given a performance in Paris in 1958, and also at La Scala Milan.

L'Olimpiade is an amorous play about the Olympic Games. Licida, the adopted son of a King of Crete, sets off for the games with his friend Megacle and an older companion Aminta; there, Aristea, daughter of King Klisthenes, is offered as the prize for the winner. Megacle is faithfully devoted to his friend because the latter once saved his life, and since Licida is not very good at sporting contests, Megacle declares himself prepared to compete in Licida's name. But Aristea loves Megacle and is disconcerted not to find his name on the list of competitors. In conversation with the shepherdess Licori, the latter tells her that her real name is Argene and that she comes from Crete. She loved Licida, but the Cretan

King had decided that Megacle should be her bridegroom. In order to escape this marriage, she fled from home. Thus Aristea hears again of her beloved, who had fled to Crete years ago because her father had opposed their union. Since she now knows that he is still alive, she tries in vain to hinder the contests. Megacle too has now found out that the prize is his beloved Aristea. Torn between love and fidelity to his friend he determines to win Aristea for his friend. On entering the stadium Aristea recognizes him and tries apparently without success to reawaken in him his former feelings. The supposed Licida becomes the victor, extolled by the people, and Klisthenes crowns him and embraces him as his future son-in-law. So as to avoid the situation he foresees, Megacle asks leave to return home immediately; Aristea can first be entrusted to the hands of his friend, whom he presents under the name of Egisto. At this moment Aristea arrives and suddenly finds herself face to face with her beloved as the victor. Now he has to admit the imposture, and Aristea rejects Licida who has just met Argene, who in turn has reproached him mightily for his lack of fidelity. Now Aminta brings the news that Megacle—who has meanwhile departed—has taken his own life by leaping into a torrential river. But he is alive, having been rescued by a fisherman. Meanwhile Licida has been led before the King, and in his desperation tries to kill him. He is brought to judgment before priests and dignitaries, and the King has to pass a sentence of death. Then Argene rushes to the scene, confesses who she is, asks to be allowed to die in place of her beloved and offers a bracelet as a pledge. Klisthenes recognizes it: it is the one his little son Filinto used to wear, before he was exiled on account of a prophecy of parricide. So it turns out that Licida is his son and Aristea's brother. The final scene unites two happy couples in marriage and reconciles them with the moved father.

Vivaldi laid out the work particularly sumptuously, and the overall plan, with changes from choral scenes to arias and duets of tenderly sustained expressions of love, up to the outburst of despair, was particularly conducive to this. Both Casella and the arranger Virgilio Mortari have commented on the problems which arose from making a version for the modern stage in 1947 in the Quaderni dell'Accademia Chigiana (No. XIII). Casella says: 'The choice of L'Olimpiade from the numerous Vivaldi operas which can be found in the National Library in Turin was influenced above all by consideration of the extremely beautiful libretto by Metastasio (which has also been set by several other composers, among them Caldara, Jommelli, Pérez and finally Pergolesi); but also on account of the unusual beauty of the music. Nonetheless the work required patient revision, above all because of the need to shorten the endless recitatives, which the public of the time would certainly not have listened to, to their bare essentials. Since besides this some important pieces were missing, these were taken from another of Vivaldi's operas, *Dorilla*, which was performed in the same year (1734) at the same Venetian theatre of S. Angelo. The Turin score of *Dorilla* bears the remark 'three acts with sinfonia and choruses which sing and dance', and the work is much richer than *L'Olimpiade* in ensembles and above all in choruses and dances. For this reason what was lacking in *L'Olimpiade* was made up from *Dorilla*, and this was done in the knowledge that it was no more than the masters of the period continually did. In my researches at the Turin National Library I have found one and the same aria in four different operas of Vivaldi.' Mortari gives technical details: 'As the man entrusted with revision and arrangement, I have wished to undertake a task both painstakingly exact and humbly faithful to the style, without however demanding of the public that they should suffer austerities and conventions which today would doubtless be intolerable. Thus the harpsichord, which accompanies all the recitatives, has been omitted from all the arias in which the orchestral writing fills out the harmony with a well-balanced sound. Not all the pieces of the original score were of equal importance, and it was considered necessary to make deletions, changes of position and substitutions. The very long recitatives were reduced to the minimum possible, because a recitative that exceeds a certain length can present an obstacle to the modern listener's appreciation. The abundant expressiveness of the music made no enrichment of the original orchestral palette necessary. The sonorities, which are a component of the style, have remained untouched in their functions.'

In contrast to this procedure of revision, which adopts a seemingly very free attitude to the score but approximates completely in the spirit of the time to a procedure to which Vivaldi himself might have had recourse in the case of a revival, is the attempt to give a totally faithful realization of the original score, as was undertaken in 1958 in Paris with *La Fida Ninfa*. In this work too the composer had written valuable music for a static, oratorio-like libretto. In doing so, he clearly showed a repeated tendency to surmount the accustomed sequence of recitative and aria and thereby to achieve a stronger dramatic impact. This concern, however, is concentrated on the single numbers, and cannot conceal the weaknesses in the text's conception. One of the essential creative traits of this late period is the increased participation of the orchestra in many arias, evident not only in the very markedly condensed conception of the ritornellos but equally in the part played by motifs in the accompaniment of the solo section. Really the word accompaniment is out of place here, and one should speak rather of a joint conception of the soloist and the orchestra (Ex. 141). Whilst in number the solo arias retreat somewhat into the background, the composer now lays greater stress on ensembles, which in general are carefully worked out. In a duet between Elpina and Osmino (Act 1, Scene 3) the two parts are often written imitatively, or closely linked in their composition by chains of suspensions. At the end of the first act a trio, very well written for the voices and with a strong finale effect, is headed 'à 3 con Istrom^{ti}'. A 'Quartetto' forms the end of the second act, and here there are very effective alternations between imitative and homophonic sections.

Contrasted with these very worthwhile sections there are successions of scenes which consist only of recitatives (without arias). This may have been well intentioned on the part of the librettist as a means of pushing along the action, but it produces almost eternal chains of recitative. Here above all an energetic pair of scissors would be necessary for the music to become suitable for an actual performance. A reproduction that was true to the score, as was offered in Paris with first-rank singers and the orchestra of the Palazzo Pitti from Florence, is now hardly tolerable in its wearisome length. About the performance, Edgar Schall wrote in the Schweizerischen Musikzeitung (1958/353): 'Opera lovers of today could not summon up sufficient interest for the totally undramatic "pastorale Drama" that was first performed in Verona in 1732, even though the singers (two female and four male) were a great credit to the Italian school. The greatest admirers of Vivaldi finally moved about restlessly in their seats, because in the course of three hours nothing at all had really happened on stage. All enlivening additions had been expressly eschewed in maintaining historical accuracy. Only very drastic cuts would have allowed the musical qualities to come out of it better.' The first performance in the year 1732 in Verona was an occasion of great pomp: the stage designer was Francesco Bibbiena, and it is noted in the libretto that the choreography was by Andrea Cattani, 'ballerino della Maestà del rè di Polonia' (solo dancer of His Majesty the King of Poland), and that 'i più insigni professori' (the most distinguished professional musicians) were working in the orchestra.

Another particularly interesting work from his late period is *Griselda*, written for Venice six years before the composer's death; and it was about the origins of this work that Goldoni wrote so graphically. The libretto introduces the singers taking part:

Gualtiero	Rè di Tessaglia. Il Sig. Gregorio Balbi Virtuoso di S.A.S. il Signor Gran Duca di Toscana
Griselda	sua Moglie. La Signora Anna Girò
Costanza	Principessa loro figlia non conosciuta dalla Madre, amante di Roberto. La Signora Margherita Giacomazzi
Roberto	Principe di Atene suo amante. Il Sig. Gaetano Valletta Virtuoso di Camera di S.A.R. il Signor Gran Duca di Toscana
Ottone	Cavalier di Tessaglia. Il Signor Lorenz Saletti Virtuoso di S.A.Serenissima la Principessa Eleonora Gonzaga di Toscana
Corrado	Fratello di Roberto, amico di Gualtiero. La Signora Elisabetta Gasparini
Everardo	figlio di Gualtiero e Griselda che non parla.

(King of Thessaly; his wife; Princess, their daughter, unknown to the mother, loved by Roberto; Prince of Athens, her lover; Thessalian nobleman; brother of Roberto, friend of Gualtiero; son of Gualtiero and Griselda, non-speaking part.)

The action takes place in Larmirio, a Thessalian city. In the libretto the following introduction is given: Gualtiero has met the shepherdess Griselda while hunting and has taken her for his wife. Because of this marriage below his station there is unrest among the people, and almost an insurrection when a daughter is born. The King makes it known that the little Costanza was killed. But he has taken her to a friendly prince in Athens who has two sons, of whom the elder, Roberto, falls in love with the adolescent girl. Meanwhile Griselda brings a son into the world, and unrest is stirred up once more, this time by Ottone, who loves Griselda. In order to make an end of the troubles Gualtiero wants to leave Griselda and marry Costanza, the apparent daughter of his friend.

The work is announced as 'atti tre con Sinfonia a principio' (three acts with overture), and this reference to the three-movement introductory music here perhaps has a special meaning; for some sinfonia had probably always been played before an opera, even if none had been specially written for it. The *Griselda* sinfonia is remarkable in that its first movement is written in clear classical sonata form. After a 16-bar C major section played f, there follows an expressively (ppp!) very contrasted C minor section with a virtuoso bridge motif to the development section. This shows all the essential elements of the classical methods of development.

The strongly accentuated recapitulation is kept short, but again brings the very characteristic subsidiary section (Ex. 142).

Griselda exhibits all the merits and weaknesses of the Vivaldi operas: the most marked participation of the orchestra in the dramatic construction of the arias, and the never-ending recitatives. Straight after the overture, the opera proper begins with a chain of recitatives covering nine pages of score, which is meant to introduce the listener to the very complicated and visually unpresentable 'story so far'. Vivaldi's conception of the intermingling of solo concerto form with the aria is most apparent in an aria from the second act. The orchestral ritornello is taken from the Bassoon Concerto in C major, P. 50 (see Kolneder, *Solokonzertform*, p. 30), whose extremely opulent construction had already led the composer to arrange this concerto for the oboe. This fresh adaptation as a soprano aria has led to a renewed concentration which gives the piece the quality of a high-point in Vivaldi's formal powers, which alone would have served to silence all talk of 'frivolity and eccentricity in composition'.

It is still not possible to make a final judgment on Vivaldi as an opera composer. Rinaldi has meritoriously brought together excellent material, though this relates more to the librettos than to the music. Pincherle intentionally left the composer's dramatic music out of his consideration. At the time he was writing his book, the task of comprehensively cataloguing and describing the instrumental music was so gigantic that one readily understands his self-imposed limitation. A dissertation by Jonathan Schiller, *The Operas of Antonio Vivaldi* has for a long time been announced as 'in progress'. But, as Harvard University informs me, the work was 'never completed' and Schiller 'has apparently abandoned his musicological work'. Thus this section of the present book represents a first attempt at the analytical investigation and assessment of the composer's operatic output. A thoroughgoing description still remains to be undertaken and might result in valuable conclusions in that Vivaldi's dramatic stage works—apart from a few exceptions—are datable and would give us an insight into the master's 'creative curve'.

SECULAR VOCAL MUSIC

In his article 'The Italian cantata from its beginnings till Handel' in the Encyclopaedia *Musik in Geschichte und Gegenwart* (Cassel, Bärenreiter), Hans Engel writes: 'A. Vivaldi too wrote about two dozen cantatas, in which he made as little use as did Albinoni of the orchestra and of concertante instruments.' A survey of the three most important source locations, however, yields no less than 59 cantatas with different types of ensemble:

THE WORK

	Turin	Dresden	Paris	Total
Soprano and continuo	24	7	—	31
Alto and continuo	2	3	—	5
Bass and continuo	1	—	—	1
Voice with solo instrument and continuo	1	1	2	4
Voice with string orchestra	9	—	5	14
Two voices with string orchestra	1	—	—	1
Voice with larger orchestra	1	—	—	1
Two or more voices with larger orchestra	2	—	—	2
	41	11	7	59

In addition there are over 100 arias in these libraries and in Schloss Wiesentheid, which for the most part are probably from preserved or lost operas by Vivaldi, but of which some were undoubtedly composed as short cantatas complete in themselves.

With regard to form, all the types of the Italian secular cantata of the time appear in these groups of works, the most frequent being the small two-movement chamber cantata, generally accompanied only by the continuo, in which two arias are juxtaposed, one in a slow tempo and the closing one in Allegro or Presto. The general rule is that they have the same key but contrasting metres (simple followed by compound time or vice versa). A shortish recitative may precede them or be sung between the arias; often the introductory aria has the character of a recitative in some sections. The two parts are contrasted in content, like those of the poem itself, though this contrast holds them together: meditation, reflection, doubt, uncertainty and fear generally dominate the first aria, whilst firmness, resolve, joy and hope are the emotional states brought into play in the second aria.

The instrumentation and formal layout are closely related insofar as the composer might expand his resources if the work were to be of larger dimensions. A cantata for alto and strings, *Cessate omai* (Cease henceforth), consists of a recitative, an aria with solo violin, a recitative and a final aria. Another for alto, strings and two hunting horns consists of two arias, two ariosos and two recitatives. The strings are given an ample share of extended ritornellos, and the single arias are constructed almost throughout as are those in the operas: in other words, they are for the most part A–B–A arias, of which the last section is not written out, but is indicated by D.C., and which, in their alternation of ritornello and solo section, come very close to solo concerto form. Basically, all the cantatas of Vivaldi and his contemporaries are small scenes from unwritten operas.

Increasing the number of singers to two or three was a natural consequence in certain circumstances which demanded a work of larger proportions. The festival cantata, often performed as a preliminary to a festival opera performance, could take on almost oratorio-like dimensions by such an increase, and then was divided into two sections, like for instance the *Serenata à 3* for two sopranos and tenor, with an orchestra augmented by hunting horns, oboes and bassoon; its first section comprises nine numbers, its second eight.

Perhaps Vivaldi's most interesting work from this group is the two-section cantata *La Sena festeggiante* (The festive Seine), a festival cantata (as the title already indicates), similar to a Te Deum for a celebration of the French legation in Venice, or perhaps even a commissioned work for the French court. The text was the brainchild of his trusted collaborator Domenico Lalli. In fact it deals with no plot, but undisguisedly provides many opportunities to sing the praises of the city of Paris: two allegorical figures, L'Età dell'Oro (The Golden Era, soprano) and La Virtù (Virtue, alto), in their desperate quest for the lost happiness of mankind, come to the bank of the Seine, which is embodied by a sort of River God (bass). There finally they are enlightened by, as the recitative has it, 'l'Astro maggior che della Gallia è il lume' (the great star which is the light of Gaul). Vivaldi composed this large-scale work, whose first part comprises 20 numbers and whose second 15, very carefully, and gave exact indications in the score. It is headed by a three-movement sinfonia, which exists in Turin with a different middle movement as a self-contained work (P. 64), though there it bears the title 'Con^to'. The first movement also bears the remark 'Alla francese' in this independent version, and as a special gesture towards France the music is written in the French rhythm (Ex. 143). A typically French 'Ouvertur' also introduces the second part; this is in three sections—an Adagio (in dotted rhythms), Presto (3/8 time, fugato) and shortened return of the Adagio. It is followed by a short Allegro molto, an independent movement perhaps conceived as a danced transitional movement leading to the second part proper. The 'Coro' after the introductory sinfonia is orchestrated with oboes and recorders, the composer asking for '2 Hautbois ò più se piace' (two oboes or more ad libitum) and '2 Flauti ò più'. This indication of doubled or even heavier woodwind was perhaps necessary for an open-air performance. In one of the work's later numbers these instruments are also used as 'soli'.

In the arias, just as in the operas, the composer makes considerable technical demands on the singers. For the *Sena* a basso profundo is needed who can reach down to a full-voiced E at several places in the 3/2-time Largo aria 'Pietà dolcezza' (Piety and sweetness mark his face, virtue and greatness his heart) (Ex. 144). But broadly flowing depth of tone is not enough for the bass, and in another aria virtuoso coloratura is required of him. The piece bears the truly Vivaldian tempo indication, given half in jest, half in earnest, 'Allegro, più ch'è possibile' (Allegro, more than is possible). Besides the already mentioned principal form, the ritornello aria, a further type sometimes appears, built in two repeated sections after the model of the dance forms. For the instrumental epilogue, the composer prescribes: 'Dopo l'Aria Gl'Istrom^ti replicano soli la seconda parte' (After the aria the instruments alone repeat the second half). An especially delightful piece is the soprano aria 'Giace languente' (Reclining, languishing). This is composed in three parts for voice, all the violins in unison and bass (Le Violette sempre con il Basso), and the composer has headed it with the instruction 'Tutti gl'Istrom^ti sempre pianiss^mo anco nelli Ritornelli' (All instruments always ppp, also in the ritornellos). For the ensemble numbers the indication 'Coro' does not necessarily mean a choral performance, but rather designates the ensemble of soloists. The work's final number too is given as 'Coro'. This is composed in four mixed parts, but in the third stave is the comment 'Sarebbe molto bene far cantare questo tenore, mà però non è necessario' (It would be very good to have this tenor part sung, but this is not necessary), in other words, the composer would like a four-part vocal performance, perhaps even with a chorus, but he does not count on it. In fact in this number the tenor is treated as obbligato almost throughout; if it was not interpreted vocally the violas would probably have to come to the rescue and take it over. In the final chorus of the first part an already highly developed finale technique is in evidence, some of its details being suggestive of Mozart. It is 233 bars long, furnished with large orchestral ritornellos, and written for three vocal parts—that is, for three soloists. The indication 'Coro' always appears when all three voices are singing together; with one or two voices, the indication is 'solo' or 'soli'. In this way a possibility of choral performance is also probably suggested.

The recitatives are characterized by a strong interplay between harpsichord and orchestral accompaniment. Sometimes this interplay takes place within a single recitative and makes vivid changes of mood possible. In both types of recitative, the bass and the strings too are also occasionally given motivic material. A peculiarity is the indication 'Arcate lunghe' (long bow strokes) which appears in the bass in several secco recitatives— a direction to hold the single long notes for their exact notated length. However, in one recitative at the beginning of which this indication appears, there is a later one: 'arcate sciolte' (literally loose, unbridled bow strokes), although here as before the usual whole note-values appear. This means in fact that Vivaldi used two methods in the performance of secco recitatives: 1) 'come sta' (as written); 2) if the dramatic expression required it, with short, detached chords, especially with regard to the stringed instruments playing the bass.

Single numbers of the work are provided with two versions of the text, the second being a modification of the first. This suggests that at least two performances took place. It is possible that Vivaldi could not always be present and had to entrust the preparation and direction of the performance to a colleague. Hence, perhaps, the exact indication of many details which makes the score of *La Sena festeggiante* a valuable document of performing practice. It is remarkable that the modern French Vivaldi movement has not yet taken up this cantata in honour of Paris.

THE MUSICA SACRA

The *Mercure de France* of October 1727 reported that on the occasion of the birth of a princess in Venice the French ambassador had organized festivities during which there was a 'very fine instrumental concert lasting almost two hours, in which the music, like that of the Te Deum, was by the famous Vivaldi'. Until the discovery of the Vivaldi collection in Turin this was the only report of church music by the composer, a few sacred works in the Dresden Library remaining virtually unheeded. The prominent place as an instrumental composer that Vivaldi was accorded first by his contemporaries and again in our own time made it natural that as soon as the Turin discovery was even glimpsed the general interest centred first of all on the instrumental music, all the more so because in any case a collection comprising so many works could only be managed by organizing and surveying it according to categories. Gentili was the first to point out the great merits of the composer's sacred music, and this at a time when he was only acquainted with the first part of the great Vivaldi collection. As early as 1927 he wrote: 'Amongst the sacred music we find above all a large volume of Vivaldi, a manuscript of exceptional interest. It contains ten large, hitherto unknown compositions, bearing Vivaldi's name, for the most part autograph copies'—then follows an enumeration of the works. In this connection Gentili gives an appreciation of the oratorio *Juditha*. His high estimation of the composer's sacred music was confirmed when the second part of the collection was available and proved to yield many more works of this kind written by Vivaldi. Then Alfredo Casella worked through the treasures of the Turin National Library for the Vivaldi Festival in Siena in 1939, and, with the eye of a connoisseur, chose works which would provide a comprehensive picture of the composer's personality. Then, on September 20, 1939, four of the master's sacred works were heard for the first time for more than 200 years in the Chiesa dei Servi in Siena: a *Stabat Mater*, a motet for soprano and strings, a *Credo* for chorus and orchestra and a *Gloria* for two sopranos, alto, chorus and orchestra. In the programme book, Casella recalled the deep impression Vivaldi's music had made on him as soon as he looked through the manuscripts: '. . . at a first (and exciting) contact with these manuscripts it was possible for me to recognize straight away that as a creator of sacred music, Vivaldi was certainly no lesser a figure than he was in the instrumental concertos'. Then in the year 1941 the oratorio *Juditha* was performed in Siena. With these two concerts a fundamental part of the composer's musica sacra was made known to the public. Unfortunately, as a consequence of the circumstances of war, these efforts were to remain without any effect, and for the great musical public as well as for professional musicians Vivaldi remained, as before, an instrumental composer. The first musicians to impart comprehensive knowledge of this group of works were the 'Circle Antonio Vivaldi' of Brussels who, supported by the tireless Angelo Ephrikian, set themselves the special aim of performing and propagating the sacred works. Today, thanks to several excellent gramophone recordings, it is possible to evaluate the composer also as an important creator of sacred music.

It seems that Vivaldi's interest in musica sacra roughly corresponded in time with the period of the illness of Gasparini, the *Maestro del Choro* at the Ospedale della Pietà, and that it was his absence that provided Vivaldi with the direct pretext for writing sacred works. Then, by a decree of March 17, 1715, the composer received an exceptional gift of 50 ducats for 'le vertuose composizioni in musica contribuite dopo l'absenza del maestro Gasparini' (for excellent musical compositions contributed after the absence of Maestro Gasparini). In an 'Inconbenza dei maestri di Choro' (Duties of the *maestri di choro*) decreed on July 6, 1710, we find under figures 2–4: '2) He must every year, at least for Easter and for the Feast of the Visitation of the Blessed Virgin Mary, to whom this new church is consecrated, write two new masses and vespers, at least two motets each month, and any other composition which might be ordered from him by those appointed to direct the church in Holy Week, in cases of Funeral ceremonies or in any other case. These compositions must be entered in the register of the principal choirgirl so that it can be examined at the assembly of church directors every six months. 3) He must be present personally in the choir at all the main Feast-days and especially at Easter, at Christmas, at the Feast of the Visitation, and during Holy Week, and in cases of Funeral ceremonies, to play the organ and supervise the instruments and the performance, so that he can give instructions to the girls, and in any other case according to the directions of the aforesaid men appointed to direct the church. 4) He must leave copies of scores to the principal choirgirl who will attend to them without any burden on the maestro.' The last clause is particularly interesting, for it ensured that the directors of the institution had the rights in perpetuity of performing all works composed to their commission and in their service. Thus Vivaldi probably helped Gasparini occasionally with a composition during the latter's illness, and then, from 1713 on, provided music for the Ospedale for the great Church Festivals. His first (not preserved) oratorio *Moyses Deus Pharaonis* was performed in 1714, and in 1716 his second oratorio *Juditha Triumphans devicta Holofernis barbarie* (Judith triumphant though defeated by the barbarian Holofernes).

Altogether, 60 sacred works by the composer have been preserved, 3 in Dresden and 57 in Turin. The latter are divided over the volumes Foà II (*Juditha*) and IV and Giordano I, II, III and V. A few further works preserved in the Turin collection could already be identified by Gentili as most probably not by Vivaldi, including a *Laudate* with the date 1690, which for a long time served as evidence for a very early dating of the composer's birth. Nine works are identified by Vivaldi himself as motets, and these are shorter pieces, generally for solo voice and strings. A series of further compositions served as interpolations in services and are entitled, for instance, 'Introduzione al Miserere'; many works obviously intended to be more extensive are incomplete. But the Turin collection also contains large-scale works, whose antiphonal structure and rich orchestral layout point to their having been used in important Feast-day celebrations.

Only the libretto of Vivaldi's first oratorio has survived, in the Library of the Conservatoire of Santa Cecilia in Rome. In this the names of the singers are entered in handwriting; all the parts, even those of masculine characters, were sung by women's voices:

Moyses	Barbara
Aaron	Candida
Elysabeth Aaron Uxor	Silvia
Maria soror Moysis et Aaron	Michielina
Pharao Egypti Rex	Anastasia
Sapiens primus	Soprana

Sapiens secundus	Meneghina
Unus ex Regis Ministris	Apollonia
Unus ex Ch. Ebraeor.	Gieltruda
Una ex Ch. Foeminar. Ebr.	detta
Nuncius	Anna

(Elisabeth, Wife of Aaron; Maria, sister of Moses and Aaron; Pharao, King of Egypt; first wise man; second wise man; one of the ministers of the King; one of the chorus of Jews; one of the chorus of Jewish women; messenger.)

The soloists of the Ospedale della Pietà were thus only known by their Christian names. It reveals something of life at the institution that one girl was simply called 'Soprana'. Three choruses, of Jews, Egyptians and Jewish women, complete the copious cast list.

The oratorio *Judith*, in the freshness of its musical ideas, the balance of its whole conception and the abundance of its well-planned instrumental colours, is a masterpiece. The libretto, written in an occasionally slightly Italianized Latin, provides a favourite type of subject matter whose combination of war-like and heroic with more erotic moments was well suited to the emotional appetites of the Baroque, and has remained effective to this day. This story was first set to music of importance by Marc-Antoine Charpentier in his *histoire sacrée 'Judith sive Bethulia liberata'*; Alessandro Scarlatti followed, and the fifteen-year-old Mozart, for his *Betulia liberata*, had at his disposal a libretto by Metastasio written by the latter for Georg Reutter jun. in 1734 as a commission from the Emperor Charles VI; within about a hundred years it was set to music about thirty times, by masters such as Jommelli, Holzbauer, Gassmann, Anfossi, Pugnani and Salieri. Finally in 1925 this well-tested material stimulated Arthur Honegger to write a biblical opera, *Judith*.

In contrast to *Moyses*, the circle of dramatis personae is kept very small; the main figure, Judith, accompanied by her maid Abra, opposes the Assyrian commander-in-chief, Holofernes, with his adjutant referred to in the score as Vagans. A 'Chorus Militum furentium in acie' (Chorus of soldiers, in storming battle formation) depicts the atmosphere in the Assyrian camp; a 'Chorus virginum canentium in Bethulia' (Chorus of maidens singing in Bethulia) embodies the people; and the high priest Ozias is their spokesman. The action takes place in the year 659 B.C. Nebuchadnezar has dispatched an army under Holofernes to carry out a punitive action against the Jews who have been slow to pay him tribute. From the beleaguered town of Bethulia, the beautiful and wise widow

Judith comes to the commander and supplicates for mercy. Holofernes, immediately inflamed with love, invites her to his tent for a festive banquet which he wishes to enjoy with her alone. As he has fallen asleep, she beheads him and the town is saved. The choice of just this subject was influenced by the fact that at the time the Venetians were in fact involved in a hard struggle with the Turks. Shortly before the end of the work the librettist clearly emphasizes the action's symbolic character. Ozias sings of the liberated town:

Gaude felix Bethulia laetare
consolare urbs nimis afflicta
Coelo amata es fortunata
inter hostes semper invicta.

(Rejoice, happy Bethulia, comfort thee, thou hard-tried city, thou art loved of heaven, fortunate, unvanquished in the midst of foes.)

and then compares it with Venice:

Ita decreto aeterno
Veneti maris Urbem
inviolatem discerno.
Sic in Asia Holoferni impio
   tyranno
Urbs virgo gratia Dei semper
   munita
erit nova Juditha . . .

(Thus I see, by an eternal decree, Venice, city of the sea, inviolate. Just as in Asia, against the heathen tyrant Holofernes, the virginal city, always protected by God's grace, will be a new Judith . . .)

If he calls Venice a new Judith in this way, his final words 'applaudite Judithae Triumphanti' (applaud the triumphant Judith) are therefore an invitation to praise also the oppressed home city.

In place of an introductory sinfonia there is an introductory chorus of Assyrian soldiers. Formally it is laid out in three sections, with D.C. al Segno, but to the middle section (in B minor) of only eleven bars is contrasted an A section of 52 bars in radiant D major, so as to make effective use of the two trumpets and timpani, which, together with two oboes, complement the string orchestra. It is indicative of the economical use of resources that this ensemble is not heard again until the final chorus 'Salve invicta Juditha formosa' (Hail, beautiful unvanquished Judith). The chorus of soldiers is here written in four mixed parts, as is also that of the maidens later. In the performance by the girls of the Pietà, the tenor part was probably sung by deep alto voices and the bass by teachers at the institution, perhaps filled out by members of church choirs. Also a distant chorus is specified in one number with the direction 'Le Voci in lontano' (voices in the distance). As in *Moyses*, the five solo parts in the work were sung by girls, those of Judith, Holofernes and Ozias being notated in the alto clef and the other two in the soprano clef. For the part of Vagans, the girl Barbara who had already taken part in *Moyses* was probably available for a later performance. Vivaldi wrote out two alternative arias for her, the score giving them in both versions, the second being designated 'Per la Sig^ra Barbara' each time.

In its succession of recitatives and arias the oratorio is laid out in exactly the same way as the composer's operas. The fact that such a work would be designated in Italy as 'azione sacra' (sacred act) indicates its proximity to the sacred opera and provides the impulse for a stage presentation. In its first modern performance the work was given in a 'riduzione scenica' (scenic arrangement) in the R. Teatro dei Rizzi in Siena; as his Plate XXIV, Rinaldi gives a design for the set by Virgilio Marchi.

What we have said about the operatic arias also holds good for those of *Judith*: they are developed as D.C. arias in A–B–A form throughout, but in their treatment of the ritornello as a framework for the structure of the vocal part they come very close to solo concerto form. The overall harmonic plan is carefully balanced with regard to the tensions yielded by the different tonalities. In the key succession of the arias there are relationships of the subdominant minor as well as links at the fifth, switches to the major key and the mediant; at one point there is the succession D major—B♭ major—G minor—A major, and at another point B♭ major E major—F major. Corresponding to the solo sections in solo concerto form, the harmonically more flexible recitatives are here the modulatory connecting links. After an aria in F major, a recitative enters in C major and modulates to F♯ minor, whereupon a D major chorus follows. In another instance two arias, in A minor and C minor, are connected by a recitative which leads from C major through C♯ minor to E♭ major. The shaping of the textual expression in the arias is very much determined by the ritornellos. In an aria of Holofernes 'Nil arma, nil bella, nil flamma furoris, si cor bellatoris est cadens in se' (Arms, war, flaming fury are nothing if the warrior's courage sinks) the heroic attitude is presented as much in the large intervals of the ritornello as in the fanfare-like treatment of the vocal line (Ex. 145). In its concentrated motif structuring, the work's pièce de résistance is probably another aria of Holofernes, that on the text 'Agitata infide flatu' (Driven by perfidious winds).

The most conspicuous feature of the score of *Judith* is the scoring, with its constantly changing instrumental colours. In an aria of Judith, 'Quanto

magis generosa' (The greater the generosity), a viola d'amore is given a
solo part, and two 'Violᶦ con piombi' (muted) take the middle and lower
parts; apart from a few bars, the aria has no bass, and the muted solo
violins provide a continuous canopy of sound, showing off the silvery
sympathetic strings of the viola d'amore to good effect. Moreover, the
latter is notated in scordatura, the aria being in E♭ major. Vivaldi drew
on the instrument's tone-colour again in a small cantata which he headed
'Conᵗᵒ di Viole all'Inglèse'. Judith stands directly faced with the decisive
act and appeals to the Creator to witness the purity of her intention. Her
recitative 'Summe astrorum Creator' (Supreme Creator of the stars) is
accompanied by a five-part group of violas reaching from the treble to
the bass; the latter is reinforced by a solo double bass (Plate XVIII). The
same ensemble accompanies the aria that follows. However, the viola
all'Inglese, the English violet, was not built in such a family. Perhaps
the upper parts were played by this instrument, and the lower ones by
viole da gamba.

When Vagans sings of his master's previous night of love, 4 'Tiorbe'
are called on (notated alternately in the tenor and bass clef, and treated
in one- to two-part writing), and the bass at this point bears the indication 'Cembali soli'. In the aria choral refrains are inserted on the
text 'Honoris amoris sit consona nox' (May the night be worthy of his
honour and his love). Theorbos were easily come by in Venice at that
time: the orchestral roll of San Marco in 1708 includes 3 theorbists, one
of them in holy orders, out of 23 musicians.

An instrument that was already very rare in Vivaldi's time, and which
the composer also used in two other works (P. 16 and P. 385), is the
salmoè, called on (and here in fact muted) for the characterization in an
aria of Judith. The choice of the instrument was probably influenced by
the textual passage 'Sponsa orbata, turtur gemo' (Robbed of my friend,
I sigh like a turtledove). Pincherle concerned himself for a long time with
interpreting the name of the instrument and on p. 101 of his book he
presents the results of his researches. The salmoè, which Vivaldi elsewhere also referred to as salmò, was very probably a shawm which was
played with a double reed, thus perhaps the folk version of the oboe so
popular in the Abruzzi. Today the production of the required sound can
be attempted on the oboe, which can be somewhat damped by the introduction of a sponge into its bell. It is in fact also possible that the salmoè
was a precursor of the clarinet; but in one of the work's soldiers' choruses
Vivaldi uses 'Clareni 2', thus clarinets. Moreover these are not clarini,
for the trumpets which are heard in two choral numbers are designated

XVII. Francesco de' Guardi (1712–1793), interior of S. Marco.

XVIII. From *Juditha*.

as 'Trombe'. The use of trombe, clareni and salmoè in a work of the year 1716, and their clear terminological differentiation, lends the score of *Judith* considerable value in connection with the history of musical instruments. The choice of the clareni for the soldiers' chorus is extraordinarily characteristic: the warriors do not sing of the battle, but of their leader's love-feast, so that whilst trumpets would have been symbolically out of place, the clarinets of the time, with their coloration between brass and woodwind, were exactly suited to the situation.

In an aria of Judith, in whose text the soul's immortality is contrasted with the transitoriness of life, Vivaldi draws on the mandoline as a solo instrument; he also in fact wrote two concertos for the instrument. The two solo parts, alto and mandoline, are supported by a bass, played by 'Violini Soli pizzicati'. As a continuo instrument the organ is once mentioned; but in one aria it is also used as a soloist in the high register that is so significant in Vivaldi's aural conception. Together with the alto (Holofernes, begging for love) and the solo oboe, it produces magical sound effects (Ex. 146). Since in an aria of Vagans before his sleeping master 'Si dominus dormit sit placida gens' (When the master sleeps may the people be restful) '2 Flauti', thus recorders, are also used, the following is the list of instruments in the orchestra: two recorders, two oboes, salmoè, two clarinets, at least two bassoons (not given, but a matter of course), two trumpets, timpani, mandoline, four theorbos, viola d'amore (perhaps two or three), viole da gamba—one alto, one tenor, one bass—strings with two violins, viola, cello and double bass, two harpsichords and organ. This copiously laid-out orchestra, however, is never used in its entirety, but the resources of the variegated palette are used differently from one scene to another: an instrumental procedure which reminds us of the intermedii of the sixteenth century and the early operas of Monteverdi. However, it is debatable whether this tradition was still a living one in 1716, and as an ingenious experimenter in sound colours Vivaldi probably arrived at such results of sonority without any direct stimulus.

Of the large number of Vivaldi's works intended for church services we shall now select four which are available either in gramophone recordings or as publications, and can thus be studied extensively:

Psalm 126 *Nisi Dominus* for alto solo, viola d'amore, strings and continuo (AMS 25)
Dixit Dominus for soloists (SATB), two choruses, strings and continuo (AVRS 5016)

Magnificat for soloists (SSAT), chorus, strings, two oboes and continuo (AMS 25, KA Ricordi 130 037)
Gloria for soloists (SSA), chorus, orchestra and continuo (KA Ricordi 125 356)

If we are to understand these works independently of modern liturgical notions, it is necessary to bear in mind the development which led to Vivaldi's conception of sacred music. Since the time of the elder Gabrieli, but particularly after 1600, the instruments that had hitherto been used only as non-obbligato supports for the chorus came more and more into their own in sacred music as independent factors of construction, and with them came elements of the new *stile concertato*. The term Concerto came into common use as a title for sacred music with instruments, and the genre 'Missa concertata'—also 'Missa da concerto'—came into being. At the same time the tendency towards musical illustration of the text, which had already been in evidence since the early Renaissance, became more marked, leading to a stronger formal division of texts which had in earlier years been conceived and composed as self contained entities. If it was natural to use contrasts such as homophony/polyphony, solo/ripieno and first choral group/second choral group to represent textual subdivisions such as Kyrie–Christe–Kyrie, it was equally natural to accord a certain independence to sections such as 'Et incarnatus' and 'Crucifixus', as had already been usual for some time in the fugal Amen. The result of this development was the cantata mass which in about 1700 offered every possibility of a personal, subjectively heightened expression in a well-contrasted succession of movements. This division of a text into smaller units of meaning, and their musical representation by those vocal and instrumental means which would best suit the text at any given point, are essential characteristics of Vivaldi's church music.

The 126th Psalm *Nisi dominus aedificaverit domum, in vanum laborant qui aedificant eam* (Except the Lord build the house, they labour in vain that build it) is a solo cantata in nine movements and is split up as follows:

1)	Nisi Dominus	alto solo and strings	Allegro	G minor
2)	Vanum est nobis	alto solo and continuo	Largo	B♭ major
3)	Surgite	alto solo and strings	Presto/Largo	B♭ major
4)	Cum dederit	alto solo and strings	Largo	G minor
5)	Sicut sagittae	alto solo and continuo	Presto	E♭ major
6)	Beatus vir	alto solo and continuo	Andante	B♭ major
7)	Gloria Patri	alto solo and viola d'amore	Larghetto	D minor

| 8) Sicut erat | alto solo and strings | Allegro | G minor |
| 9) Amen | alto solo and strings | Allegro | G minor |

At the beginning there is an aria in Vivaldi's best operatic style, whose ritornello might be from any solo concerto movement (Ex. 147). Virtuoso mastery of coloratura is demanded of the solo voice. The same music is used in No. 8 to the text 'Sicut erat in principio' (As it was in the beginning), and this reprise rounds off the work's form in a pronounced way. Numbers 2, 5 and 6 are accompanied only by the continuo. If this is performed in church with an organ, one should not neglect to include a cello so as to provide an expressive counterweight to the solo voice in the bass, for which the impersonal tone of the organ would not be sufficient. The line 'Sicut sagittae in manu bellatoris' (As arrows are in the hand of a mighty man) is given a corresponding construction by motivic symbols in the vocal line, as happens in the composer's operas. No. 3 is constructed entirely from the direct illustration of the text. The three calls of 'Surgite' (rise up) with agitated semiquaver runs in the violins lead into a calm arioso accompanied only by the continuo, and the same sequence returns several times. There follows directly the 'Cum dederit dilectis suis somnum' (for so he giveth his beloved sleep). The key word, sleep, provided the suggestion for music flowing in a very peaceful Siciliano rhythm, such as may be found occasionally in sacred music of the time in Christmas scenes at the crib. Between tender string ritornellos there are far-flung, expressive melodic arches which show Vivaldi to have been a melodist of the first rank. The musical construction of the 'Gloria Patri' is unusual: not a brilliant glorification, but an inward-turning contemplation in a Larghetto aria whose ritornello is played by a solo viola d'amore.

In the invention, construction and deployment of compositional as well as instrumental and vocal means, there is no real difference between this cantata and a Vivaldi opera. However, this is not said with the intention of detracting from the composer's church music from a puritanical point of view. If the similarity of Vivaldi's and his contemporaries' church music to their operas has been and still is constantly taken by liturgical zealots as an indication and criterion for a negative evaluation, it could be asked with equal justification whether on the other hand the operatic music of this time was a less valuable example of its genre because, at least in opera seria, structural elements of sacred music had found their way into it. Basically of course both questions are false: Vivaldi's music comes from an emotive centre which radiated over all the spheres of creation. Whether it be instrumental music, opera or sacred music, all the composer's music presents a stylistic unity. The fact that his church music is of such high quality that the best of it could confidently be placed alongside that of Bach goes to show that, in keeping with his religious attitude, it was precisely the best music that he considered good enough to glorify God. In Vivaldi this glorification comes from the same area of existence as his other music, and he did not make the stylistic distinction of many masters of his time who if they occasionally wrote church music would switch to a tighter use of their craft in the 'stile antico'; he succeeded—even with regard to his technique of composition—in combining both spheres into a unity.

The 109th Psalm *Dixit* 'in due Cori' is written—both in its musical forces and their compositional exploitation—for great festive occasions; here the composer apparently took into account the possibilities of musical exposition offered by the two antiphonal choirs of St. Mark's, where the work would certainly have been performed. The ensemble used is particularly well-furnished. So-called 'Introduzioni' were usual as a sort of vocal and instrumental overture for such compositions. Vivaldi has left us five with the title 'Introduzione al Gloria', two more are headed 'Introduzione al Miserere', and a further two 'Introduzione al Dixit'. One of these Dixit introductions is a three-movement work for solo voice and strings, in which two shortish arias are joined by a transitional recitative. The text of the psalm itself is split up into ten sections; they are clearly differentiated and generally clearly distinguished from each other not only by contrasting ensembles (solo arias, duets, choruses), but also as regards tempo, time signature, and key signature. Here Vivaldi, allegedly so one-sided an instrumental composer, proves himself a master of choral writing: he writes for the eight voices sometimes in block chords and sometimes in unison; in the 'Donec ponam inimicos' (until I make thine enemies . . .) he spins out extensive lines against each other in polyphony and subdivides the choral body; in the 'Judicabit' (He shall judge), at the passage 'implebit ruinas' (he shall fill the places), there are crowd-like dramatic interjections; and the closing 'Sicut erat in principio' (As it was in the beginning) is constructed in cantus firmus technique with lively virtuoso embellishments in the upper voices.

Virtuoso singing technique is demanded above all of the soloists, the duet 'Dominus a dextris tuis' (The Lord at thy right hand—tenor/bass) and the soprano aria 'De Torrento' (of the brook) requiring the singers to give their all. However, it is not enough for the singers to have a mastery of coloratura; they must also be able to make it convincing as a necessary means of expression. The composer makes much use of echo effects, but this is not only done by means of alternating choral and orchestral groups. The 'Judicabit', whose text is a sort of portrayal of the Last Judgment, is introduced by a duet of trumpets; one of the two instruments is heard in the distance as an echoing trumpet (Ex. 148). The two solo sopranos in 'Virgam virtutis' (the rod of thy strength) would also probably have been sung in different choirs at St. Mark's. The *Dixit* (The Lord said) is a grandiose work in every respect. Gian Francesco Malipiero does not exaggerate when he calls it 'Vivaldi's *St. Matthew Passion*'.

The *Magnificat*, extant in two versions, also belongs to the group of absolute masterpieces. The composer divided the text (from the first chapter of St. Luke) into nine sections and in the first version gave no less than seven to the chorus, including one ('Sicut locutus est'—as he spoke) for a three-part group (SAB):

1)	Magnificat	Chorus (with strings, unless otherwise stated)
2)	Et exultavit	Soprano solo
	Quia respexit	Alto solo
	Quia fecit	Tenor solo
3)	Et misericordia	Chorus
4)	Fecit potentiam	Chorus
5)	Deposuit	Unison chorus
6)	Esurientes	Two solo sopranos with continuo
7)	Suscepit	Chorus
8)	Sicut locutus est	Three-part chorus, 2 oboes and strings
9)	Gloria patri	Chorus
	Sicut erat	
	Amen	

The introductory chorus is reminiscent of Monteverdian concision; the broad arches in the repetition of the text, though, were stretched by the composer by means of the harmonic resources of his time. What was said in the section on the harmonic style of Vivaldi's church music is to a large extent applicable to this opening chorus (Ex. 149).

The 'Et exultavit' (And my spirit has rejoiced) is a typical solo concerto movement, the three solo sections—enclosed by a well thought-out ritornello—here being entrusted in sequence to the solo voices soprano, alto and tenor, and in the second solo the chorus has affirmative interjections at two points.

Vivaldi's harmonic language and his intervallic technique, in the sense of intensive expression of the text, are shown by the 'Et misericordia' (And his mercy). After a four-bar string introduction the chorus enters

(Ex. 150). Note the rising major seventh (misericordia!) in the answer (Bars 6 and 8), the augmented sixth in bars 7 and 9 and the Neapolitan effect of the D♭ in bar 9! The unison of chorus and orchestra throughout the 39 bars of the 'Deposuit' (He hath put down) is a magnificent idea. For the 'Gloria Patri' the music of the opening chorus is taken up again and condensed, and the closing choral section plainly betrays the tendency to round off the structure in a comprehensive way. Thus the 'et in saecula saeculorum' (world without end) from the section 'Sicut erat' is taken over as a counterpoint in the cantus-firmus-like Amen (Ex. 151).

In this version the work was presumably not composed for performance within the Ospedale, but was only later adapted for it. The score contains five further arias which are given with the names of the star singing pupils of Vivaldi's institution, namely: Et exultavit per l'Apollonia; Quia respexit per la Bolognesa; Quia fecit per la Chiaretta; Esurientes per l'Ambrosina; Sicut locutus per l'Albetta. In this way the solo tenor is eliminated and the ensemble of soloists rearranged for the female performing resources of the Ospedale. The new arias provide evidence of the high degree of training of Vivaldi's soloists in the institution. Passages like the following lend weight to the report that singers from the Venetian theatres regularly attended the performances of the Ospedali in order to hear good models (Ex. 152). The second version, however, is interesting for another reason as well. Vivaldi split up the 'Et exultavi' into three sections so as to derive from it texts for three arias. In order to provide sufficient material for three arias the text naturally had to be stretched out by repetitions; and with an eye to making use of and displaying his singers' abilities, the composer decided on a procedure strongly suited to his liking for the portrayal of details. Moreover a duet for two sopranos, 'Esurientes' (the hungry), became an alto aria; it is notated in the tenor clef; perhaps Ambrosina possessed a quite exceptionally deep alto voice and was accustomed to singing tenor parts. Further, Vivaldi composed the three-part choral number 'Sicut locutus est' afresh as an alto aria. In the first version the emphasis is on the chorus; the alterations create a more equal balance between soloists and chorus, and the second version has a more rounded effect.

What has been said about the quality of the church works dealt with so far, is to a great extent valid in connection with the *Gloria* too; this is a large-scale composition in eleven movements:

1) Gloria	4/4	Allegro	Chorus	D major
2) Et in terra	3/4	Andante	Chorus	B minor

3) Laudamus te	2/4	Allegro	two sopranos	G major
4) Gratias agimus	C		Chorus	E minor
5) Domine Deus Propter magnam			Chorus	E minor
6) Domine, Fili unigenite	3/4	Allegro	Chorus	F major
7) Domine Deus	C	Adagio	alto solo & chorus	D minor
8) Qui tollis peccata mundi, suscipe	C	Adagio	Chorus	A minor
9) Qui sedes	3/8	Allegro	alto solo	B minor
10) Quoniam tu solus Sanctus	C	Allegro	Chorus (as Gloria, shortened)	D major
11) Cum sancto		Allegro	Chorus	D major

Notice the carefully weighed sequence of keys, metres, tempi and vocal groupings! The resplendent trumpets naturally appear only at the beginning and the end in the principal tonality. The extremely contrasting way in which the composer handles the chorus can be seen in the second 'Qui tollis' (Thou that takest away) and in the broad melodic arches of the 'Propter magnam gloriam' (For thy great glory) (Exx. 153 and 154). The first 'Qui tollis' is a chorus juxtaposed in dialogue with the soloist's 'Agnus'.

Because of the similarity of such works to those of Bach, and also the fact that in the Gloria of the B minor Mass Bach split up the text extensively in the same way, the conclusion has been drawn that Bach had direct knowledge of Vivaldi's sacred music, especially since we know of transcripts of Vivaldi's vocal works in Bohemia. In all Bach composed five Glorias, of which three split up the text into five sections (Masses in F, A and G), one into six (Mass in G minor), and in the Mass in B minor, which in fact represents his first setting of the mass, it is in nine sections. Robert Stevenson was the first to assert this supposed influence on Bach in the latter Gloria; others have since followed suit. In his book *Music before the classic era* he says on p. 146: 'As he used Vivaldi frequently for a model, and learned from him, it may be instructive to compare the Gloria of the B minor Mass with Vivaldi's Gloria Mass. It will be found that Bach followed Vivaldi not only in the division of the text, but also in the assignment of certain sections to solo voices and others to chorus.' Both are incorrect. Straight away in the first two sections a unity is formed in Bach, so that 'Gratiam' and 'Propter'—which in Vivaldi are clearly separated after a fermata by contrasting textures, homophonic and poly-phonic—were through-composed by Bach as a unity. The difference is most marked in the next movement: Bach composed 'Domine Deus rex', 'Domine Fili' and 'Domine Deus Agnus' as one movement, Vivaldi in three movements; the 'Qui tollis', treated in two lines of text by Vivaldi, is also through-composed by Bach. Finally the 'Quoniam' is a bass solo in Bach, but a choral number in Vivaldi. However, the technique of dividing up large textual complexes in the manner of a cantata was already such common practice in the first half of the eighteenth century, and such uniform pretexts for the distribution between solo and chorus could be found in the subject matter, that seen from this angle all large-scale and hence considerably compartmentalized liturgical compositions show certain formal similarities. As opposed to such rather superficial similarities which are rooted in the practices of the times and are probably somewhat fortuitous, it is necessary, if we are to compare the church music of the two masters, once again to emphasize the strong spiritual affinities between Bach and Vivaldi. These were already present before Bach came to know Vivaldi's music. Then, as he studied Vivaldi's works, they deepened and led to an adoption of certain stylistic details. His further development, continuing on the basis of his whole spiritual make-up, then apparently led Bach away from Vivaldi again, though only from the hitherto known Vivaldi of the instrumental music. But acquaintance with his church music shows that the relationship goes deeper, even though whereas in Bach the predominant impulse is towards meditative brooding, in Vivaldi it is towards communication.

An essential factor of their relationship is perhaps hinted at by a remark which I heard and concurred with many times when I introduced uninitiated listeners to Vivaldi's church music without naming the composer: 'This music is not by Bach, certainly, but it is so good that really only Bach could have written it.'

VIVALDI RESEARCH IN
RECENT YEARS

It is in the nature of research that our knowledge in any given area is constantly on the move, and publications begin to be in need of complementation from the moment of their appearance onward.

In 1965, the year in which the German edition of this book was printed, a dissertation was read at Rostock University towards an inventory of the work, which is still far from concluded (Karl Heller, *Die deutsche Vivaldi-Überlieferung*: Researches into the manuscript concertos and sinfonias of Antonio Vivaldi preserved in German libraries. Two volumes, the second being a thematic catalogue). The author was able to correct quite a number of errors which had previously found their way from one publication to another, besides drawing attention to some new sources. This study is complemented by an American dissertation 'An Historical Survey of Thematic Catalogs with Special Reference to the Instrumental Works of Antonio Vivaldi' by Lenore Coral (Univ. of Chicago, 1965). The Vivaldi legacy in the Nordic countries has occupied the young Danish musicologist Peter Ryom; his work, 'A propos de l'inventaire des œuvres d'Antonio Vivaldi . . . découverte, en Scandinavie, de 45 manuscrits inconnus', is at present being printed. In view of Vivaldi's relations with the Danish court, evident from the dedication of the Op. II violin sonatas to King Frederick IV of Denmark and Norway, the results should be eagerly anticipated.

Remo Giazotto's book on Vivaldi also appeared in 1965 (Milan). The author has made use of documents hitherto barely noticed in connection with Vivaldi, found in the Venetian archives under the headings Segretario alle Voci, Notarile, Inquisitori di Stato, Dispacci ambasciatori, etc., and he thus contributes especially to our knowledge of the composer's private life.

VIVALDI RESEARCH IN RECENT YEARS

Perhaps the most important contribution to research has been made by Tomislav Volek and Marie Skalická with the essay 'Vivaldis Beziehungen zu den böhmischen Ländern' (*Acta Musicologica*, 1967). They have been able to show that in the years 1726–32 Vivaldi's operas flourished in Prague; for this, the impresario 'Antonio Denzio Venetiano', who in 1716 had sung in the first performance of Vivaldi's *La Costanza* . . . in Venice, was responsible. Since the composer had demonstrably been in correspondence not only with Denzio, but also with members of the Bohemian nobility, and since besides a fair number of Vivaldi's works are to be found in Bohemian libraries, it is quite possible that Vivaldi was in Prague with his father, and he may have staged some of his operas there himself. This seems to be the explanation for the journey in view of which Vivaldi's father applied for leave in 1729. Lasting connections with the Bohemian nobility are also confirmed by a voucher dated '28 giugno 1741' which, just a month before the day of his burial, Vivaldi gave as a receipt for money received in payment for some music he had sold.

Vivaldi's operatic works have been the object of increasing interest. Lewis E. Rowell jr. has made a study of 'Four Operas of Antonio Vivaldi' (Dissertation, University of Rochester, 1959). In 1964 Raffaele Monterosso published an edition of the opera *La Fida Ninfa* (Cremona, Ateneo Cremonese) which might serve as a model for all practical realizations of Baroque opera had this de luxe edition not been too expensive, and had the performing material been provided.

As far as opera is concerned, the great surprise has come from research in the Bentivoglio archive, which is housed in the Ferrara National Archives. Adriano Cavicchi discovered five letters of Vivaldi and also the drafts of his patron's replies. They all date from the critical years after 1736 and relate to operatic performances in Ferrara. On January 2, 1739, Vivaldi complains bitterly that his reputation in Ferrara as an operatic composer is in ruins, and says:

> 'Con tutto che al mio nome, et alla mia riputazione mi stà avanti tutta un'Europa, ad ogni modo doppo 94 Opere da me composte, non posso soffrire inconveniente simile'.

Here, then, Vivaldi gives an exact number for his operatic works which is almost twice that of the dramatic works of which we had evidence hitherto. If Vivaldi had said 'a hundred', such an expression would not be taken so seriously, for it could well be a deliberate exaggeration. But the number 94 is astonishing and, even if one counts works later performed with slight alterations and under different titles, it must still be reckoned that a whole series of Vivaldi operas remains to be discovered, even if only by name.

Finally the Union Theological Seminary School of Sacred Music in New York has announced that Robert E. Fort jr. is at work on a dissertation, 'The Sacred Choral Music of Antonio Vivaldi in the Foà and Giordano Collections'. Thus the master's church music, long neglected in favour of the instrumental music, has once more attracted scholarly research.

EPILOGUE

The immense accumulation of what in a general fashion we call the intellectual wealth of mankind is continually changing without our ever becoming aware of these changes in themselves. According to laws yet undiscovered, and doubtless undiscoverable, we choose from the new accretions offered to us daily, and make room for them by forgetting, by an unconscious process of disposal. Manners and fashions basically have little influence on this process, and at most can delay its effect. Much is excluded, thus losing its emanatory intellectual force, but its preservation in the mind of only one man prevents the total suppression of the material to which it is bound. Attempts to revive it founder if they happen at untimely moments. Only when that mysterious fluid that Goethe called selective affinity becomes effective does the time come, as if of its own accord, when the long-blocked sources begin to flow once again.

For Vivaldi's music the process of rejection had already begun in the composer's lifetime, and a few decades after his death it was completely forgotten. When in the nineteenth century the composer was rediscovered as a figure in Bach's environment—almost as if fortuitously—he was considered more as a curiosity than as a creative personality; early Vivaldi research was undertaken but little for the sake of the composer himself and it seemed more of a 'hobby' for one or two men than a task of any contemporary urgency. Many of Vivaldi's violin concertos were useful for pupils who had just learnt the third position. . . .

In fact it is possible that Conte Giacomo Durazzo was fully aware of the meaning and importance of his deal when he bought up the gigantic repertoire in Venice and incorporated it in his library. During his life he had had so many opportunities to observe genuine creativeness from the closest proximity and to exert a beneficial influence on the circumstances of creation that he may well have had an inkling of the imperishability of great art, whose preservation he felt himself pledged to guarantee as a collector, precisely because the tastes of the time ran counter to these works. And perhaps one and a half centuries later his descendant in Genoa fought so obstinately for his music manuscripts because he did not consider the world he was about to leave sufficiently worthy to rejoice in the contents of these documents?

When, more than thirty years ago, Alberto Gentili concerned himself with the composer's work, the time for a Vivaldi revival was not yet ripe. But the way was prepared for it equally by Conte Chigi dei Saracini, Alfredo Casella, Marc Pincherle and many others. The fact that it set in completely after the last war seems symbolic: after so much horror and devastation mankind yearned for music in which pure beauty seemed to be without anything at all problematic. This was perhaps not so much a flight from day-to-day life as rather a search for strength from the music to reshape that life. After the war, Antonio Fanna too began his edition of the composer's works with admirable tenacity, and today it is published by Ricordi. The fact that from the outset it was planned as a complete edition has brought into the light of day a lot of music that even Vivaldi himself would surely not have intended for posterity, at any rate insofar as such considerations would have been possible in the world as he saw it. Today Vivaldi's popularity has taken on such dimensions that it almost threatens that of other good music. The performance of so many superfluous works of the composer has provoked such a critical mind as Stravinsky's. In his *Conversations with Igor Stravinsky* Robert Craft asks 'Are you interested in the current revival of eighteenth-century Italian masters?', and Stravinsky replies: 'Not very. Vivaldi is greatly overrated—a dull fellow who could compose the same form so many times over.'* And in a review of gramophone recordings of Vivaldi's music Paul Henry Lang uses the expression 'run-of-the-mill music'. Stravinsky's dismissive judgment is also ascribed to Dallapiccola. It makes little difference who was first here, for this is in fact only a paraphrase of a well-known comment on Bruckner's symphonies. Whether a successful composer of today, who can sit back tranquilly on his fat bank account and wait for the next radio or festival commission, should thus express himself about a colleague of pre-copyright times is questionable and must in the last resort be attributed to a complete ignorance of the circumstances of a creator in the eighteenth century. All the notorious fast or prolific writers like Pergolesi, Telemann, Scarlatti, Graupner, Vivaldi, Bach, Stamitz, Haydn and Mozart did not work their fingers sore for the fun of it

---

* *Conversations with Igor Stravinsky* by Igor Stravinsky and Robert Craft, London, 1959, p. 76.

but because it was contractually required of them or because they were pressed by a concern for their very existence. Even the great masters could often turn out 'run-of-the-mill' music which owed more to a practised hand than to inspiration. But one might have expected some feeling of gratitude towards the older masters from the same Stravinsky who, in times when things were not going so well for him as they are today, did not scorn to put his name on Baroque music in order to make himself royalties from it.

The author of this book has regarded it as his special task to find a happy mean between extravagant idolization and irrelevant criticism. The picture of the master who, like hardly anyone else, was the motive force behind the development of music in the early eighteenth century, has been drawn from sober analysis of the music, from the few verbal documents by him that we possess, and also from reports by his contemporaries. Whilst with every ounce of his being he lived in his time and fulfilled its claims on him, he created works which have survived that time and will, all being well, tell unborn generations of the splendour and beauty of his native Venice.

BIBLIOGRAPHY

ABBADO, Michelangelo:
Antonio Vivaldi (Turin 1942)
ADLER, Guido:
Handbuch der Musikgeschichte (Frankfort/M 1924)
ALTMANN, Wilhelm:
'Thematischer Katalog der gedruckten Werk Antonio Vivaldis' (AfM IV, 1922, p. 262)
BABITZ, Sol:
'A problem of rhythm in baroque music' (MQu 1952, p. 533)
BAIGNÈRES, Claude:
Vivaldi, vie, mort et résurrection (Paris 1955)
BARBLAN, Gugliemo:
Francesco A. Bonporti (Florence 1948)
BENINCASA, Conte Bartolomeo:
Descrizione della raccolta di stampe di S. Conte Jacopo Durazzo, eposta in una dissertazione sull'arte dell'intaglio a stampa (Parma 1784)
BERNARDI, Gian Giuseppe:
La musica a Venezia nell'età di Goldoni (Venice 1908)
BERRI, Pietro:
'La malattia di Vivaldi' (*Musica d'oggi*, January 1942)
Indice discografico Vivaldiano (Milan 1953)
BESSELER, Heinrich:
'Bach als Wegbereiter' (AfM 12, 1955, p. 1)
'Die Meisterzeit Bachs in Weimar' (in: *J. S. Bach in Thüringen*, Weimar 1950)
'Zur Chronologie der Konzerte Joh. Seb. Bachs' (in: *Festschrift Max Schneider*, Leipzig 1955, p. 115)
BONACCORSI, Alfredo:
'Contributo alla storia del concerto grosso' (RMI 1932, p. 467)
BOYDEN, David D.:
'When is a concerto not a concerto?' (MQ 1957/220)
BRAUNSTEIN, Joseph:
'Vivaldi. The Discovery of the Turinese Vivaldi Manuscripts' (Library of recorded Masterpieces, New York 1961)
BRENET, Michel:
'La librairie musicale en France de 1653 à 1790' (SIMG VIII)
BROSSES, Charles de:
Lettres familières sur l'Italie (new edition, Paris 1931)

213

BIBLIOGRAPHY

BRUERS, Antonio:
'Antonio Vivaldi. Discorso pronunziato il 15 Settembre 1947 . . .' (*Quaderno dell' Acc. Chig.* XV/7, Siena 1947)

BUKOFZER, Manfred F.:
Music in the Baroque Era (New York 1947)

BUNTING, Christopher:
'The Violoncello' (in Baines, *Musical Instruments Through the Ages*, London 1966)

BURNEY, Charles:
The Present State of Music in France and Italy (London 1771)
The Present State of Music in Germany, the Netherlands, and United Provinces (London 1773)
A General History of Music from the Earliest Ages to the Present Period (London 1776–89)

CAFFI, Francesco:
Storia della Musica sacra nella già Cappella Ducale di San Marco in Venezia (Venice 1855)

CASELLA, Alfredo:
'Come sono state scelte ed elaborate le musiche della 'Settimana'' (*Antonio Vivaldi, note e documenti*, Siena 1938, p. 11)
'Le composizioni sacre e vocali di Antonio Vivaldi' (*A.V., note e documenti*, Siena 1939, p. 15)

CASELLA / LUCIANI / RUDGE:
'Note sulle opere eseguite durante la prima Settimana senese Settembre 1939' (*A. V.*, Siena 1947, p. 28)

CASELLA / FRAZZI / LUCIANI / TORREFRANCA:
'Note sulle opere eseguite nel 1941 e 1942' (*A. V.*, Siena 1947, p. 40)

CHORON et FAYOLLE:
Dictionnaire historique des Musiciens (Paris 1810/11)

CUCUEL, George:
'Quelques documents sur la librairie musicale au XVIIIe siècle' (SIMG XIII 1911/12)

DELLA CORTE, Andrea:
'L'Olimpiade' (*La Stampa* 20.8.1939)

DEUTSCH, Otto Erich:
Music Publishers' Numbers (London 1946)

DITTERSDORF, Karl Ditters von:
Lebensbeschreibung, seinem Sohne in die Feder diktiert (new edition, Regensburg 1940)

DOUNIAS, Minos:
Die Violinkonzerte G. Tartinis als Ausdruck einer Künstlerpersönlichkeit und einer Kulturepoche (Wolfenbüttel 1935)

EINSTEIN, Alfred:
Foreword to the edition of Vivaldi's Op. III, No. 8 (Eulenburg Score No. 762)

ELLER, Rudolf:
'Nationale Bedingtheiten des europäischen Instrumentalstils' (Congress Report, Bamberg 1953, p. 259)
'Zur Frage Bach-Vivaldi' (Congress Report, Hamburg 1956, p. 80)
'Die Konzertform Antonio Vivaldis' (Inaugural Dissertation, Leipzig 1957)
'Vivaldi—Dresden—Bach' (*Beiträge zur Musikwissenschaft*, Berlin 1961, p. 31)
'Die Entstehung der Themenzweiheit in der Frühgeschichte des Instrumentalkonzerts' (*Besseler-Festschrift* 1962, p. 323)

ENGEL, Hans:
Das Instrumentalkonzert (Leipzig 1932)
'Johann Sebastian Bachs Violinkonzerte' (*Festschrift zum 175jährigen Bestehen der Gewandhauskonzerte*, Leipzig 1956, p. 40)
'Die italienische Kantate von den Anfängen bis zu Händel' ('Kantate' in *Musik in Geschichte und Gegenwart*)
Das Concerto grosso (Cologne 1962)

BIBLIOGRAPHY

FARGA, Franz:
Geigen und Geiger (Zurich ²1940)
FEDOROV, Vladimir:
'Lettres de quelques voyageurs russes du XVIIIᵉ siècle' (*Festschrift Friedrich Blume*, Cassel 1963, p. 112)
FISCHER, Wilhelm:
'Instrumentalmusik von 1600–1750' (in: Adler, *Handbuch der Musikgeschichte*, Frankfort/M 1924, p. 482)
FORKEL, Johann Nikolaus:
Über Johann Sebastian Bachs Leben, Kunst und Kunstwerke (Leipzig 1802)
GALLO, Rodolfo:
'Antonio Vivaldi, il Prete Rosso, la famiglia, la morte' (*Ateneo Veneto* Venice, 1938, Vol. XII)
GANASSI, Sylvestro:
Opera intitulata Fontegara (Venice 1535)
GENTILI, Alberto:
'La raccolta di rarità musicali "Mauro Foà" alla Biblioteca Nazionale di Torino' (*Accademie e Biblioteche d'Italia*, Rome, July/August 1927)
'La raccolta Mauro Foà nella Biblioteca Nazionale di Torino' (RIM 1927, p. 356)
'Vivaldi and Stradella. A recent find' (*Musical Times*, 1.6.1927)
'Vivaldi' (Programme note, Teatro di Torino, 28.1.1928).
'Die Mauro-Foà-Sammlung alter Musikwerke in der Nationalbibliothek von Turin' (translated by Roslin Charlemont; *Italien, Monatsschrift für Kultur* . . . 1929, Vol. 4)
'La raccolta di antiche musiche "Renzo Giordano" alla Biblioteca Nazionale di Torino' *Accademie e Biblioteche d'Italia*. Rome, September 1930)
GENTILI, Verona:
'Storia delle collezioni Foà e Giordano della Biblioteca Nazionale di Torino' (Ms)
GERBER, Ernst Ludwig:
Historisch-biographisches Lexicon der Tonkünstler (Leipzig 1790/92)
Neues historisch-biographisches Lexicon der Tonkünstler (Leipzig 1812/14)
GERSTENBERG, Walter:
'Die Zeitmasse und ihre Ordnungen in Bachs Musik' (Lecture given at the Ansbach Bach Festival; yearbook of *Freunde der Bachwoche Ansbach*, 1952)
GIAZOTTO, Remo:
Tomaso Albinoni (Milan 1945)
Vita di Alessandro Stradella (Milan 1962)
GIEGLING, Franz:
Giuseppe Torelli. Ein Beitrag zur Entwicklungsgeschichte des italienischen Konzerts (Cassel 1949)
GOLDONI, Carlo:
Commedie. Preface to the XIIIth Vol. (Venice 1761)
Memorie (Venice 1798)
GOLDSCHMIDT, Hugo:
Die Musikästhetik des 18. Jahrhunderts (Zurich 1915)
GRADENIGO:
Commemoralihs. (Venice, Museo Correr)
GRUNSKY, Karl:
'Bachs Bearbeitungen und Umarbeitungen eigener und fremder Werke' (*Bach Jb.* 1912, p. 61)
GUERRINI, Guido:
Vivaldi (Florence undated [1951])
HAAS, Robert:
Gluck und Durazzo im Burgtheater (Vienna 1925)

BIBLIOGRAPHY

Die Estensischen Musikalien (Regensburg 1927)
Die Musik des Barocks (Potsdam 1929)
'Durazzo' (*Musik in Geschichte und Gegenwart*)
HILGENFELDT, C. L.:
Johann Sebastian Bach's Leben, Wirken und Werke (Leipzig 1850)
HILLER, Johann Adam:
Wöchentliche Nachrichten und Anmerkungen die Musik betreffend (Leipzig 1766–69)
Lebensbeschreibungen berühmter Musikgelehrter und Ton künstler neuerer Zeit (Leipzig 1784)
HUTCHINGS, Arthur:
The Baroque Concerto (London 1961)
JUNG, Hans Rudolf:
'Die Dresdener Vivaldimanuskripte' (AMW 1955, p. 314 ff.)
KAHL, Willi:
Selbstbiographien deutscher Musiker im 18. Jahrhundert (Cologne 1948)
KELLER / UNVERRICHT / JONAS / KREUTZ / ZIMMERMANN:
Die Bedeutung der Zeichen Keil, Strich und Punkt bei Mozart (Cassel 1957)
KNÖDT, Heinrich:
'Zur Entwicklungsgeschichte der Kadenzen im Instrumentalkonzert' (SIMG XV, 1913/14)
KOLNEDER, Walter:
'Die Klarinette als Concertino-Instrument bei Vivaldi (Mf 1951, p. 185; Dutch translation: *Symphonia* 1951, Nov./Dec.)
'Biographisches um Antonio Vivaldi' (ÖMZ 1952, p. 53)
'Vivaldi als Bearbeiter eigener Werke. Ein Fagottkonzert, eingerichtet für Oboe' (AM 1952, p. 45)
'Das Frühschaffen Antonio Vivaldis' (Congress Report, Utrecht 1952, p. 254)
'Antonio Vivaldis pädagogische Tätigkeit in Venedig' (Mf 1952, p. 341)
'Il concerto per due trombe di Antonio Vivaldi' (RMI 1953, p. 54)
'Zur Frage der Vivaldi-Kataloge' (AfM 1954, p. 323)
'Antonio Vivaldi' (Riemann *Musik-Lexikon*, 12th impression)
'Noch einmal: Vivaldi und die Klarinette' (Mf 1955, p. 209)
'Antonio Vivaldi. Neue Studien zur Biographie und zur Stilistik der Werke: 1. Der heutige Stand der Erforschung der Lebensgeschichte Vivaldis; 2. Der Aufführungsstil; 3. Melodietypen bei Vivaldi; 4. Doppelfassungen Vivaldischer Werke; 5. Die Solokonzertform bei Vivaldi' (Inaugural Dissertation, Univ. of Saarland 1956), printed separately:
   Aufführungspraxis bei Vivaldi (Leipzig 1955)
   De Solokonzertform bei Vivaldi (Strasbourg/Baden-Baden 1961)
'The Solo Concerto'
'The Rise of Orchestral Music'
'Orchestral Music in the Early 18th Century'
(Three Chapters for *The Oxford History of Music*, Vol. 6)
'Antonio Vivaldi e la forma del concerto solistico' (*Convegno Vivaldiano*, Venice 1958)
'Dynamik und Agogik in der Musik des Barock' (Congress Report, Cologne, 1958, p. 343)
'Fagott' (*Musik in Geschichte und Gegenwart*)
'Ausdrucksdynamik im Lehrwerk von Quantz' (*Zs. Hausmusik* 1959, p. 73)
'Der Aufführungsstil Vivaldis' (ÖMZ 1964, p. 574)
'Vivaldis Aria-Concerto' (*Deutsches Jahrbuch der Musikwissenschaft für 1964*)
KOOLE, Arend:
Pietro Antonio Locatelli (Amsterdam 1949)

BIBLIOGRAPHY

KRETZSCHMAR, Hermann:
'Beiträge zur Geschichte der venezianischen Oper' (Peters Yearbook 1907)

KRÜGER, Walther:
Das Concerto grosso in Deutschland (Wolfenbüttel 1933)

LAURENCIE, Lionel de la:
L'école française de violon de Lully à Viotti (Paris 1922–4)

LANDSHOFF, Ludwig:
Forewords to the editions of the A major Concerto P. 228, Peters Ed. 4206, and Two short sinfonias by Vivaldi, Peters Ed. 4206.

LEBERMANN, Walter:
'Zur Besetzungsfrage der Concerti grossi von A. Vivaldi' (Mf 1954, p. 337)

LESURE, François:
'La Datation des Premières Editions d'Estienne Roger' (Congress Report, Bamberg 1953, p. 273)

LOESER, Norbert:
Vivaldi (Haarlem 1959)

LORENZETTI, Giulio:
Venezia e il suo estuario (Rome 1956)

LUCIANI, S. A.:
'I Concerti' (in: *Antonio Vivaldi, Note e documenti*, Siena 1939)
'La Juditha e messa in scena' (*Quaderno dell'Acc. Chig.* Siena 1947)

MALIPIERO, Gian Francesco:
'Un frontespizio enigmatico' (in: *Bollettino biografico-musicale*, Milan 1930)
Antonio Vivaldi, Il Prete rosso (Milan 1958)

MARCELLO, Benedetto:
Il Teatro alla Modo (Venice 1720)

MICHEL, Antoine:
'Antonio Vivaldi et François de Lorraine' (*Annales de l'Est*, Nancy 1954)

MORTARI, Virgilio:
"L'Olimpiade" e il teatro musicale di Antonio Vivaldi' (in: *A.V., Note e documenti*, Siena 1939)

NEWMAN, William S.:
'The Sonatas of Albinoni and Vivaldi' (JAMS 1952)
The Sonata in the Baroque Era (Chapel Hill 1959)

PASTORELLO, Ester:
Tipografi, editori, librai a Venezia nel secolo XVI (Florence 1924)

PAUL, Emil:
'La date de naissance d'Antonio Vivaldi' (*Convegno Vivaldiano*, Brussels 1963)

PINCHERLE, Marc:
'Antonio Vivaldi, saggio biografico' (RM 1929)
'La naissance du Concerto' (*Courrier Musical* 1930)
Corelli et son temps (Paris ²1954)
'Vivaldi e gli Ospedali di Venezia' (RM 1937)
'Note sur E. Roger et M. C. Le Cène' (RBM 1947)
Antonio Vivaldi et la musique instrumentale (Paris 1948)
Vivaldi (Paris 1955)
translated as *Vivaldi, Genius of the Baroque*, New York 1957

PRAETORIUS, Ernst:
'Neues zur Bachforschung' (SIMG VIII 1906/7, p. 95)

PREUSSNER, Eberhard:
Die musikalischen Reisen des Herrn von Uffenbach (Cassel 1949)

BIBLIOGRAPHY

QUANTZ, Johann Joachim:
Versuch einer Anweisung die flute traversière zu spielen (Berlin 1752)
'Herrn Johann Joachim Quantzens Lebenslauf von ihm selbst entworfen' (in: Marpurg *Historisch-kritische Beiträge* . . ., Berlin from 1754)
RARIG, Howard R. Jr.:
The Instrumental Sonatas of Antonio Vivaldi (Diss., University of Michigan 1958)
RINALDI, Mario;
Antonio Vivaldi (Milan 1943)
Catalogo numerico tematico delle composizioni di A. Vivaldi (Rome undated [1945])
RUDGE, Olga:
'Catalogo tematico delle opere strumentali di Antonio Vivaldi esistenti nella Biblioteca Nazionale di Torino' (in: *A.V.*, *Note e documenti* . . ., Siena 1939)
'Opere vocali attribuite a Antonio Vivaldi nella R. Biblioteca Nazionale Torino' (in: *La Scuola Veneziana* Siena 1941)
RÜHLMANN, Julius:
'Antonio Vivaldi und sein Einfluß auf J. S. Bach' (NZfM 1867 No. 45-47)
SALVATORI, Arcangelo:
'Antonio Vivaldi (il Prete Rosso), note biografiche' (*Riv. mens. della Città di Venezia*, August 1928)
SCHERING, Arnold:
'Zur Bach-Forschung I, II' (SIMG IV, 1902/03 and V, 1903/04)
Geschichte des Instrumentalkonzerts (Leipzig 1905)
'Zur instrumentalen Verzierungskunst im 18. Jahrhundert' (SIMG VII, 1905/6)
'Die freie Kadenz im Instrumentalkonzert des 18. Jahrhunderts' (Congress Report, Basel 1906)
Aufführungspraxis alter Musik (Leipzig 1931)
SCHNEIDER, Max:
'Das sogenannte "Orgelkonzert d-moll von Wilhelm Friedemann Bach" ' (*Bach JB* 1911 p. 23)
SCHWEITZER, Albert:
J. S. Bach, le musicien poète (Leipzig 1905)
German edition (Leipzig 1908)
SIEGELE, Ulrich:
Kompositionsweise und Bearbeitungstechnik in der Instrumentalmusik J. S. Bachs (Diss., Tübingen 1957)
SMITH, William C.:
A Bibliography of the musical works published by John Walsh during the years 1695-1720 (London 1948)
SPITTA, Philipp:
J. S. Bach (Leipzig 1873/80)
STEFANI, Federigo:
Sei lettere di Antonio Vivaldi veneziano (Venice 1871)
STEVENSON, Robert:
Music before the classic era (London ²1962)
SZABOLCSI, Bence:
'Tre composizioni sconosciute di Antonio Vivaldi' (*Quaderno dell'Acc. Chig.*, Siena 1947)
TAGLIAVINI, Luigi Ferdinando:
Foreword to W. A. Mozart "Betulia liberata" (New collected edition I/4/2)
TORREFRANCA, Fausto:
'Antonio Vivaldi' (*Enc. Ital.* Vol. XXXV)
'Modernità di Antonio Vivaldi' (*Nuova Antologia* 1.8.1942)
'Problemi Vivaldiani' (Congress Report, Basel 1949, p. 195)

218

BIBLIOGRAPHY

VATIELLI, Francesco:
'Primordini dell'arte del Violoncello',
'La genesi del Concerto strumentale e Giuseppe Torelli' (in: *Arte e vita musicale a Bologna* Bologna 1927)
'Un ritratto di Antonio Vivaldi?' (RMI 1938)

VEINUS, Abraham:
The Concerto (London 1948)

WALDERSEE, Paul Graf:
'Antonio Vivaldis Violinconcerte unter besonderer Berücksichtigung der von Johann Sebastian Bach bearbeiteten' (VfM I, 1885 p. 356)

WRIGHT, Edward:
Some observations made in travelling through France, Italy . . . (London 1730)

ZEIM, Eleonore:
Sinfonia und Ritornello als Intermedien in der Kirchenmusik der ersten Hälfte des 17. Jahrhunderts (Diss., Halle 1950)

ZOBELEY, Fritz:
Rudolf Franz Eberwein Graf von Schönborn und seine Musikpflege (Würzburg 1949)

MUSIC EXAMPLES

MUSIC EXAMPLES

MUSIC EXAMPLES

227

MUSIC EXAMPLES

MUSIC EXAMPLES

233

80
Op. X No. 2
P. 342
from the 1st movement
Flute Vl. I

81
Op. VIII No. 3
P. 257
1st movement

120
P. 75
from the 1st movement

121
P. 75
from the 3rd movement

126
P. 87
from the 1st
movement

Harpsichord I

Harpsichord 2

127
P. 36
from the 1st
movement

Organ

Organ

128
P. 53
1st movement
2 Solo Oboes

Vl. I, II

Vla

Bass

(without tempo indication)

130
P. 74
from the 3rd
movement,
Clarinets
Oboes

(All⁰)
Bar 21

(with Continuo)

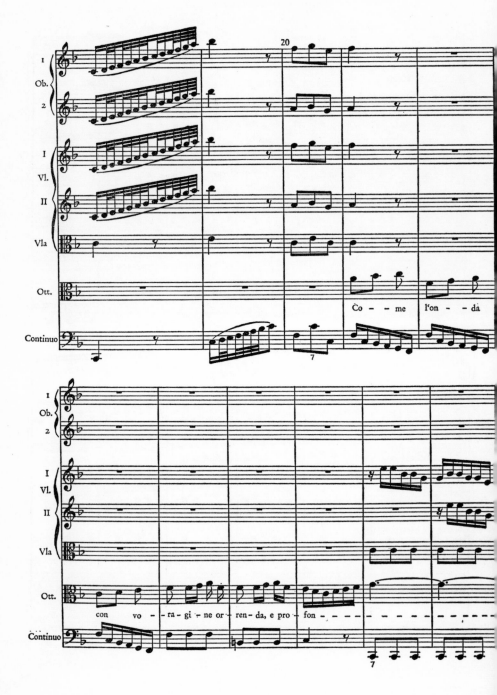

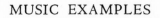

40
om *L'Incoronazione*
Dario

141

La Fida Ninfa

Act I, Scene 9

44
a Sena festeggiante
art 2, No. 3

148
from *Psalm 109*

149
from *Magnificat*

(with strings doubling the chorus)

152
from *Magnificat*
per l'Apollonia

153
from *Gloria*

GENERAL INDEX

279

GENERAL INDEX

GENERAL INDEX

GENERAL INDEX

INDEX OF WORKS

(Music examples listed in italic numerals)

INDEX OF WORKS

41568